Business Writing

2nd Edition

by Natalie Canavor

for dummies®
A Wiley Brand

Business Writing For Dummies®, 2nd Edition

Published by: **John Wiley & Sons, Inc.**, 111 River Street, Hoboken, NJ 07030-5774, www.wiley.com

Copyright © 2017 by John Wiley & Sons, Inc., Hoboken, New Jersey

Published simultaneously in Canada

For general information on our other products and services, please contact our Customer Care Department within the U.S. at 877-762-2974, outside the U.S. at 317-572-3993, or fax 317-572-4002. For technical support, please visit https://hub.wiley.com/community/support/dummies.

Wiley publishes in a variety of print and electronic formats and by print-on-demand. Some material included with standard print versions of this book may not be included in e-books or in print-on-demand. If this book refers to media such as a CD or DVD that is not included in the version you purchased, you may download this material at http://booksupport.wiley.com. For more information about Wiley products, visit www.wiley.com.

Library of Congress Control Number: 2017936222

ISBN 978-1-119-36900-4 (pbk); ISBN 978-1-119-36901-1 (ebk); ISBN 978-1-119-36903-5 (ebk)

Manufactured in the United States of America

10 9 8 7 6 5 4 3 2 1

Contents at a Glance

Table of Contents

CHAPTER 3: Making Your Writing Work: The Basics 45

CHAPTER 4: Self-Editing: Professional Ways to Improve Your Work 67

Introduction

Writing was invented around 5,000 years ago, and the rest is . . . well, history. Before writing evolved, people couldn't record events or anything they learned, so they had no means of sharing information other than in person. Without a way to build upon knowledge, people were limited by their own experience and what they learned from those immediately around them.

Writing changed all that. With it, human beings created civilizations. But for many millennia, the rich governing classes owned the ability to both read and write. A few culture and technology revolutions later, and now we all own those powers. With a simple click you can share an opinion with the whole world. Reach decision-makers and influencers. Create a market for a product or service, or a community of followers or friends.

One result of owning this magical power is that like Superman, you're obliged to use it! More opportunities are open to you than any of your ancestors, even your parents. But because everyone has the power, whatever your goals, competition is guaranteed. Whether you're a job applicant, a manager who wants to rise, an entrepreneur who hopes to do it *your* way, a professional or a specialist of any kind, writing well is today's imperative.

If you're reading this book, you already know that. But I think you'll be surprised by how many more ways good writing can reward you than you now suspect. Good writers are increasingly at a premium in every industry and in every kind of enterprise. And everybody must write. It's no longer a responsibility that can be delegated to assistants or PR professionals. Nor is it a side task that most employees, entrepreneurs, or independent workers can sidestep.

Today we all stand on our own: for everyday messaging that gets the job done, builds relationships, and prevents problems. For strong reports, proposals, and marketing materials that may be make or break events. For playing a role in the online world and using websites, blogs, networking sites, and social media to our advantage.

Whenever a new communication medium emerges and we have more ways to deliver messages, the writing challenge grows. The Internet turns the worlds of journalism, marketing, public relations, advertising, and business-building upside down. It's all become "democratized" — one big open field. The ticket is good writing backed by strategic planning, or strategy backed by writing. Properly seen, they are two sides of the same coin.

About This Book

I wrote this book to give you a high-stakes tool for accomplishing your own goals and dreams. While I aim to show you how to think and write strategically, the methods are totally pragmatic. Every idea and technique is ready to use and fully demonstrated. I base everything on my own decades of trial and error as a journalist, magazine editor, corporate communications director, and consultant. The methods I show you have been field-tested in hundreds of my workshops and courses for businesspeople, public relations professionals, corporate communicators, and nonprofit leaders.

This book gives you a complete foundation for effective business writing as well as guidelines to instantly improve everything you write. I hope the following chapters inspire you to keep improving, a process I see as an endlessly rewarding quest.

Foolish Assumptions

Do you assume any of the following?

>> Writing well is a talent you're born with — or not.

>> Improving poor writing is difficult.

>> Good writing is defined by correct grammar and spelling "rules."

>> Expressing complex thought demands complex language.

>> Writing dense copy with long words makes you look more intelligent and educated.

>> Visual media like video and images diminishes the need for writing well.

>> Reserving your best skills for "important" material makes sense.

Every one of these assumptions is false. I debunk all of them in this book. For now, the important truth is that *you can write better*, whether you need basic grounding or are already a good writer and want to become better yet.

This book gives you down-to-earth, easy-to-use techniques. It does not give you grammar lessons. Many of the ideas and thinking processes are drawn from the toolkits of professional writers who in large part learn by long trial and error. I want to save you that time. My mission is to show you how to know what to say and how to say it, whatever the challenge. I also leave you with ways to recognize how to determine if you're succeeding, and if not, how to fix the problems.

How This Book Is Organized

As the author, naturally I'm happy if you read the whole book in the sequence I created for it and build your skills step by step. However, you can equally choose to dip into chapters and sections as you need them or the spirit moves you. Use the table of contents or index to find what you want and after you're there, you may see options for delving further into subjects elsewhere in the book.

I organize the book into six parts.

Part 1: Winning with Writing

This part gives you the whole groundwork for writing everything well. Discover a planning structure that helps you strategize your message in every medium and a set of techniques for writing it the best possible way. Apply practical approaches to edit and revise your own work, which empower you to fine-tune your writing and enjoy the process more.

Part 2: Applying Your Skills to Business Messages and Documents

Email and letters remain important communication staples. Everyday messaging helps you build your business relationships and professional image while accomplishing your day-to-day goals. More formal business materials like reports and proposals can be turning-point opportunities. This part shows you how to identify your own writing problems and correct them, and practice a thinking structure that lets you find your best content every time.

Part 3: Writing to Present Yourself Effectively

Strategic thinking based on writing helps you succeed in person as well as in media. This part shows you the how-to you need to create effective elevator speeches and presentations, find and craft your personal story, produce video, and develop talking points to guide you in face-to-face situations, plus tips and techniques for the job hunt: résumés, cover letters, and networking messages.

Part 4: Evolving Your Writing for Online Media

Content is king . . . but today's online reader and consumer have infinite choices, and you need your contributions to engage quickly and deliver substance. Writing is the cornerstone of online media. This part shows you how to adapt your writing style for digital readers, adopt effective techniques, and plan and build blogs and websites. This part also shows you how to create a social media program to build your audience, reputation, authority, and networks.

Part 5: Extending Your Writing Skills

Both in-house workers and independents — business owners, consultants, and freelancers — benefit from thinking like entrepreneurs. This part covers the tools of persuasion, marketing yourself, pitching the media, communicating with teams and bosses, and writing tough messages when you're the boss.

Part 6: The Part of Tens

Many readers find this section the most fun section of the *For Dummies* book series. Look here for ten punchy ideas to advance your career with writing, how to produce quality video, and how to energize your résumé.

Icons Used in This Book

To help you focus on what's most important and move it into memory, look to the icons.

These are practical ideas and techniques you can put to work immediately — and amaze yourself with good results!

This icon keys you in to guidelines and strategies to absorb and use for everything you write.

This icon signals thin ice, don't take the risk! Observe these cautions to avoid endangering your business, image, or cause.

You'll also find sections that begin with, **Try This:**. Why leave all the work to me? Take these opportunities to try your own hand or apply an idea. Nothing builds your skills like practice — and I think you'll enjoy it, and feel more confident.

Beyond the Book

In addition to what you're reading now, this book also comes with a free access-anywhere Cheat Sheet that gives you even more pointers on how to write effectively in the business world. To get this Cheat Sheet, simply go to www.dummies.com and search for "*Business Writing For Dummies* Cheat Sheet" in the Search box.

Where to Go from Here

Starting at the beginning gives you a foundation that applies to everything you write. But if you prefer diving right in for help on a specific challenge, by all means do so. The advice may suggest other sections for more depth and you can follow up as you choose.

Everyone learns differently. Grown-ups enjoy the advantage of knowing their own learning style. Furthermore, we all have our own writing problems to recognize and address. I tell you freely that I have my own, and many of the examples of transforming blah wording to a more powerful version come from editing my own first drafts. To be most useful, I offer choices — different ways to identify problems and improve everything you write.

Build a personal repertoire of techniques that work for you, then take this toolkit on the road with you. Doing so brings you a more successful journey, new confidence, and a lot more fun along the way.

1

Winning with Writing

IN THIS PART . . .

Learn the core elements of good business writing to solve your most pressing communication challenges.

See how a goal-plus-audience strategy will never fail you, no matter how hard the writing challenge seems.

Learn how you can make people care about your message by connecting with your reader, highlighting the benefits, and showing them "what's-in-it-for-me."

Understand how to write for readability and impact in today's business world using the tools of writing — words, sentences, and structure — to say what you mean in a way most likely to earn respect, support, and agreement.

Learn how to switch into the editor's role and fix common writing problems so that your messages accomplish what you want.

Chapter **1**

Make Writing Your Not-So-Secret Weapon

Delivering your message well and being heard. What could be more important in today's world of over-communication?

If your career ladder involves applying for jobs, you need strong résumés, letters, and face-to-face skills. To earn a promotion, your everyday communication must signal your reliability, judgment, and resourcefulness. If you run your own business, or work as a consultant or other professional, I bet your success depends on proposals and presentations. And today, whatever our aspirations, most of us want to create an effective online presence. We want to team successfully with others and advocate for our own needs and ideas.

The foundation for all of this, of course, is . . . writing! Surprisingly few people realize this. When they think about polishing their communication skills, most people jump straight to presentations. Knowing how to give a good speech may seem sexier than writing, but it leapfrogs past the reality: Even a 20-second elevator pitch needs to be written before it's spoken. Good websites, videos, Twitter campaigns, blogs, and most other communication tools start with the written word.

There's a simple reason for this. Human beings think in language. No matter how big a role visuals play in a communication "product," whether print or digital, writing provides the indispensable support structure for planning. And if even a few words appear in the ultimate message, they must be just the right ones.

In this chapter, I highlight the core elements of good business writing and introduce a planning structure that enables you to figure out what to say and how to say it in just about every circumstance. This step-by-step approach to writing works for every communication platform with just a little adaptation for each one. You'll find that improving your writing offers even more benefits than you may suspect, and that you've already begun to build the foundation for it. In later chapters, I show you how to apply these ideas to all your business communication.

Putting Good Writing to Work for You

Can you imagine building relationships without language? Today we initiate most relationships — especially in business — through the written word. In-person contact may follow, or it may not. When the first contact is successful, we continue to rely on writing to build the connection and collaborate.

From everyday email to reports, letters, and digital platforms, today's working world runs on writing. Therefore, the rewards of good writing have never been more extraordinary. The Internet enables us to reach beyond our personal geographic and social reach to almost anyone we want to sell to, collaborate with, or learn from. Almost anyone with time and dedication can start a business and sell a product or service, post her artwork, publish a book, or establish his authority as an expert on a subject.

There's just one catch. Because anyone can do this, unless you are a narrow specialist, the competition is overwhelming.

Consider these statistics:

>> 112.5 billion business email messages are sent daily. (That's 122 messages per user!)

>> There are 130 million active Twitter users, and 303 million tweets per day are sent.

>> The Internet holds 1 billion websites.

>> There are 300 million blogs.

Of course, you're not competing with all of these email messages, tweets, web-sites, and blogs, or reading more than an infinitesimal fraction of them yourself in each medium. But people today — just like you — are extremely selective about what they choose to read because so many options vie for their attention.

REMEMBER

There are few captive audiences in today's world. Check how many messages you've recently received that you *must* read. Even if you hold top-down authority, there's no assurance that your message will be read. Attention, along with respect, must be earned. Writing a message that someone will actually read is an achieve-ment. Writing messages that people will act on demands not just writing that is clear and direct, but also content that is well thought-out and framed to the reader's own perspective. In other words, today's business writing needs to be strategic.

What is *strategic writing?* Planned communication that achieves a set of goals — your goals, and often the goals of your employer and clients. The good news is that you already have a solid base for knowing how to write strategically. You're in command of the three imperatives:

>> **Your subject:** You are invested in your field and possess in-depth knowl-edge of it.

>> **Your audience:** You know who your audience is, such as prospective employers, coworkers, and target markets for your business.

>> **Your goal:** You know what you want, now and in the bigger-picture future.

Here are some of the things you may *not* know yet:

>> How to choose the right communication tool for the job

>> How to capture and retain reader attention

>> How to make people care about your message

>> How to select the right content to make your case

>> How to use writing techniques that make your material persuasive and convincing

>> How to use every single thing you write to build relationships and advance your cause

>> How to understand other people's perspective and predict their responses

>> How to sharpen your ear and eye so you can spot your own writing problems and fix them

I show you how to do all these things in this book.

TIP

Notice that almost every item in this list relates to the *thinking* part of writing, not the technical part. Master the art of thinking your content through and you move way ahead of the competition. But of course, the technical side of writing — how you use language — matters, too. I cover that as well. You'll find a whole resource of practical tips for improving your sentences, word choice, and organization. Instead of grammar lessons, I give you a broad resource of practical tips for improving your sentences, word choice, and organization. Try them out and discover the techniques that work best for you.

Let's start with a planning structure that will help you figure out what you want to say and how to say it. You may be surprised at how much better your messages are received, and how much more often you get a positive response, once you start applying it.

Planning and Structuring Every Message

Faced with a blank page and something to accomplish, many people freeze at the first question: *Where do I start?* The answer? Start with the three components of strategic writing. You already know them:

>> **Your subject:** What you're writing about

>> **Your audience:** Whom you're writing to

>> **Your goal:** What you specifically want to accomplish

To create a good message and get the result you want from your reader, you need to think about all of these things more systematically than you ordinarily might.

REMEMBER

You must "read" your audience in an organized way — I show you how. And you benefit from visualizing your goal in a broad way. Consider that for almost every message you write, you actually have a whole set of goals beyond the immediate: communicating your own professional image, for example. When you combine your knowledge of the audience with your set of goals, it becomes easy to translate what you know about the subject into content that supports your message.

For example, suppose you want to ask your supervisor for a plum assignment you see on the horizon. You can simply write:

> *Jane, I'd like to present myself as a candidate for the lead role on the Crystal Project. You know my work and qualifications. I'll really appreciate the opportunity, and I'll do a great job. Thanks, Jake*

This is maybe okay insofar as it's clear and contains no obvious errors. But it's definitely not compelling. All Jane learns from the message is that Jake wants the opportunity and thinks he's qualified.

Jake would fare better if he first looked at his own goals more in depth. Perhaps he wants a chance to:

Exercise more responsibility

Show off his capabilities and be noticed

Expand his know-how in regard to the project's subject

Add a management credential to his résumé

But he also has the longer term to consider. Jake almost certainly will find it useful to:

Strengthen his position for future special assignments

Remind his boss of his good track record

Build his image as a capable, reliable, resourceful leader

Build toward a promotion or higher-level job in his current organization or elsewhere

From this vantage point, Jake can see the pitch itself as a building block for his overall career ambitions, which calls for a better message than the perfunctory one he dashed off. He must think through the actual assignment demands and how his skills match up. Then there's Jane — his audience — to consider. What qualifications does she, the decision–maker, most value? What does she care about?

After some thought, Jake may come up with a list like this:

Job requires: Planning skills; ability to meet deadlines; knowledge of XYZ systems; experience in intra-departmental coordination; good judgment under pressure

Jane values: Collaborative teaming; people skills; department reputation; effective presentation. She is weak in systems planning and insecure with new technology.

This bit of brainstorming helps Jake produce a blueprint for persuasive content. His email can briefly cite his proven track record in terms of the job requirements, his ability to deliver results as a team leader, his awareness that success will enhance the department's reputation, and that he'll use his excellent presentation skills to ensure this result.

The weaknesses he pinpoints for Jane give Jake another avenue for presenting himself as the best choice. He can suggest a planning system he'll use to make the most of staff resources and/or a specific way to incorporate new easy-to-use technology. These aspects of his message are likely to catch Jane's attention.

All Jake's points must be true, needless to say. I don't suggest ever making up qualifications, but rather, that you take the trouble to communicate the best of what is real and what matters in a particular situation.

Further, never assume people understand your capabilities or remember your achievements, even if they're colleagues who know you well. Other people don't have time to put you in perspective. They're thinking about themselves. That's why doing it yourself has such power.

Even if Jake doesn't get the assignment, writing a good email contributes to his longer-range goals of presenting himself as ready, willing, and able to take on new challenges and to be seen as more valuable.

What Jake's message illustrates is how to use a simple structure for everything you write. My shorthand for this is simply Goal + Audience = Content. When you define what you want to accomplish with a specific message, and think about the specific person you're writing to, content decisions help make themselves.

When you use this structured thinking to plan your messages, whether they're email messages or proposals or anything in between, you move far toward the real heart of good writing — real and relevant substance. Writing is not a system for manipulating words, and don't ever expect it to camouflage a lack of thought, knowledge, or understanding. Good writing is good thinking presented clearly, concisely, and transparently in ways that make sense to your readers.

I make you a rash promise: For every fraction you improve your writing, you'll improve your thinking along with it. Plus, you will improve your ability to understand other people, which will help you build better relationships and achieve what you want more often.

Chapter 2 gives you an in-depth demonstration of this planning structure and shows you how to translate it into successful messages. While you may pick and choose which sections of the book to read and draw upon them at need, I encourage you to invest in Chapter 2. It gives you the entire foundation for deciding *what* to say in any circumstance. Remember that the ideas apply equally to communications that appear to be dominated by visuals or spoken language.

The other essential groundwork for successful writing is *how* to say what you want. Chapters 3, 4, and 5 demonstrate common-sense techniques that professionals use to spot problems and fix them with the least effort.

Try This: To quickly upgrade anything you write, use the *say-it-aloud diagnosis.* When you read your own copy aloud (or whisper it to yourself if you're not alone), you get immediate signals that something isn't working or can work better. You may be forcing your sentences into a sing-song cadence that denotes awkward construction, unnecessary words, and overly long sentences. You may hear repetitive sounds or inappropriate pauses created by poor punctuation. You can easily fix all these problems, and many more, once you identify them this way. Many professional writers use this approach. It works beautifully for business writing, because when well done, your writing sounds conversational.

Chapters 3 through 5 give you a host of down-to-earth strategies for monitoring your own work and improving it. These include computer resources like Microsoft Word's easy-to-use Readability Index, which provides helpful clues for making your writing clear.

WHY LEARNING TO WRITE BETTER MAKES SENSE

If good writing is a skill that can be developed — and based on teaching hundreds of adults, I know it can — you may wonder why you don't currently write as well as you'd like. You already learned to write in school, correct?

Actually, few people did. Unless you were lucky and ran across an unusual teacher, the people who taught you to write never worked on practical writing themselves. Unlike the business world, the academic system is not geared to getting things done, but rather to thinking about them. Writing for school mostly aims to demonstrate your understanding of what you learned, or contribute to the store of human knowledge. Academia traditionally rewards dense, complicated, convoluted writing full of expensive words. This *is* changing, but not very fast.

Business writing, on the other hand, invariably has a goal and is geared toward action. And whatever the goal, it is always best accomplished by being accessible, direct, clear, concrete, and simple. What you write should be conversational as well as engaging and persuasive.

Imitating nineteenth-century writing traditions in your work makes little sense, and striving to produce empty, cliché-ridden twenty-first-century blog posts is just a recipe for boring your readers. However, even though no one wants to read such messages, they surround us. (Why this is true remains a mystery to me.) Therefore, learning to write well gives you a major competitive advantage, and helps set you apart from the crowd.

No matter where you now see yourself on the writing spectrum, I guarantee there's room for improvement. Most journalists, corporate communicators, bloggers, and public relations specialists are obsessive about discovering better ways to write and build their skills. They want to create material that's ever more interesting, persuasive, informative, and engaging.

REMEMBER

For people inhabiting any part of the business, nonprofit, or government worlds, the rewards of better writing are often immediate. Your email and letters get the results you want much more often. Your proposals are more seriously considered and your reports are more valued. You are perceived as more authoritative, credible, and capable. People accord you more respect, often without knowing exactly why. And you move toward your goals faster.

You also find yourself actively building relationships that benefit you over the long run. If a negative relationship hampers you at work, the structured thinking I show you in Chapter 2 even provides a tool for turning that relationship around.

Applying the Goal-Plus-Audience Strategy to All Business Needs

You may have felt challenged at times to write differently for so many forms of communication, or may even have avoided using new or unfamiliar media. Here's the best encouragement I can give you to experiment and venture forth: The strategizing process is the same for all media, present and future. Planning a brief effective email is very much the same as planning a proposal or blog post, presentation, or resume. The Goal + Audience = Content structure will never fail you, no matter how hard the writing challenge seems.

For this reason, I begin with "small" messages like email. Once you absorb the thinking process for this everyday workhorse, you're well prepared to tackle more formal business documents and strategize your digital presence and face-to-face communication.

Succeeding with email, letters, and business documents

Email remains the dominant everyday communication medium at work for most people. In many ways, email is also the most basic, so it's a natural starting point for improving your writing. Even if you don't use email much, it makes a good demonstration medium. So, read the examples knowing the ideas apply to most other writing tasks.

TIP

Don't underestimate the importance or overall impact of email! This workhorse offers a hard-to-beat chance to build your reputation and image, incrementally. You can actually decide how you want to be perceived: Confident? Creative? Inventive? Responsible? Steady? A source of ideas? A problem-solver? Make up your own list and write everything from inside this persona!

REMEMBER

Understanding your audience pays off hugely with email. Analyzing the person who reads your message shows you how to ask for what you want, whether you're requesting an opportunity, inviting someone to a meeting, or pitching something. Further, knowing your audience in-depth enables you to anticipate your reader's response and build in answers to objections he's apt to raise.

Framing the right content at the intersection of goal and audience works equally well for a wide range of business materials (as you find in Chapter 7). You may be surprised to see how the same principles also give you the foundation for long-form materials that often feel like make-or-break opportunities: proposals, reports, and executive summaries. They also equip you to create effective marketing messages and write media releases.

Writing for the spoken word

From a 20-second "elevator speech" to introduce yourself to hosting a webinar, the best system is: plan, write, rehearse, *then* deliver. Chapter 8 shows you how to strategize, write, and prepare for an oral presentation whether formal or less so. Learn how to guide yourself with *talking points,* an essential technique that enables politicians and CEOs to speak effectively and respond to challenges on their feet. It can work wonders for your own preparation and confidence.

You'll find that writing for speech purposes relies on the same structure as writing email, letters, and other business documents — Goal + Audience = Content — but the medium suggests tighter technical guidelines than print. You need to aim for simple, clear language based on short, everyday words in natural speaking patterns. Simplicity takes thought!

The basic planning process applies to scripting your own videos and visual-style social media as well. In most cases, ideas must first be shaped in words, even if the core idea is expressed in a single sentence. And even if words end up playing a minor role on screen.

WARNING

For business purposes, never leave your meaning to people's imagination. Ambiguity invites the audience to make up what they don't understand. Use language to plan, provide context, and connect your visuals, as covered in Chapter 8, along with more traditional scripting techniques.

Writing online: From websites to blogs to tweets

People often assume that when it comes to online content, they can toss all the old writing rules out the virtual window. Big mistake! Digital media with its lightning delivery speed and infinite reach does upend many traditional ideas about communication — top-down thinking, most notably, whereby authoritative figures issue "the word." Today anyone can market a business, entertain the world, and become a journalist or author. But this democratization makes the need to write well more imperative than ever.

WARNING

There are simply too many websites, blogs, tweets, and all the rest to compete against if you don't provide first-rate material people want. The wide-open pioneering days of social media are in some ways over, even though new platforms keep emerging. Any digital guru will tell you that only the very best "content" gains an audience anymore. Translated to concrete terms, that means content that is well-planned, well-worded, and well-edited. Write blogs and posts marred by poor thinking, grammar, or spelling, and you lose credibility and readers. Fail to plan your website from the audience's perspective, and the site won't contribute to your goals. Use Twitter or LinkedIn or Pinterest or Instagram without a business strategy, and you might damage your cause (and reputation) rather than advance it. Chapters 11 and 12 give you the writing know-how you need to communicate in today's digital world and integrate your chosen media into a unified program.

The online world is the great leveler. Never before has there been so much opportunity for individuals, or small enterprises, to make an impact. Equip yourself to use it effectively and the possibilities are boundless. Practice crystallizing your ideas and information into concise, zingy copy. And of course, digital media introduce new demands for interactivity — you want people to respond and share, which demands inventive thinking.

As you read this, I'm sure new technologies are emerging to dazzle and intrigue us. But the newest technology is basically one more delivery system for your messages. You will need clear thinking and good writing to succeed. The techniques presented in this book will not go out of date! But adapt them with imagination.

Special purpose writing

You may or may not remember, depending on your age, the days when a career job meant a nearly lifetime commitment for both employer and employee. That's far from the norm now. In fact, the U.S. government estimates that someone entering the workplace now will hold ten different jobs by the age of 40. People in general stay in jobs an average of 4.4 years. So, for most of us, applying for jobs is an ongoing fact of life. This is especially true if you're part of the Millennial generation, under the age of 35, and share with your cohorts a quick-exit tendency when a job doesn't satisfy you.

Therefore, you need be an outstanding job applicant. I devote a full chapter (Chapter 10) to writing not just résumés and cover letters, but also successful networking messages. You'll also find a special section on how to define and explain your own value and equip yourself for interviews.

If you ultimately hope to take a management role, I've got you covered in Chapter 14. Learn to establish trust, communicate with staff, share your vision, and write inspiring messages. Great leaders often have a particular skill — storytelling. Using stories as well as anecdotes, examples, and testimonials are within your reach, too. Chapter 9 shows you how to find your own story and shape it to your business needs.

Taking the global perspective

This book is based on American business writing style and practice. North Americans are singularly lucky in that their English has become the international language of business, reflecting the United States' economic dominance of the past century. But if you run a cross-national business or work for one, it's a mistake to assume that your audiences in other cultures will read your writing in the way you wish.

Someone who learned English as a second, third, or fourth language may not find your email, letters, and websites easy to understand. Spoken language skills are much easier to acquire than written ones. Further, cultural differences may be much bigger than you think.

WARNING

It's often remarkably hard to realize that everyone is *not* on the same wavelength. Every country and culture has distinct values and perspectives. For writing, this means taking into account factors that include preferred degree of formality, attitude toward business relationships, priorities such as courtesy versus efficiency, specific ways of opening a conversation, and an expectation of directness versus indirectness. In some countries, saying yes may mean no!

REMEMBER

Even if cross-border communication doesn't concern you, most workplaces are increasingly diverse. People don't leave their cultural perspective at home when they come to the office. Your coworkers, partners, and customers may have grown up anywhere in the world.

As with all writing, the challenge should be met on the technical level: How can you write in ways that works for other people, in this case those with limited English-speaking skills? The second aspect is psychological: How can you communicate well with someone whose goals, values, background, and experience are unlike your own, though invisible?

This question relates to the most basic premise of this book. So often we overlook how different people are from each other. You feel that you are unique — and you are. So is everyone else. We each see the world through our own filters, unconsciously constructed of innate characteristics, personal experience, cultural values, and everything we grow up with and that happens to us.

TIP

Taking the trouble to see through other people's filters is what enables you to communicate powerfully and at the same time, understand yourself better. We take for granted how we see things until we notice contrasts, whether cultural, personal, or situational. Your supervisor, for example, has different goals and priorities than yours, as well as different values and problems. Taking this into account helps you communicate authentically and productively.

REMEMBER

Really good business writing is not about formulas, smart responses, and clever manipulation of other people. It is best based on understanding individual people and seeing the world within each one's framework. What does he or she care about? Hope for? Worry about? Writing this way is especially challenging when you communicate with people you've never met and with large unseen audiences, such as through a website or blog.

The syntax of writing — the arrangement of words, phrases, and sentences — is a tool for delivering your messages. Like all tools, it must be used well. But the message is what matters. Understanding your own goals and practicing empathy enables you to build meeting points for true communication and relationships.

Improving your writing will open up your perceptions and sharpen your thinking. There's an aphorism that says, "How do I know what I think until I write it?" In my view, writing is the best imaginable way to grow your understanding of other people, foster your business relationships, and work toward becoming your best and most successful self.

What could be more rewarding or interesting?

You now know *why* improving your writing will benefit you and have already begun building the foundation to do it. The next chapter shows you exactly how to strategize every message to accomplish your goals.

IN THIS CHAPTER

» **Strategizing for success before you write**

» **Knowing your goal and audience**

» **Making people care about your message**

» **Using the correct tone**

» **Finding opportunities to build relationships**

Chapter **2**

Planning Your Message Every Time

Think for a minute about how you approached a recent writing task. If it was an email message, how much time did you spend considering what to write? A few minutes? Seconds? Or did you just start typing?

Now bring a more complex document to mind: a challenging letter, proposal, report, marketing piece, blog post, or anything else. Did you put some time into thinking about and shaping your message before you began writing, or did you just plunge in?

This chapter demonstrates the power of taking time before you write to consider *whom* you're writing to, *what* you truly hope to achieve, and *how* you can generate the right content.

Adopting the Plan-Draft-Edit Principle

Prepare yourself for one of the most important pieces of advice in this book: Invest time in planning your messages. And that means every message. Even an everyday communication such as an email can have a profound impact on your success. Everything you write shows people who you are.

I can't count the times I've received an email asking for a referral or an informational interview that was badly written and full of errors. I didn't respond. Would you? Or a long, expensively produced document with an email cover note that's abrupt and sloppy. A poorly written email message doesn't help the cause — whatever the cause may be.

REMEMBER

I'm not suggesting that prior to writing every email you lean back in your chair and let your mind wander into blue-sky mode to see what emerges. The planning I recommend is a step-by-step process that leads to good decisions about what to say and how to say it. It's a process that will never fail you, no matter how big (or small) the writing challenge. And it's quite simple to adopt — in fact, you may achieve surprisingly quick results. You may also find that after applying this process, you enjoy writing much more.

This strategic approach has no relation to how you learned to write in school, unless you had an atypical teacher who was attuned to writing for results. Start by tossing out any preconceived ideas about your inability to write, because in my experience, *everyone* can learn to write better.

When you have a message or document to write, expect your time to be divided equally between these tasks:

>> Planning

>> Drafting

>> Editing

TIP

Spend one-third of your time deciding what to say (planning), one-third to writing your first draft (drafting), and finally, one-third to sharpening what you wrote (editing).

You probably wonder if this system helps you write faster or slower. For most people it's a time shift. When you take a write-first-then-think approach, you probably get lost in the middle, then stare at your important messages for a while with vague questions about whether they could read better or be more persuasive. Planned messages are easy to organize, and the effectiveness is built in because you've already customized the content to your goal and reader.

What about the editing time at the end? If you don't review your messages at all before sending them, you are doing yourself a disservice. A professional writer with decades of writing experience would *never* send a business communication — even a simple-looking email — without careful review and improvements. Nor should you. The stakes are too high. You need to be your best in everything you write.

The real issue is less about time and more about results. Planned messages bring you what you want much more often. Try the strategy I recommend and see what happens. My money is on more success. Also, this approach quickly becomes a habit and more — it becomes a problem solver. Practice it every day with routine messaging, and you'll be ready to field big challenges with confidence.

Fine-Tuning Your Plan: Your Goals and Audience

A well-crafted message is based on two key aspects: your goal and your audience. The following section shows you how to get to know both intimately.

Defining your goal

Your first priority is to know exactly what you want to happen when the person you're writing to reads what you've written. Determining this is far less obvious than it sounds.

Consider a cover letter for your résumé. Seen as a formal but unimportant necessity toward your ultimate goal — to get a job — a cover letter can just say:

Dear Mr. Blank, Here is my résumé. —Jack Slade

Intuitively you probably know that this isn't sufficient. But analyze what you want to accomplish and you can see clearly why it falls short. Your cover letter must:

>> Connect you with the recipient so that you become a person instead of another set of documents.

>> Make you stand out from the competition in a positive way.

>> Persuade the recipient that your résumé is worth reading.

>> Show that you understand the job and the company.

>> Set up the person to review your qualifications with a favorable mind-set.

You also need the cover letter to demonstrate your personal qualifications, especially the ability to communicate well. If you see that accomplishing your big goal, getting a shot at the job, depends on this set of more specific goals, it's obvious why a one-line perfunctory message won't do well against the competition.

A cover letter for a formal business proposal has its own big goal: help convince an individual or an institution to finance your new product, for example. To do this, the cover letter's role is to connect with the prospective buyer, entice him to actually read at least part of the document, predispose him to like what he sees, present your company as better than the competition, and show off good communication skills.

How about the proposal itself? If you break down this goal into a more specific subset, you realize ideally the proposal must demonstrate:

>> The financial viability of what you plan to produce

>> A minimal investment risk and high profit potential

>> Your own excellent qualifications and track record

>> Outstanding backup by an experienced team

>> Special expertise in the field

>> In-depth knowledge of the marketplace, competition, business environment, and so on

REMEMBER

Spelling out your goals is extremely useful because the process keeps you aligned with the big picture while giving you instant guidelines for effective content. Because of good planning on the front end, you're already moving toward *how* to accomplish what you want.

To reap the benefit of goal definition, you must take time to look past the surface. Write *every* message with a clear set of goals. If you don't know your goals, don't write at all.

Try This: Invariably one of your goals is to present yourself in writing as professional, competent, knowledgeable, creative, empathetic, and so on, but don't let me tell you who you are or want to be! Create a list of the personal and professional qualities you want other people to perceive in you. Then remember, every time you write, be that person. Ask yourself how that individual handles the tough stuff. Your answers may amaze you. This technique isn't mystical, just a way of accessing your own knowledge base and intuition. You may be able to channel this winning persona into your in-person experiences, too.

Defining your audience

You've no doubt noticed that people are genuinely different in countless ways: what they value, their motivations, how they like to spend their time, their attitude toward work and success, how they communicate and make decisions, and much more. One ramification of these variables is that they read and react to your messages in different and sometimes unexpected ways

TIP

As part of your planning you need to anticipate people's reactions to both your content and writing style. The key to successfully predicting your reader's response is to address everything you write to someone specific, rather than an anonymous, faceless "anyone."

When you meet someone in person and want to persuade her to your viewpoint, you automatically adapt to her reactions as you go along. You respond to a host of clues. Beyond interruptions, comments, and questions, you also perceive facial expression, body language, tone of voice, nervous mannerisms, and many other indicators.

REMEMBER

Obviously, a written message lacks all in-person clues. For your message to succeed, you must play both roles — the reader's and your own. Fortunately, doing this isn't as hard as it may sound.

Unless you're sending a truly trivial message, begin by creating a profile of the person you're writing to. There's a really big payoff in doing this for people who are important to you, such as your boss. You emerge with illuminating guidelines on how to improve all your interactions with him or her, as well as knowing what to say and how to say it. This helps you with your face-to-face interaction as well as writing.

When the situation involves someone you don't deal with often, or don't know at all, the depth of the profile you create depends on how important the results are to you. If you're responding to a customer query, you don't need to know his decision-making style. If you're writing to the department head with a request, you might want to find out how much information he prefers to have, what his priorities are, and more.

Before you try profile building, it might seem daunting to characterize someone when so much that drives each person is invisible. Trust me, you know much more about your audience than you think. In the case of a person already familiar to you, your observations, experience, and intuition go a long way. It's a matter of drawing on these resources in a systematic manner, especially your memory of how she reacted to previous interactions.

Try This: Here's the system I recommend. For now, suppose the person is someone you know. Begin with the usual suspects: demographics. Write down what you already know about the person, or take your best guess:

>> How old?

>> Male or female?

>> Occupation?

>> Married, single, or some other arrangement?

>> Member of an ethnic or religious group?

>> Educated to what degree?

>> Social and economic position?

After demographics, consider *psychographics*, the kind of factors marketing specialists spend a lot of time studying. Marketers are interested in creating customer profiles to understand and manipulate consumer buying. For your purposes, some psychographic factors that can matter are:

>> Lifestyle

>> Values and beliefs

>> Opinions and attitudes

>> Interests

>> Leisure and volunteer activities

You also need to consider factors that reflect someone's positioning, personality, and, in truth, entire life history and outlook on the world. Some factors that may directly affect how a person perceives your message include the following:

>> Professional background and experience

>> Position in the organization: What level? Moving up or down? Respected? How ambitious? Happy in the job and with the organization?

>> Degree of authority

>> Leadership style: Team-based? Dictatorial? Collaborative? Indiscernible?

>> Preferred communication style: In-person? Brief or detailed written messages? Telephone? Texting? PowerPoint? Facebook or other social media?

>> Approach to decision-making: Collaborative or top-down? Spontaneous or deliberative? Risk-taker or play-it-safer?

>> Information preferences: Broad vision? In depth? Statistics and numbers? Charts and graphs?

>> Work priorities and pressures

>> Sensitivities and hot buttons: What makes her angry? Happy?

>> Interaction style and preferences: A people person or a numbers, systems, or technology person? Good team member or not?

>> Type of thinking: Logical or intuitive? Statistics-based or ideas-based? Big picture or micro-oriented? Looking for long-range or immediate results?

>> Weaknesses (perceived by the person or not): Lack of tech savvy? Poor people skills? Lack of education and training? No experience?

>> Type of people the person likes, feels comfortable with, and respects, and the reverse: Who likes and gets along with him?

>> Sense of humor, personal passions, hobbies

TIP

Do you know, or can you figure out, what your reader worries about? What keeps him up at night? His biggest problem? When you know a person's concerns, you can create more compelling messages. I am not suggesting your aim should be manipulative. Taking the trouble to think within another person's framework is respectful. Wouldn't you rather be addressed in a way that acknowledges what matters to you most when you need to make a decision, for example?

And of course, your precise relationship to the person matters, as well as your relative positioning and the degree of mutual liking, respect, and trust — the *simpatico* factor.

TIP

I'm sure you're wondering how you can possibly take so much into consideration, or why you would want to. The good news: When your message is truly simple, you usually don't. More good news: Even when your goal is complex or important, only some factors matter. I'm giving you a lengthy list to draw on because every situation brings different characteristics into play. Thinking through which ones count in your specific situation is crucial and rarely hard.

For example, say you want authorization to produce a video explaining your department's work to show at an employee event. Perhaps your boss is someone who's enthusiastic about video. Or you may report to someone who values relationships and wants to cultivate a positive environment. This boss would probably welcome a way to show staff members they are valued. Or she may be a person who likes innovation and the chance to be first in the neighborhood. To gain approval, it's best to frame the story differently for the specific decision-maker. I'm not saying you should distort the facts or omit any: The story you tell must be true and fair. But the focus and emphasis can be adapted.

REMEMBER

You succeed when you take the time to look at things through another person's eyes rather than solely your own. Doing so doesn't compromise your principles. It shows that you're sensible and sensitive to the differences between people and helps your relationships. It tells you how to frame what you're asking for.

GENERATION GAPS: UNDERSTANDING AND LEVERAGING THEM

In almost every workplace employing more than a few people, generational differences present some major challenges. Sweeping generalizations based on when people were born may seem suspect, but we are all shaped by the culture and time period we grow up in. Our beliefs, communication and decision-making styles, interaction patterns, and expectations of each other can be at odds. Misunderstandings flourish. In response, consultants are at work explaining the groups to each other, marketers are researching the young people they must market to, and human resource specialists try to smooth cross-generational conflicts so their companies can function better.

Whatever age group you belong to, you will benefit from some empathy for the other cohorts. Supplement the following ideas with your own observations and you'll discover ways to make subordinates and higher-ups happy without the risk of compromising your own values. Here are some tips to support sympathetic workplace relationships:

- **Baby Boomers** (born 1946 to 1964) are highly competitive and define themselves by achievement. Many are workaholics. Although Boomers wanted to change the world and fought for change (civil rights, women's role), on the whole they respect authority, loyalty, position, and hard work that creates upward progress. They would like today's young people to advance the same way they did: earning rewards (and confidence) gradually over time.

  Communication style: Good with confrontation and face-to-face; hold meetings often; like the telephone, email, and detailed information; get information from newspapers and television; many use Facebook, LinkedIn, and Twitter.

  React badly to: Younger people's perceived lack of respect, low commitment level, expectations of fast progress, constant need for mentoring, arrogance about their own superior technology skills, and careless writing!

  React well to: A can-do attitude, willingness to work hard and overcome obstacles, respect for their achievements and knowledge, and well-planned and proofed messages.

- **Generation X** (born 1965 to 1980) is a relatively small generation literally caught in the middle. They are often middle managers and must translate between those they report to and those who report to them. They are hard-working, individualistic, committed to change, and seeking life balance. They value opportunities to build skills.

  Communication style: Depend on email, preferably short and efficient, would prefer to skip meetings; comfortable with new technology and social media (especially Facebook) to varying degree, but without the full enthusiasm of younger people; refer to television and to a lesser extent, newspapers, for information.

  React badly to: Autocratic, unappreciative managers; an air of entitlement from subordinates and subordinates' need for constant attention, encouragement, and supervision, and unwillingness to go the extra mile and adapt to workplace needs; impatience; "unearned" confidence.

  React well to: Resourcefulness, independence, sense of responsibility, attention to detail, willingness to take on "uninteresting" assignments, good communication.

- **Millennials** (also known as Generation Y) (born 1981 to 1996) belong to an especially large generation and face strong competition but fewer opportunities. They are highly social and communal-minded, preferring to work in teams and in close touch with everyone else inside and outside the office. They want responsibility — quickly — plus intensive mentoring. They expect to spend their careers job-hopping and experimenting with other income sources. They are non-materialistic and typically leave jobs quickly when unengaged, even without another in sight. Accord high value to active experience, inclusiveness, and tolerance.

  Communication style: Digital all the way; prefer to interact through texting, instant messaging, and social media, especially Facebook; draw news and information from the Internet; use email only as required; unenthusiastic about telephone contact, meetings, and confrontation.

  React badly to: Lack of respect; insufficient encouragement, appreciation, inclusion, and fast rewards; not being given reasons for assignments; not being accommodated in lifestyle preferences; being required to work with old technology.

  React well to: Coaching, opportunities to learn and grow, sense of purpose, being valued, explanations, new experiences, constant communication, teaming, and insights into the big picture.

- **Generation Z** (also known as the Homeland Generation) (born 1997 to 2010) is an unknown element of the workplace as yet. Growing up with the experience of a Great Recession and the War on Terror, this most parent-protected group of all shows signs of being more conservative, fearful, pragmatic, and concerned with privacy. They are the first "true digital natives" and use their smartphones for all information, entertainment, and communication, but few phone calls. In social media, they prefer the ephemeral Snapchat and Instagram.

Brainstorming the best content for your purpose

Perhaps defining your goal and audience so thoroughly sounds like unnecessary busy-work. But doing so helps immeasurably when you're approaching someone with an idea, product, or service that you need him to buy into.

Suppose your department is planning to launch a major project that you want to lead. You could write a memo explaining how important the opportunity is to you, how much you can use the extra money, or how much you'll appreciate being chosen for the new role. But unless your boss, Mark, is a totally selfless person without ambition or priorities of his own, why would he care about any of that?

You're much better off highlighting your relevant skills and accomplishments. Your competitors for the leadership position may equal or even better such a run-down, so you must make your best case. Think beyond yourself to what matters most to Mark.

A quick profile of Mark reveals a few characteristics to work with:

>> He likes to see good teamwork in people reporting to him.

>> He's a workaholic who is usually overcommitted.

>> He likes to launch projects and then basically forget about them until results are due.

>> He's ambitious and always angling for his next step up.

Considering what you know about Mark, the content of your message can correspond to these traits by including:

>> Your good record as both a team player and team leader

>> Your dedication to the new project and willingness to work over and beyond normal hours to do it right

>> Your ability to work independently and use good judgment with minimal supervision

>> Your enthusiasm for this particular project, which, if successful, will be highly valued by the department and company

Again, all your claims must be true, and you need to provide evidence that they are. For example, you could include a reminder of another project you successfully directed and handled independently.

Your reader profile can tell you still more. If you wonder how long your memo needs to be, consider Mark's communication preferences. If he prefers brief memos followed by face-to-face decision-making, keep your memo concise, but still cover the major points to secure that all-important meeting. However, if he reacts best to written detail, give him more information up front.

Creating a reader profile enables you to create a blueprint for the content of all your messages and documents. After you've defined what you want and analyzed your audience in relation to the request, brainstorm the points that may help you win your case *with that person.* Your brainstorming gives you a list of possibilities. Winnowing out the most convincing points is easy, and you can organize simply by prioritizing, as I show you how to do in Chapter 3.

TIP

Thinking through how to profile your reader works equally well when you're writing a major proposal, a business plan, a report, a funding request, a client letter, a marketing piece, a blog, a Microsoft PowerPoint presentation, networking message, or website copy. Know your goal. Know who your intended audience is and what that person or group cares about. Then think widely within that perspective.

REMEMBER

Another way to think about your content is to consider that everything you write is an "ask." Even a message that just conveys information is asking your audience to read it and act upon it in some way, if only to absorb or file it. An event announcement asks the recipient to take note and usually, you're asking her to feel motivated to participate. A "congratulations on your promotion" note asks the lucky person to notice that you're on her side.

Try to think of a written communication that doesn't ask for something. It's pretty tough. There's an advantage to seeing every message as a request: Doing so sets you up to frame your message with the right content for the person to whom you're writing.

Writing to groups and strangers

Profiling someone you know is relatively easy, but you often write to groups rather than individuals, as well as to people you haven't met and know nothing about. The same ideas covered in the preceding section apply to groups and strangers, but they demand a little more imagination on your part.

TIP

Here's a good tactic for writing messages addressed to groups: Visualize a single individual — and/or a few key individuals — who epitomize that group. The financier Warren Buffet explained that when writing to stockholders, he imagines he's writing to his two sisters: They are intelligent, but not knowledgeable about finance. He consciously aims to be understood by them. The results are admirably clear financial messages that are well received and influential.

Like Buffet, you may be able to think of a particular person to represent a larger group. If you've invented a new item of ski equipment, for example, think about a skier you know who'd be interested in your product and profile that person. Or create a composite profile of several such people, drawing on what they have in common plus variations. If you're a business strategy consultant, think of your best clients and use what you know about them to profile your prospects.

Imagining your readers

Even when an audience is entirely new to you, you can still make good generalizations about what these people are like and even better, their needs. Suppose you're a dentist who's taking over a practice and writing to introduce yourself to your predecessor's patients. Your basic goal is to maintain that clientele. You needn't know the people to anticipate many of their probable concerns. You can assume, for example, that your news will be unwelcome because long-standing patients probably liked the old dentist and dislike change and inconvenience, just like you probably would yourself.

You can go further. Anticipate your readers' questions. Just put yourself in their shoes. The dental patients may wonder:

>> Why should I trust you, someone I don't know?

>> Will I feel an interruption in my care? Will there be a learning curve?

>> Will I like you and find in you what I value in a medical practitioner — aspects such as kindness, respect for my time, attentiveness, and experience?

TIP

Plan your content to answer the questions your readers would ask, and you won't go wrong. You'll save time, too. How many memos do you send or receive daily, asking for clarification or trying to sort out some kind of confusion? Careless communication is a huge concern for business leaders. One badly written email sent to ten people can waste many hours of collective work just to retrieve the situation. An even bigger worry is the impact of mistakes generated by poor communication. Recently an auto company's engineers failed to clearly describe a safety problem to upper management, with disastrous consequences. On an everyday basis, minor variations on this theme occur everywhere.

TIP

Notice that in addition to being "me"-centered, nearly all the questions asked by the dental patients are emotional in nature rather than factual. Few patients are likely to ask about a new doctor's training and specific knowledge. They take that for granted. They're more concerned with the kind of person he is and how they'll be treated. This somewhat counterintuitive truth applies to many situations.

Good salesmen don't pitch themselves — they pitch their ability to make the customer's life better. Notice also that the questions would be essentially the same for a new accountant or any other service provider.

When writing, you may need to build a somewhat indirect response to some of the questions you anticipate from readers. Writing something like "I'm a really nice person" to the dental patients is unlikely to convince them, but you can comfortably include any or all of the following statements in your letter:

I will carefully review all the records so I am personally knowledgeable about your history.

My staff and I pledge to keep your waiting time to a minimum. We use all the latest techniques to make your visits comfortable and pain-free.

I look forward to meeting you in person and getting to know you.

I'm part of your community and participate in its good causes such as . . .

REMEMBER

Apply this audience analysis strategy to job applications, business proposals, online media, and other important materials. Ask yourself, whom do I want to reach? Is the person a human resources executive? A CEO? A prospective customer for my product or service? Then jot down a profile covering what that person is probably like and what her concerns and questions may be.

Everyone has a problem to solve. What's your reader's problem? The HR executive must fill open jobs in ways that satisfy other people. The CEO can pretty well be counted on to have one eye on the bottom line and the other on the big picture — that's her role. If you're pitching a product, you can base a prospective customer profile on the person for whom you're producing that product.

Making People Care

Sending your words out into today's message-dense world is not unlike tossing them into the sea in a bottle. Worse, your message is now among a trillion bottles, all of which are trying to reach the same moving and dodging targets. So, your competitive edge is in shaping a better bottle . . . or rather, message.

Any message you send must be well crafted and well-aimed, regardless of the medium or format. The challenge is to make people care enough to read your message and act on it in some way. The following sections explore the tools you need to ensure your bottle reaches its target, that the target is moved to take the message out, and that the message makes the impact you desire.

Connecting instantly with your reader

Only in rare cases do you have the luxury these days of building up to a grand conclusion, one step at a time. Your audience simply won't stick around.

REMEMBER

The opening paragraph of anything you write must instantly hook your readers. The best way to do this is to link directly to their central interests and concerns within the framework of your purpose.

Suppose you're informing the staff that the office will be closed on Tuesday to install new air conditioning. You can write:

> *Subject: About next Tuesday*
>
> *Dear Staff:*
>
> *As you know, the company is always interested in your comfort and well-being. As part of our company improvement plan this past year, we've installed improved lighting in the hallways, and in response to your request that we . . .*

Stop! No one is reading this! Instead, try this:

> *Subject: Office closed Tuesday*
>
> *We're installing new air conditioning! Tuesday is the day, so we're giving you a holiday.*
>
> *I'm happy the company is able to respond to your number one request on the staff survey and hope you are, too.*

TIP

One of the best ways to hook readers is also the simplest: Get to the point. The technique applies even to long documents. Start with the bottom line, such as the result you achieved, the strategy you recommend, or the action you want. In a report or proposal, the executive summary is often the way to do that, but note that even this micro version of your full message still needs to lead off with your most important point.

Notice in the preceding example that the subject line of the email is part of the lead and planned to hook readers as much as the first paragraph of the actual message. Chapter 6 has more ideas of ways to optimize your email communication.

Focusing on what's-in-it-for-me

In marketers' terms, the acronym is WIIFM (what's-in-it-for-me). The air-conditioning email in the preceding section captures readers by telling them first that they have a day off, then follows up by saying that they're getting something they wanted. Figuring out what's going to engage *your* readers often takes a bit of thought.

To make people care, you must first be able to answer the question yourself. Why *should* they care? Then put your answer right in the lead or even the headline.

If you're selling a product or service, for example, zero in on the problem it solves. Rather than your press release headline saying,

> *New Widget Model to Debut at Expo Magnus on Thursday*

Try:

> *Widget 175F Day-to-Night VideoCam Ends Pilfering Instantly*

If you're raising money for a nonprofit, you may be tempted to write a letter to previous donors that begins like many you probably receive:

> *For 25 years, Freedom's Path has helped incarcerated women transition to the outside world by providing job training, counseling, and support services. Your donations have been essential to equipping young transgressors to . . .*

This sounds worthy but yawn-inducing. Would you respond better to a letter that opens more like this?

> *When we talked to 19-year-old Jenny Y., she was holding back tears. "Sure, I'll get out in six months, but so what? Where's my life? No family. No education. I'll be right back on the street and what else can I do than go back with the friends who got me here. I don't want to. But I don't have a choice."*
>
> *Against the odds and for the first time in her life, Jenny was lucky. We picked her for the Second Chance Program and gave her a new start . . .*
>
> *We want to help more Jennys. And with your help we can . . .*

The second version works better not just because it's more concrete, but because it takes into account two factors that all recipients probably share: (1) a concern for disadvantaged young people, and (2) a need to be reassured that their donations are well used.

Highlighting benefits, not features

People care about what a product or service can do for them, not what it is.

>> *Features* describe characteristics: a car having a 200-mph engine; an energy drink containing 500 units of caffeine; a hotel room furnished with priceless antiques.

>> *Benefits* are what features give us: the feeling that you can be the fastest animal on earth (given an open highway without radar traps); the ability to stay up for 56 hours to make up all the work you neglected; the experience of high luxury for the price of a hotel room, at least briefly.

Benefits have more to do with feelings and experiences than actual data. Marketers have long understood the power of benefits, but psychologists now confirm that most buying decisions are made emotionally rather than logically. You choose a car that speaks to your personality instead of the one with the best technical specs, and then you try to justify your decision on rational grounds. You buy a dress that makes you feel beautiful, not because the seams are cleverly designed.

REMEMBER

The lesson for business writing is clear: People care about messages that are based on what really matters to them. Don't get lost in technical detail. Focus on the impact of an event, idea, or product. You can cover the specs, but keep them contained in a separate section or as backup material. Approach information the way most newspapers have always done (and now do online as well). Put what's most interesting or compelling up front and then include the details in the back (or link to them) for readers who want more.

Finding the concrete, limiting the abstract

The Freedom's Path example in the previous section demonstrates that focusing on a single individual delivers a more effective message. One concrete example is almost always better than reams of high-flown prose and empty adjectives. Make things real with techniques like these:

>> **Tell stories and anecdotes.** They must embody the idea you want to communicate, the nature of your organization, or your own value. An early television show about New York City used a slogan along the lines, "Eight million people, eight million stories." A good story is always there, lurking, even in what may seem mundane or ordinary. But finding it can take some thinking and active looking.

>> **Use specific examples.** Tell customers how your product was used or how your service helped solve a problem. Give them strong case studies of implementations that worked. Inside a company, tell change-resistant staff members how another department saved three hours by using the new ordering process, or how a shift in benefits can cut their out-of-pocket healthcare costs by 14 percent. And if you want people to use a new system, give them clear guidelines, perhaps a step-by-step process to follow.

>> **Use visuals to explain and break up the words.** Readers who need to be captured and engaged generally shy away from uninterrupted type. Plenty of studies show that people are much more drawn to read material like blogs,

articles, and social posts when there is a good visual element. When you're depending on words, look for ways to graphically present a trend, a change, a plan, a concept, or an example. Incorporate photographs, illustrations, charts, graphs, and video to suit your purpose. When you must deliver your message primarily in words, use graphic techniques like headlines, subheads, bullets, typeface variations, and icons — like this book!

>> **Give readers a vision.** Good leaders know that a vision is essential, whether they're running companies or running for public office. You're usually best off framing your message in big-picture terms that make people believe the future will be better in some way. Don't make empty promises; instead, look for the broadest implications of what you want to communicate and use details to back up that central concept and make it more real. Will your product or service save readers time or money? Make them healthier or more attractive? Those are bottom-line messages for everyone. Framing a complicated document within a broad vision also makes it more organized and more memorable — both big advantages.

>> **Eliminate meaningless hyperbole.** What's the point of saying something such as, "This is the most far-reaching, innovative, ground-breaking piece of industrial design ever conceived"? Yet business writing is jampacked with empty, boring claims.

WARNING

Today's audiences come to everything you write already jaded, skeptical, and impatient. If you're a service provider and describe what you do in words that can belong to anyone, in any profession, you fail. If you depend on a website and it takes viewers 20 seconds to figure out what you're selling or how to make a purchase, you lose. If you're sending out a press release that buries what's interesting or important, you're invisible. The antidote: Know your point and make it fast!

TIP

Go for the evidence! Tell your audience in real terms what your idea, plan, or product accomplishes in ways they care about. Show them

>> How the product improves their lives

>> How the nonprofit is helping people and prove it

>> How the service solves problems

>> How you personally helped your employer make more money or become more efficient

Proof comes in many forms: statistics, data, images, testimonials, surveys, awards, promotions, case histories, biographies, social media followers and likes, and video and audio clips. Figure out how to track your success and prove it. You end up with first-rate material to use in all your communication.

Choosing Your Written Voice: Tone

Presentation trainers often state that the meaning of a spoken message is communicated 55 percent by body language, 38 percent by tone of voice, and only 7 percent by the words. Actually, this formula has been thoroughly debunked and denied by its creator, the psychologist Albert Mehrabian, because it misinterpreted a very limited study. However, it does suggest some important points for writing.

WARNING

Written messages come without body language or tone of voice. One result is that humor in written messages — particularly sarcasm or irony — is risky. When readers can't see the wink in your eye or hear the playfulness in your voice, they take you literally. So, refrain from subtle humor unless you're really secure with your reader's ability to "get it." Better yet: Be cautious at all times because such assumptions are dangerous.

But even lacking facial expression and gesture, writing does carry its own tone, and this directly affects how readers receive and respond to messages. Written tone results from a combination of word choice, sentence structure, and other technical factors.

Also important are less tangible elements that are hard to pin down. You've probably received messages that led you to sense the writer was upset, angry, resistant, or amused, even if only a few words were involved. Sometimes even a close reading of the text doesn't explain what's carrying these emotions, but you just sense the writer's strong feelings.

REMEMBER

When you're the writer, be conscious of your message's tone. Consistently control the tone so that it supports your goals and avoids undermining your message. You've probably found that showing emotion in the workplace rarely gives you an advantage, usually the opposite. Writing is similar. Tone conveys feelings, and if you're not in control of your emotions when you write, tone betrays you. The following sections explore some ways to find and adopt the right tone.

Aligning tone with the occasion, relationship, and culture

Pause before writing and think about the nature of the message. Obviously if you're communicating bad news, you don't want to sound chipper and cheery. Always think of your larger audience, too. If the company made more money last month because it eliminated a department, best not to treat the new profits as a triumph. Current staff members probably aren't happy about losing colleagues and are worried about their own jobs. On the other hand, if you're communicating about a staff holiday party, sounding gloomy and bored doesn't generate high hopes for a good time. The same is true if you're offering an opportunity or assigning a nuisance job: Find the enticing side.

REMEMBER

Just as in face-to-face situations, the moods embedded in your writing are contagious. If you want an enthusiastic response, then write with enthusiasm. If you want people to welcome a change you're announcing, sound positive and confident, not fearful or peevish and resentful, even if you don't personally agree with the change.

TIP

Make conscious decisions about how formal to sound. After you work in an organization for a while, you typically absorb its culture without really noticing. In fact, most people don't realize their organizations have a culture until they run into problems when introducing change or a high-level hire. If you're new to the place, observe how things work so you can avoid booby-trapping yourself. Read through files of correspondence, email, reports, as well as websites and online material. Analyze what your colleagues feel is appropriate in content and in writing style. What communication media are used? How formal is the tone? Adopt the guidelines you see enacted.

WARNING

Every passing year seems to decrease the formality of business communication. Just as in choosing what to wear to work, people are dressing down their writing. This less formal style can come across as friendlier, simpler, and more direct than in earlier years — and should. But business informal doesn't mean you should address an executive or board member casually, use abbreviations or emoji your reader may not like, or fail to edit and proofread every message. Those are gaffes much like wearing torn jeans to work or to a client meeting.

And you want to be especially careful if you're writing to someone in another country, even an English-speaking one. Most countries still prefer a more formal form of communication than American business English.

Writing as your authentic self

Authentic means being a straightforward, unpretentious, honest, trustworthy person — and writer. It doesn't mean trying for a specific writing style. Clarity is always the goalpost. This absolutely holds true even for materials written to impress. A proposal, marketing brochure, or request for funding gains nothing by looking or sounding pompous and weighty.

TIP

Never try to impress anyone with how educated and literate you are. Studies show that in reality people believe that those who write clearly and use simple words are smarter than those whose writing abounds in fancy phrases and complicated sentences.

Smiling when you say it

People whose job is answering the phone are told by customer service trainers to smile before picking up the call. Smiling physically affects your throat and vocal chords, and your tone of voice. You sound friendly and cheerful and may help the person on the other end of the phone feel that way, too.

The idea applies to writing as well. You need not smile before you write (though it's an interesting technique to try), but be aware of your own mood and how easily it transfers to your messages and documents.

REMEMBER

I'm not saying your feelings of anger, impatience, or resentment aren't well-grounded, but displaying them rarely helps your cause. Nobody likes to get negative, whiny, nasty messages that put them on the defensive or make them feel under attack. Suppose you've asked the purchasing department to buy a table for your office and were denied without explanation. You could write to both your boss and the head of purchasing a note such as the following:

> *Hal, Jeanne: I just can't believe how indifferent purchasing is to my work and what I need to do it. This ignorance is really offensive. I'm now an Associate Manager responsible for a three-person team and regular meetings are essential to my . . .*

Put yourself in the recipients' places to see how bad the impact of such a message can be — for you. At the least, you're creating unnecessary problems, and at worst, perhaps permanent bad feelings. Why not write (and just to the purchasing officer) this, instead:

> *Hi, Hal. Do you have a minute to talk about my request for a small conference table? I was surprised to find that it was denied and want to share why it's important to my work.*

REMEMBER

The best way to control your tone is to let emotion-laden matters rest for whatever time you can manage. Even a ten-minute wait can make a difference. Overnight is better, if possible, in important situations. You're far more likely to accomplish what you want when you come across as logical, reasonable, and objective. Positive and cheerful is even better.

Try This: If you don't have the luxury of waiting for a good mood to hit before writing, try a method I often use. I churn out the basic document regardless of my spirits, and later when I'm feeling bouncier, inject the energy and enthusiasm I know the original message is missing. Typical changes involve switching out dull passive verbs and substituting livelier ones, picking up the tempo, editing out the dead wood, and adding plusses I overlooked when I felt gray. Chapter 3 is chock-full of ideas to energize your language.

People naturally prefer being around positive, dynamic, enthusiastic people, and they prefer receiving messages with the same qualities. Resolve not to complain, quibble, or criticize in writing. People are much more inclined to give you what you want when you're positive — and they see you as a problem-solver rather than a problem-generator.

Using Relationship-Building Techniques

REMEMBER

Just about everything you write is a chance to build relationships with people you report to and even other people above them in the chain, as well as peers, colleagues, customers, prospects, suppliers, and members of your industry. More and more, people succeed through good networking. In a world characterized by less face-to-face contact and more global possibilities, writing is a major tool for making connections and maintaining them.

As with tone, awareness that building relationships is always one of your goals puts you a giant step ahead. Ask yourself every time you write how you can improve the relationships with that individual. A range of techniques is available to help.

Showing active caring and respect

REMEMBER

Never underestimate or patronize your audience, regardless of educational level, position, or apparent accomplishment. People are quite sensitive to such attitudes and react adversely, often without knowing why or telling you. In *all* work and business situations, take the trouble to actively demonstrate respect for your reader. Specifically:

>> Address people courteously and use their names.

>> Close with courtesy and friendliness.

>> Write carefully and proofread thoroughly; many people find poorly written messages insulting.

>> Avoid acronyms, jargon, emoji, and abbreviations that may be unfamiliar to some readers.

>> Never be abrupt or rude or demanding.

>> Take the trouble to consider cultural differences.

Apply these guidelines whether you're writing to a superior, a subordinate, or peer. You don't need to be obsequious to an executive higher up the chain than you are (in most cases), though often you should be more formal. Nor should you condescend to those lower down. Consider, for example, how best to assign a last-minute task to someone who reports to you. You could say,

> Terry, I need you to research consultants who specialize in cultural change and send me 10 names tomorrow. Thanks.

Or:

> Terry, I need your help. The CEO called a surprise meeting for tomorrow afternoon to discuss ideas for making some organizational changes. I'd like to be ready to describe some consultants we might call on. Can you do the groundwork by morning and come up with 10 possible specialists? I'll appreciate it very much. Thanks!

Either way, Terry may not be thrilled at how his evening looks, but treating him respectfully and explaining *why* you're giving him this overtime assignment accomplishes a lot: He'll be more motivated, more enthusiastic, more interested in doing a good job and happier to be part of your team. At the cost of writing a few more sentences, you improve your subordinate's attitude and perhaps even his long-range performance.

TIP

Explaining how assignments fit into the bigger picture and why they matter is especially inspiring to Millennials. If you have people under 35 reporting to you, take note.

Whatever their age, people who report to you are doing your work and helping you perform better and look good. Why not make them feel as important as they are, in ways that matter to them?

Personalizing what you write

In many countries, business email and letters that get right down to business seem cold, abrupt, and unfeeling. Japanese writers and readers, for example, prefer to begin with the kind of polite comments you tend to make when meeting someone in person: "How have you been?" "Is your family well?" "Isn't it cold for October?" Such comments or questions may carry no real substance, but they serve an important purpose. They personalize the interaction to better set the stage for a business conversation.

TIP

In any culture, creating a sense of caring or at least interest in the other person gives you a much better context within which to transact business. If you've thought about your audience when planning what to write (see "Defining your audience" earlier in this chapter), you can easily come up with simple but effective personalizing phrases to frame your message. You can always fall back on the old reliables: weather and general health inquiries. If communication continues, you can move the good feelings along by asking whether the vacation mentioned earlier worked out well, or if the weekend was good — whatever clues you can follow up on without becoming inappropriate or intrusive. The idea works when you address groups, too: You can, for example, begin, "I hope you all weathered the snowstorm okay."

Some techniques you can use to make your writing feel warm are useful, but they may not translate between different cultures. For example, salutations like *Hi, John* set a less formal tone than *Dear John*. Starting with just the recipient's name — *John* — is informal to the point of assuming a relationship already exists. But both ways may not be appropriate if you're writing to someone in a more formal country than your own. A formal address, such as Mr. Charles, Ms. Brown, Dr. Jones, General Frank, may be called for. In many cultures, if you overlook this formality and other signs of respect, you can lose points before you even begin. Or not even get the chance to begin.

Framing messages with "you" not "I"

Embrace this basic concept: People care infinitely more about themselves, their problems, and what they want than they do about you. This simple-sounding premise has important implications for business communication.

Suppose you're a software developer and your company has come up with a new template for creating a home page. Your first thought for an announcement on your website might be:

> *We've created an amazing new home page template better than anyone ever imagined was possible.*

Or you could say:

> *Our great new Template X helps people build beautiful home pages with the least effort ever.*

The second example is better because it's less abstract and it makes the product's purpose clear. But see if you find this version even more effective:

> *Want a faster way to create a knock-out home page in half the time, with resources you already own? We have what you need: Template X.*

When you look for ways to use the word *you* more, even implicitly (the first sentence of the last pitch omits the "you"), and correspondingly decrease the use of *I* and *we*, you put yourself on the reader's wavelength. In the case of the new template, your readers care about how the product can help them, not that you're proud of achieving it.

The principle works for everyday email, letters, and online communication, too. For example, when you receive a customer complaint, instead of saying,

We have received your complaint about . . .

You're better off writing:

Your letter explaining your disappointment with our product has been received . . .

Or, much better:

Thank you for writing to us about your recent problem with . . .

Coming up with a "you frame" can be challenging. It may draw you into convoluted or passive-sounding language, such as, "Your unusual experience with our tree-pruning service has come to our attention." Ordinarily I recommend a direct statement (like, "We hear you've had an unusual experience with . . ."), but in customer service situations and others where you need to instantly relate to your reader, figuring out a way to start with "you" can be worth the effort and a brief dip into passive voice.

In every situation, genuinely consider your reader's viewpoint, sensitivities, and needs. Think about how the message you're communicating affects that person or group. Anticipate questions and build in the answers. Write within this framework and you will guide yourself to create successful messages and documents.

Before sending a message, always ask yourself: How will it make the person feel? When you care, it shows. And you succeed.

In Chapters 3, 4, and 5, I give you a full set of techniques to draw on for delivering your message clearly and powerfully. Discover how to use the tools of writing — words, sentences, and structure — to say what you mean in a way most likely to earn respect, support, and agreement.

Chapter **3**

Making Your Writing Work: The Basics

Your writing style probably took shape in school where literary traditions and formal essays dominate. This experience may have led you to believe that subtle thoughts require complex sentences, sophisticated vocabulary, and dense presentation. Perhaps you learned to write that way — or maybe you didn't. Either way: Get over it. The rules of academic writing don't apply to the business world.

Real-world business writing is more natural, reader-friendly, and easier than academic writing — especially after you learn the essential techniques covered in this chapter.

Stepping into Twenty-First-Century Writing Style

REMEMBER

In business, you succeed when you achieve your goals. You need to judge business writing the same way — by whether it accomplishes what you want. What works is:

» **Clear and simple language:** Except for technical material directed at specialists, no subject matter or idea is so complex that you cannot express it in clear, simple language. You automatically move forward a step by accepting this basic premise and practicing it.

>> **A conversational tone:** Business writing is reader-friendly and accessible, far closer to spoken language than the more formal and traditional style. It may even come across as casual or spontaneous. This quality, however, doesn't give you a free pass on grammar, punctuation, and the other technicalities.

>> **Accuracy:** Noticeable mistakes interfere with your reader's ability to understand you. Further, careful writing is critical to how people evaluate your credibility and authority. Every reader responds, consciously or not, to the clues that tell him or her whether to take you seriously. Carelessness loses you points. However, good contemporary writing allows substantial leeway in observing grammatical niceties.

>> **Friendly persuasion:** When you dig beneath the surface, most messages and documents ask something of the reader. This request may be minor ("Meet me at the coffee shop at 4") to major ("Please fund this proposal; $1 million will do"). Even when you're just asking someone to provide information, frame your message to suit that person's viewpoint. This is covered in Chapter 2.

All these indicators of successful business communication come into play in everything you write. The following sections break down the various components of style into separate bits you can examine and adjust in your own writing.

Aiming for a clear, simple style

Clarity and simplicity go hand in hand. It means your messages communicate what you intend with no room for misunderstanding or misinterpretation. Your reason for writing, and what you want the reader to do as a result of reading the message, are equally clear. This requires using:

>> Words your reader already knows and whose meanings are agreed upon — no forcing readers to look up words; no trying to impress

>> Sentences centered on simple, active verbs in the present tense when possible (for example, "Jane wrote the report" rather than "the report has been written by Jane")

>> A sentence structure that readers can easily follow

>> Well-organized, logical, on-point content without anything unnecessary or distracting

>> Clear connections between sentences, paragraphs, and ultimately ideas, so your statement is cohesive

>> Correct spelling and basic grammar

Writing with the preceding characteristics is transparent — nothing stands in the way of the reader absorbing your information, ideas, and requests. Good business writing for most purposes doesn't call attention to itself. It's like a good makeup job. A woman doesn't want to hear, "Great cosmetology!" She hopes for, "You look beautiful." Similarly, you want your audience to admire your thinking, not the way you phrased it.

One result of meeting these criteria is that people can move through your material quickly. This is good! A fast read is your best shot at pulling people into your message and keeping them from straying off because they're bored. These days we are all so overwhelmed and impatient that we often don't bother to invest time in deciphering a message's meaning. We just stop reading.

Creating an easy reading experience is hard on the writer. Just like a simple dress or suit is often more expensive than a fussy one, a message that seems simple is a bigger investment, but in terms of thought. When you write well, you do all the readers' work for them. They don't need to figure out anything because you've already done every bit of it. Leave out information or connections, and they will leap the gap in any way they choose. So, take the trouble to be unambiguous and complete, because that's how you win what you want.

Applying readability guidelines

Guidelines for business writing are not theoretical. They're practical, and moreover, supported by research studies on how people respond to the written word. Fortunately, you don't have to read the research. Most word-processing software, including Microsoft Word, and several websites have already digested all the data and offer easy-to-use tools to help you quickly gauge the readability of your writing.

Several readability indexes exist (see the sidebar "Readability research: What it tells us" later in this chapter). In this section, I focus on the Flesch-Kincaid Readability Index because it's the one Microsoft Word uses. A readability index predicts the percentage of people likely to understand a piece of writing and assigns it a grade level of reading comprehension. The grade-level scores are based on average reading ability of students in the U.S. public school system. The algorithm for a readability index is primarily based on the length of words, sentences, and paragraphs.

Microsoft Word's version of the readability index also shows you the percentage of passive sentences in a selection, which is a good indicator of flabby verbs, indirect sentence structure, and cut-worthy phrases. See the section "Finding action verbs" later in this chapter for more on energizing your sentences.

Match reading level to your audience

TIP

Whatever readability index you use, your target numbers depend on your audience (one more reason to know your readers). Highly educated readers can certainly comprehend difficult material, which may lead you to strive for text written at a high educational level for scientists or MBAs. But generally, this isn't a good idea. For most business communication — email, letters, proposals, websites — we are all lazy readers and prefer "easy" material. Don't you?

At the same time, usually you don't want to gear your use of language to the least literate members of your audience. So, take any calculations with many grains of salt and adapt them to your audience and purpose. And just so you know, the "average reader" in the United States is pegged at a seventh- to ninth-grade reading level, depending on which study you look at.

TIP

When you want to reach a diverse group with a message, you can segment your audience, just like marketers, and craft different versions for each. If a company needs to inform employees of a benefits change, for example, it may need different communications for top managers, middle managers, clerical staff, factory workers, and so on. Beyond assuming varying reading comprehension levels, you often need to rethink the content for each as well. A manager needs to know the financial impact for his department; a clerical or factory worker is more interested in the impact on his own budget.

Assess readability level

Finding the Flesch-Kincaid Readability Index varies a little based on which version of Microsoft Word you use. Generally, go to Word's Spelling and Grammar Preferences screen and make sure the "Show readability statistics" checkbox is selected. Thereafter, whenever you complete a spelling and grammar check, you see a box with readability scores: the Flesch Reading Ease score, which rates how difficult the text is to read, and the Flesch-Kincaid Grade Level, which assigns an approximate U.S. grade level to the text.

Several readability tests are available free online, including at www.readability-score.com. On most sites, you simply paste a chunk of your text into a box and the readability information pops right up.

My personal *print media* readability targets for general audiences are as follows:

>> Flesch Reading Ease: 50 to 70 percent

>> Flesch-Kincaid Grade Level: 8th to 12th grade

- **»** Percentage of passive sentences: 0 to 8 percent
- **»** Words per sentence: 14 to 18, *on average* (some sentences can consist of one word, while others a great many more)
- **»** Sentences per paragraph: Average three to five

For online media, my readability targets are even tighter. Reading from a screen — even a big one — is physically harder for people so they are even less patient than with printed material. Sentences for online media work best when they average 8 to 12 words, and interspersing short sentences — sometimes just a single word — adds punch. Paragraphs should contain one to three sentences.

On the other hand, somewhat longer paragraphs work better for books, if you wonder why I'm bending my own rules at times.

READABILITY RESEARCH: WHAT IT TELLS US

Serious studies to figure out what produces easy reading began in the early twentieth century and continue to be done in many languages in addition to English. The most influential researchers have been Rudolph Flesch, whose name is borne on the Flesch-Kincaid Readability Index, and Robert Gunning, whose measurement system is more picturesquely called the Fog Index. Both worked with American journalists and newspaper publishers in the late 1940s to lower the reading grade level of newspapers, and sure enough, newspaper readership went up 45 percent.

Recent grade-level ratings of what we read are illuminating. Overall, the simpler and clearer the language, the higher the readership. Here are a few examples of grade-level measurements found by testers:

- Popular music: Grades 2.6 to 5.5
- Popular authors, including Stephen King, Tom Clancy, and John Grisham: Grade 7
- *The New York Times* and *The Wall Street Journal:* Grade 11
- *London Times:* Grade 12
- *The Guardian:* Grade 14
- *Times of India:* Grade 15
- Academic papers: Grades 15 to 20
- Typical government documents: Higher than grade 20

To check out how a readability index works, select a section or a whole document of something you wrote recently in Microsoft Word and run a spelling and grammar check. (Or copy and paste a selected passage into an online readability checker.) When the spelling and grammar check is completed, review the Readability Statistics to find out if you need to simplify your writing. If the statistics say that at least a 12th-grade reading level is required (in many Word versions, the index doesn't show levels above 12), and less than 60 percent of readers will understand your document, consider rewriting. Do the same if you used more than 10 percent passive sentences. You'll find lots of suggestions for rewriting in the next section, but consider any or all of the following:

>> Substitute short, one or two syllable words for any overly long words.

>> Shorten long sentences by breaking them up or tightening your wording.

>> Break paragraphs into smaller chunks so that you have fewer sentences in each.

>> Look for weak verbs that are forms of "have" or "to be" ("is," "are," "will be," and so on). These verbs produce a passive effect and complex structures.

>> Review the rewrite to make sure your message still means what you intended and hasn't become even harder to understand.

Then recheck the statistics. If the figures are still high, repeat the process. See if you can get the grade level down to grade 10, then grade 8. Try for less than 8 percent passive voice. Compare the different versions. Which do you prefer? Which do you think best serves your purpose?

Finding the right rhythm

You may wonder whether basing your writing on short simple sentences produces choppy and boring material reminiscent of a grade school textbook. Aiming for clear and simple definitely should not mean dull reading.

TIP

Become aware of rhythm in what you read and what you write, and you will improve your writing dramatically. Like all language, English was used to communicate orally about 100,000 years before writing was invented, so sound and rhythm patterns are critical to how written forms as well as spoken ones are received.

Think of the worst public speakers you know. They probably present in a series of long, complex sentences in an even tone that quickly numbs the ear. Good speakers, by contrast, hold your attention by varying the length of sentences, inflection, and intonation. As a writer, you want to do the same.

In everything you write, aim to build in a natural cadence. Rhythm is one of the main tools for cajoling people to stay with you and find what you write more interesting. Just begin each sentence differently from the previous one and try alternating short, plain sentences with longer ones that have two or three clauses, usually marked by commas. Like good public speakers, you can also inject short punchy words and phrases, but dole them out carefully

Fix the short and choppy

Even a short message benefits from attention to sentence rhythm. Consider this brief message:

> *Kim: The video crew didn't show up again yesterday. We waited all morning. They never came. We just sat there twiddling our thumbs. What a waste of time. It's just unaccept-able. Please advise. —Ted*

And an alternate version:

> *Kim: The video crew let us down again yesterday. Waiting all morning cost us a lot of time, and as a result, we are at risk of missing the target deadline. Do you have a suggestion on how to move ahead? Thanks. —Ted*

Notice how the tone shifts in the more readable message. The writer sounds more professional and focuses on the challenge rather than his personal resentment. The same information is delivered, and paying attention to sentence structure makes all the difference. For long documents, varying your sentence length and structure is even more critical. Few people will stay with multiple pages of stilted, mind-numbing prose.

Notice, too, that when you combine some short sentences to alternate the rhythm, easy ways to improve the wording and content emerge. Ted may be inspired to go a step further and write a third version of the same message:

> *Kim: I'm sorry to report that the video crew failed to show up again yesterday. Losing a whole morning makes it hard to meet our deadline, August 14th, which keys off the annual meeting. I've looked into some alternative resources — the shortlist is attached. Do you have a few minutes to talk about how to move ahead? Thanks. —Ted.*

Notice how much more connected the thoughts seem, and how much more authoritative the overall message feels. Yes, the content shifted — but this happens when you write thoughtfully! In everything you write, what you say and how you say it are inextricable.

Figuring out how to express something well in words often pushes your thinking to higher levels. In the first message, Ted comes across as a complainer who can't solve a problem. The second moves him up to at least sound more articulate and on point. The third message communicates that he is a take charge, efficient professional — someone reliable, someone who cares about the whole operation and takes initiative, rather than a cog who goes through the motions and waits for direction.

This is the magic of good writing. It clarifies problems. It enables you to discover solutions that didn't occur to you at first thought. It equips you to look more effective and to *be* more effective. Good writing is always worth the time it takes, and once you adopt this belief and absorb the structure I'm providing, you can become an efficient writer as well as a powerful one.

Fix the long and complicated

Many people have a problem opposite to creating short, disconnected sentences. Maybe you tend to write lengthy complicated sentences that end up with the same result: dead writing.

The solution to never-ending strings of words is the same — alternate sentence structures. But in this case, break up the long ones. Doing this produces punchier, more enticing copy.

A number of potentially good writers don't succeed as well as they might because they fall into a pattern that repeats the same rhythm, over and over again. Here's an example taken from an opinion piece written for a workshop:

> *I strongly support efforts to improve the global economy, and naturally may be biased toward the author's position. While this bias may be the reason I responded well to the piece in the first place, it is not the reason why I consider it an exceptional piece of writing. Not only is this article extremely well researched, its use of cost-benefit analysis is an effective way to think about the challenges.*

The monotonous pattern and unending sentences serve the ideas poorly. One way to rewrite the material:

> *I strongly support efforts to improve the global economy and this probably inclined me to a positive response. But it's not why I see it as an exceptional piece of writing. The article is extremely well researched. Further, its cost-benefit analysis is an effective way to think about the challenge.*

Again, simply varying the sentence length and structure quickly improves the overall wording and flow. Notice that you can take liberties with the recommended short-long-short sentence pattern and use two short sentences, then two more complex ones, for example.

REMEMBER

Everyone has particular habits of writing that leave room for improvement. Strive to recognize your own weaknesses, because then you can counter them with one of the practical fix-it techniques in Chapter 4.

Achieving a conversational tone

New business writers are often told to adopt a "conversational" tone, but what does that actually mean?

Business correspondence written during the nineteenth century and even most of the twentieth, seems slow, formal, and ponderous when you read it now. Today's communication needs to move as fast as our lives, and we want it to feel natural.

REMEMBER

Conversational tone is something of an illusion, however. You don't really write the way you talk, and you shouldn't. But you can echo natural speech in various ways to more effectively engage your audience.

Rhythm, discussed in the preceding section, is a basic technique that gives your copy forward momentum and promotes a conversational feeling. Additional techniques for achieving conversational tone include:

>> **Infuse messages with warmth.** Think of the person as an individual before you write and content that's appropriate to the relationship and subject will come to you, and the tone will be right.

>> **Choose short simple words.** Rely on the versions you use to *talk* to someone, rather than the sophisticated ones you use to try and impress. See "Choosing reader-friendly words" later in this chapter for examples.

>> **Use contractions as you do in speech.** Go with "can't" rather than "cannot," "I'm" rather than "I am."

>> **Minimize the use of inactive forms.** Carefully evaluate every use of the "to be" verbs — *is, was, will be, are,* and so on — to determine if you can use active, interesting verbs instead.

>> **Take selective liberties with grammatical correctness.** Starting a sentence with "and" or "but" or "or" is okay, for example, but avoid mismatching your nouns and pronouns.

>> **Adopt an interactive spirit.** As online media embodies, one-way, top-down communication is "so yesterday." Find ways in all your writing to invite active interest and input from your reader. Today's readers, especially younger ones, want to be part of the experience, not passive recipients of someone else's ideas. Many online techniques have been adapted to traditional media, and you want to incorporate them as appropriate.

If you ignore the preceding guidelines — and want to look hopelessly outdated — you can write a long-winded and lifeless message like the following:

Dear Elaine:

I regret to inform you that the deadline for the Blue Jay proposal has been advanced to an earlier point in time, namely, August 14. Will this unexpected eventuality present insurmountable difficulties to your department? Please advise and inform my office of your potential availability at 3 p.m. on the 2nd to discuss. —Carrie

Yawn — and also a bit confusing. Or you can write a clear, quick, crisp version like this:

Elaine, I'm sorry to say the Blue Jay deadline has been moved up to August 14. Bummer, I know. What problems does this create? Let's talk. Thursday at 3? —Carrie

TIP

Although the second example feels casual and conversational, these aren't the actual words Carrie would say to Elaine in a real phone conversation. This exchange is more likely:

Hi. How are you? Listen, we got a problem. The Blue Jay deadline — would you believe — it's now August 14th. Yeah, I know, total bummer. We should talk about the problems. Is Thursday at 3 good?

Online copy often works best when it carries the conversational illusion to an extreme. Pay attention to the jazzy, spontaneous-style copy on websites you love. The words may read like they sprang ready-made out of some genie's lamp, but more than likely they were produced by a team of copywriters agonizing over every line for weeks or months or years. Spontaneous-reading copy doesn't come easy: It's hard work. Some people — frequent bloggers, for example — are good at writing conversationally because they practice this skill consciously.

Energizing Your Language

Written communication starts with words, so choose them well. But the most important guideline for selecting the best words for business writing may seem counterintuitive: Avoid long or subtle words that express nuance. These may serve as the staple for many fiction writers and academics, but you're not aiming to sound evocative, ambiguous, impressive, or super-educated. In fact, you want just the opposite.

Relying on everyday wording

The short everyday words you use in ordinary speech are almost always best for business writing. They're clear, practical, and direct. They're also powerful enough to express your deepest and widest thoughts. They're the words that reach people emotionally, too, because they stand for the most basic and tangible things people care about and need to communicate about. "Home" is a whole different story than "residence"; "quit" carries a lot more overtones than "resign."

Make a list of basic one- and two-syllable words and almost certainly, they come from the oldest part of the English language, Anglo-Saxon. Most words with three or more syllables were grafted onto this basic stock by historical invaders: the French-speaking Normans and the Latin-speaking Romans for the most part, both of whom aspired to higher levels of cultural refinement than the Britons.

If you were raised in an English-speaking home, you learned Anglo-Saxon words during earliest childhood and acquired the ones with Latin, French, and other influences later in your education. Scan these previous two paragraphs and you know immediately which words came from which culture set.

REMEMBER

For many reasons, then, readers are programmed to respond best to simple, short, low-profile English words. They trigger feelings of trust (an Anglo-Saxon word) and credibility (from the French). Obviously, I don't choose to write entirely with one-syllable words. Variety is the key — just as with sentences. English's history gives you a remarkable array of words when you want to be precise or produce certain feelings. Even in business English, a sprinkling of longer words contributes to a good pace and can make what you say more specific and interesting. But don't forget your basic word stock.

TIP

If you're writing to a non-native English-speaking audience, you have even more reason to write with one- and two-syllable words. People master the same basic words first when learning a new language, no matter what their original tongue, so all new English-speakers understand them. You know this if you've ever had a conversation in with someone whose native language is not English, in a language foreign to both of you. For example, if you converse with a Russian speaker who studied two years of French like you did, you can communicate quite well with each other.

In many workplaces today, you need to communicate with culturally diverse audiences all the time as well as with people with different educational levels. Make simple, straightforward language the general rule.

This principle holds for long documents like reports and proposals as much as for emails. They should never read pretentiously no matter how big a job you're pitching and no matter how impressive the company. And short word guidelines are also important for online writing such as for websites and blogs. When we read onscreen, we have even less patience with multi-syllable, sophisticated words. Reading (and writing) on smartphones and other small devices usually makes short words the *only* practical choice.

Choosing reader-friendly words

Using short, friendly words may seem like common sense, so why do you see so much business messaging with all those long, highly educated words in dense sentences? I have no idea. If everyone wrote the way he prefers to read, I'm sure we'd have a more collegial, efficient, and productive world.

Consciously develop your awareness of short-word options. Clearer writing gives you better results. In most circumstances, opt for the first and friendlier word in the following pairs.

Use. . .	Rather than. . .
help	assistance
often	frequently
try	endeavor
need	requirement
basic	fundamental
built	constructed
confirm	validate
rule	regulation
create	originate
use	utilize
prove	substantiate
show	demonstrate
study	analyze
fake	artificial
limits	parameters
skill	proficiency
need	necessitate

I don't mean that the longer words are bad — in fact, they can often be the better choice. But generally, be sure you have a reason for going long. Observe your writing and identify the three or more syllable words you use often and think about shorter alternatives. An online thesaurus can help.

Focusing on the real and concrete

Concrete nouns are words that denote something tangible: a person or any number of actual things, such as dog, nose, dirt, house, boat, balloon, computer, egg, tree, chair, and so on. They are objects that exist in real space. You can touch, see, hear, smell, or taste them.

Abstract nouns typically represent ideas and concepts. They may denote a situation, condition, quality, or experience, such as catastrophe, freedom, efficiency, knowledge, mystery, observation, irritability, intemperance, analysis, research, love, democracy, and many more.

REMEMBER

When you use concrete nouns in your writing, readers bring these physical associations to your words, and this lends reality to your thoughts. Moreover, you can expect most people to take the same meaning from them. This isn't true of abstract words. Two people are unlikely to argue about what an apple is, but they may well disagree on what exactly "independence" or "education" means.

TIP

When you build your writing on a lot of abstract nouns, you are generalizing. Even when you're writing an opinion or philosophical piece, too much abstraction doesn't fire the imagination. A lot of business writing strikes readers as dull and uninspiring for this reason.

Suppose at a pivotal point of World War II Winston Churchill had written in the manner of many modern business executives:

> *We're operationalizing this initiative to proceed as effectively, efficiently, and proactively as possible in alignment with our responsibilities to existing population centers and our intention to develop a transformative future for mankind. We'll employ cost-effective, cutting-edge technologies and exercise the highest level of commitment, whatever the obstacles that materialize in various geographic situations.*

Instead he wrote and said:

> *We shall not flag or fail. We shall go on to the end. We shall fight in France, we shall fight on the seas and the oceans, we shall fight with growing confidence and growing strength in the air, we shall defend our island, whatever the cost may be. We shall fight on the beaches, we shall fight on the landing grounds, we shall fight in the fields and in the streets, we shall fight in the hills; we shall never surrender.*

Which statement engages the senses and therefore the heart, even three-quarters of a century after this particular cause was won? Which carries more conviction? Granted, Churchill was writing a speech, but the statement also works amazingly when read.

TIP

While you probably won't be called on to rouse your countrymen as Churchill was, writing in a concrete way pays off for you, too. It brings your writing alive. Aim to get down to earth in what you say and how you say it.

Notice how many words of the mock business-writing piece contain three or more syllables. Churchill's piece uses only three. And running both passages through readability checks (see the previous section, "Applying readability guidelines") predicts at least a 12th-grade reading level to understand the business-speak with only 2 percent of readers understanding it. By contrast, Churchill's lines require only a 4th-grade reading level and 91 percent of readers understand them.

WARNING

You may often find yourself tempted to write convoluted, indirect, abstract prose — because it's common to your corporate culture or your technical field or the Request for Proposal you're responding to. Don't do it. Remind yourself that nobody likes to read that kind of writing, even though he may write that way himself. Take the lead in delivering lean lively messages and watch the positive response this brings.

Finding action verbs

Good strong verbs invigorate. Passive verbs, which involve a form of the verb "to be," deaden language and thinking, too. Consider some dull sentences and their better alternatives:

> *The whole company was alarmed by the stock market loss.*
>
> *The stock market loss alarmed the whole company.*

> *Every summer the entire staff is invited to a barbecue at the CEO's country cottage.*
>
> *Every summer the CEO invites the entire staff to a barbecue at his country cottage.*

> *A decision to extend working hours was reached by the talent management office.*
>
> *The talent management office decided to extend working hours.*

The first sentence in each set represents what grammarians call the passive voice: a form of the verb "to be" followed by a word ending in "-ed." Other constructions also use non-active verbs that tell you to take a second look. One clue:

sentences that rely on the phrases "there is" and "there are," which often bury meaning. Compare the following pairs:

There is a company rule to consider in deciding which route to follow.

A company rule tells us which route to follow.

There are guidelines you should use if you want to improve your writing.

Use the guidelines to improve your writing.

TIP

For most dull inactive verbs, the solution is the same: *Find the action.* Be clear about *who* did *what* and then rework the sentence to say that.

You may need to go beyond changing the verb and rethink the entire sentence so it's simple, clear, and direct. In the process, take responsibility. Passive sentences often evade it. A classic example:

Mistakes were made, people were hurt, and opportunities were lost.

Who made the mistakes, hurt the people, and lost the opportunities? The writer? An unidentified CEO? Mystery government officials? This kind of structure is sometimes called "the divine passive": Some unknown or unnamable force made it happen.

To help you remember why you generally need to avoid the passive, here's my favorite mistake. I asked a group of people to write about their personal writing problems and how they planned to work on them. One person contributed:

Many passive verbs are used by me.

REMEMBER

Take the time to identify the passive verbs and indirect constructions in all your writing. Doing so doesn't mean that you must always eliminate them. You may want to use the passive because no clearly definable active subject exists — or it doesn't matter:

The award was created to recognize outstanding sales achievement.

Or you may have a surprise to disclose that leads you to use the passive for emphasis:

This year's award was won by the newest member of the department: Joe Mann.

TIP

Using the passive unconsciously often undermines your writing success. Substitute active verbs. They can be short and punchy, such as *drive, end, gain, fail, win, probe, treat, taint, speed.* Or they can be longer words that offer more precise meaning, such as *underline, trigger, suspend, pioneer, model, fracture, crystallize, compress, accelerate.* Both word groups suggest action and movement, adding zing and urgency to your messages.

Crafting comparisons to help readers

Comparisons help your readers understand your message on deeper levels. You can use similes and metaphors, which are both analogies, to make abstract ideas more tangible and generally promote comprehension. These devices don't need to be elaborate, long, or pretentiously literary. Here are some simple comparisons:

> *Poets use metaphors like painters use brushes — to paint pictures that help people see under the surface.*
>
> *Winning this award is my Oscar.*
>
> *Life is like a box of chocolates.*
>
> *The new polymer strand is 10 nanometers in width — while the average human hair is 90,000 nanometers wide.*
>
> *From 15,000 feet up, the world looks like a harmonious quilt of peace and tranquility.*

Whatever device you use, effective comparisons

>> **Create mental images.** You can give readers a different way to access — and *remember* — your ideas and information.

>> **Align things from different arenas.** Using the familiar to explain the unfamiliar can be especially helpful when you introduce new information or change.

>> **Heighten the impact of everyday practical writing.** Just as in well-written fiction, a great comparison in a business document engages the reader's imagination.

>> **Make intriguing headlines that grab attention.** A blog post caught me with the title, "How Learning to Ride a Bike is Like Working at Home." I read it just to find out what the two things have in common.

MAKING UP FRESH COMPARISONS

Playing with comparisons is a classic schoolroom game you can use to generate new ways to express your ideas. Simply think about bringing together two different things so readers are led to see one differently.

Take a few minutes and assemble a short list of things, activities, or experiences on the left-hand side of a page of blank paper or screen. For example, you can list your new project, writing your résumé, making your boss happy, the new product you're selling, playing a computer game, and so on.

Think about what that item is like — how you can describe it visually or through the other senses. Think about how it makes you feel. Brainstorm about other things that have similar characteristics. Try to avoid clichés and come up with something you find interesting.

Write your idea for each item on your list on the right side of the paper. Come up with an idea for every item just to give yourself the practice, without worrying whether some of your comparisons are less than brilliant. Use your new skill when you're writing an important document, trying to explain something difficult, or making your best persuasive argument.

For example, you might brainstorm for a comparison by "finishing" statements, such as:

Winning this contract is as good as . . .

This new service will change your thinking about life insurance just like X changed Y.

Saving a few dollars by investing in Solution A instead of Solution B is like . . .

Employing Reader-Friendly Graphic Techniques

Good written messages and documents are well thought out and presented clearly and vividly, as covered in this chapter and the preceding one. But I have one more aspect to highlight. Your writing must not only meet audience needs and read well; it also must look good.

Whether your material appears in print or online, every message and document you create is a visual experience. More than readability is at stake; readers judge your message's value and credibility by how it looks. Whether you want to write an effective résumé, proposal, report — or just an email message — design can make or break your writing.

The following sections show you how to use various graphic techniques to maximize your message's appeal. And rest assured, you don't need to purchase special software or other tools to easily implement these good design principles.

Building in white space

To coin a comparison (see the sidebar "Making up fresh comparisons"):

Add white space to your writing for the same reason bakers add yeast to their bread — to leaven the denseness by letting in light and air.

Help your writing breathe by providing plenty of empty space. The eye demands rest when scanning or reading. Don't cram your words into a small tight space by decreasing the point size or squeezing the space between characters, words, or lines. Densely packed text is inaccessible. If you have too many words for the available space, cut them down. You'll find many ways to do that while also improving your impact in Chapter 4.

Always look for opportunities to add that valuable white space to your message. Check for white space in everything you deliver. Factors that affect white space include the size of the typeface, line spacing, margin size and column width, and graphic devices such as subheads, sidebars, and integrated images.

Choosing a typeface

Type has numerous graphic aspects and effects. Following are some of the most significant, as well as easiest to adjust.

Fonts

Using an easy-to-read simple typeface (or font) is critical. For printed text, *serif fonts* — fonts with feet or squiggles at the end of each letter, like the font used in this book — are more reader-friendly because they make every letter distinct and unambiguous. They also guide the eye smoothly from letter to letter, word to word. However, *sans-serif fonts* (ones without the little feet) are often favored by art directors because they look more modern and classy. Some sans serifs leave room for confusion — for example, it can be hard to distinguish between a small "l" and "l." The sans-serif font Verdana was specifically designed to be readable on small screens at low resolution and is often used for digital media.

TIP

Choose your font according to your purpose. For long print documents, serif remains the better choice for the same reason that books still use it — ease of reading. But you can to some extent mix your faces. Using sans-serif headlines and subheads can make a welcome contrast. (For example, Times New Roman and Helvetica work nicely together.) But generally, resist the temptation to combine more than two different typefaces.

WARNING

Avoid fancy or cute typefaces for any purpose. They're not only distracting but also may not transfer well to someone else's computer system. They can end up garbled or altogether missing in action. Recruitment officers sometimes find a candidate's name entirely missing from a résumé because their systems lack a corresponding typeface and end up omitting these very important words.

And never type a whole message in capitals or bold face, which gives the impression that you're shouting. Avoid using italics on more than a word or two because the copy is hard to read.

Point size

Like font choice, the best point size for text depends on the result you're trying to achieve. Generally, somewhere between 10 and 12 points works best, but you need to adjust according to your audience and the experience you want to create. Small type may look great, but if you want readers 55 and older to read your annual report, 8-point type will kill it.

Online text suggests a similar 10- to 12-point range for body copy, but calculating the actual onscreen experience for a wide range of monitors and devices is complicated. Online text often looks different on different platforms. Err on the side of a generous point size.

Never resort to reducing the size of your typeface to fit more in. I once had to persuade the top boss to cut back his "Message from the CEO" because it was longer than the allocated space. He didn't want to sacrifice more than a few words. Then I showed him what his message would look like in the 6-point type we'd need to run the whole thing. He quickly found his red pen.

Margins and columns

For both online and print media, avoid making columns of type so wide that the eye becomes discouraged in reading across. If breaking the copy into two columns isn't suitable, consider widening one or both margins. Also, avoid columns that are only three or four words wide, because they're hard to read and annoying visually.

Think carefully before you fool with justifying text. Justified type has a straight edge vertically. This paragraph is justified on the left, which is almost always your best choice for body copy. When text is left uneven on the right, this is called "rag right" in printer parlance. Copy that's justified right and rag left is difficult to read because each new line starts in a different spot. The text in this book is fully justified on both the left and right, which can be a tricky style choice, especially for online media. Sometimes fully justified copy can visibly distort words and spacing to make your words fit consistently within a block of text.

Keeping colors simple

Using color to accent a print document makes for happier eyes, but stay simple. One color, in addition to black used for the text, is probably plenty. See whether an accent color sparks your message by using it consistently on headlines and/or subheads. Full color is much less expensive than it used to be, but often is best applied to photographs and other graphics rather than to making rainbow copy.

WARNING

Even online, where you face no limit on using as many colors as you like, seeing a lot of different colors strikes people as messy and amateur these days. Designers prefer simple, clean palettes that combine a few colors at most. So should you. And avoid placing any type against a color background that makes it hard to read. This means that backgrounds should be no more than a light tint. *Dropped or reversed-out type* — for instance, white type on a black or dark background — can look terrific, but only in small doses, such as a caption or short sidebar. A whole page of reversed-out type, whether in print or onscreen, makes a daunting read.

REMEMBER

If you're producing a substantial document or website in tandem with a graphic designer, never allow graphic impact to trump readability and editorial clarity. To most designers, words are just part of a visual pattern. If a designer tells you the document has too many words, certainly listen; it's probably true and you do want the piece to look good. But "just say no" if playing second fiddle to the visual undermines your message. Graphics should strengthen, not weaken, its impact and absorbability.

Adding effective graphics

If you've got good images and they're appropriate, flaunt them. Increasingly this principle is applied to email as well as long documents, because so much research demonstrates the strength of visual material in drawing and holding reader attention. Visuals are beginning to dominate relatively older online media like Twitter and *are* the story with newer tools like Pinterest and Instagram, not to mention video powerhouse, YouTube.

Appropriateness of graphics depends on your purpose. A proposal can benefit from charts and graphs to make financials and other variables clear and more easily grasped. A report may include photographs of a project under way. A blog with a fun image related to the subject is more enticing. Additional possibilities for various media include images of successful projects to support credibility, illustrations of something yet to be built, change documentation, and visualizations of abstract ideas.

Of course, your own resources and time may be limited. But when visual effect matters — to attract readers or when you're competing for a big contract, for example — take time to brainstorm possibilities. Wonderful online resources proliferate, and many are free. Your computer aided by software, and even your smartphone plus apps, can help you produce a good infographic, chart, or graph. It may take some imagination as well as research.

WARNING

Images must feel appropriate to your readers. If not, you create a negative reaction. Even with websites, research shows that contrary to popular assumption, people value the words most and are put off by images unrelated to the subject. Ready-made clip art is available from a wide range of online sources today, and is much better than it used to be. But choose carefully and customize it when you can to avoid cheapening your message in the viewer's eye. Generally, it's best to keep visual style consistent — all cartoons, or all photographs, for example.

For websites, resist the temptation to use generic stock photos of people: those depictions of good-looking models meeting, talking, or working carefully balanced for age, gender, and ethnicity. No one believes those are your staff members or clients. "Real" people are more interesting and convincing even though imperfect by model standards. If your business doesn't lend itself to showing people, exercise imagination to come up with other visual representation of what you do or what you mean.

Breaking space up with sidebars, boxes, and lists

Print media in the past decade have increasingly used graphic techniques to draw readers in with as many ways as they can come up with. Today's readers are scanners first. Think of your own behavior when opening up a newspaper or magazine. You most likely scout for what interests you and then read the material, in whole or at least in part, if it appeals to you. When you get bored, you quickly stop reading and start scanning again.

Good headlines and subheads are critical to capture readers' attention and guide them through a document. But you must also pay major attention to writing the following:

>> Captions to accompany photos and other images

>> Sidebars and boxes offering additional background, sidelights, or information

>> Interesting quotes or tidbits used as "pullouts" or "pull quotes" in the margins or inside the text

>> Small tight summaries of the article, or introductions, at the beginning

>> Bulleted or numbered lists of examples or steps

>> Icons (such as the Tip and Remember icons in this book) that denote something of special interest

All these devices serve three important purposes. Along with images, they

>> **Break up unrelieved blocks of type that discourage the eye.** Some print editors use the "dollar bill test": If you can lay down a bill on a page and it doesn't touch a single graphic device, then add one in.

>> **Capture reader attention in different ways.** A summary, a caption, or a box may draw someone to read the whole piece, or at least some of it.

>> **Help to convey ideas and information more clearly and effectively.** People absorb information in different ways. Taking lessons from the online world, today's editors offer readers choices of what they want to read, and where they want to start.

REMEMBER

Good graphic techniques should be part of your writing repertoire. Do you need them for every email you write? Of course not, but if you're delivering a sales pitch, they certainly provide more impact. Classic strategies like using subheads and bullets can help get your message across. For long documents and materials whose goal is persuasion, draw on all the techniques that suit your goals, audience, nature of your message, and the medium.

The next chapter introduces you to the editing stage of writing. If like most people you've never given much thought to this process, or it strikes fear into your heart, not to worry. Common sense can take you a long way and a batch of professional tricks does the rest. Once you discover how magically self-editing can strengthen your messages, I think you'll become a believer.

Chapter **4**

Self-Editing: Professional Ways to Improve Your Work

I f you expect to create a successful email, letter, or business document in just one shot, think again. Don't ask so much of yourself. Very, very few professional writers can accomplish a finished piece — whether they write novels, plays, articles, websites, or press releases — with their first draft. This especially includes writers known for their simplicity and easy reading.

Editing is how writers write. For them, the writing and editing processes are inseparable because they wouldn't dream of submitting work to anyone that is less than their very best. Unfortunately, many people are intimidated by the notion of editing their own work. But equipped with effective methods and techniques, you can edit with confidence.

Mastering hundreds of grammar rules is not necessary to becoming a good editor. Know the clues that reveal where your writing needs work, and you can sharpen what you write so it accomplishes exactly what you want. This chapter gives you the groundwork.

Changing Hats: From Writer to Editor

The writer and editor roles reinforce each other.

>> In writing, you plan your message or document based on what you want to accomplish and your analysis of the reader (which is discussed in Chapter 2), brainstorm content possibilities, organize logically, and create a full draft. Always think of this piece as the *first draft* because every message, whatever its nature and length, deserves editing and will hugely benefit from it.

>> In editing, you review your first draft and find ways to liven word choice, simplify sentences, and ensure your ideas hang together. You also evaluate the "macro" side: whether the content and tone deliver the strongest message to your audience and help build relationships. Furthermore, as you make a habit of regularly editing your messages, your first-draft writing improves as well.

>> In proofreading, you review your writing in nitty-gritty detail to find and correct errors — mistakes in spelling, grammar, punctuation, facts, references, citations, calculations, and more as relevant to the material. Never skip this step because mistakes that look like mistakes undermine all your good thinking and credibility with the reader.

TIP

Don't expect to bypass the whole editing process down the line as you further refine your writing abilities. Professional writers never stop relying on their editing skills, no matter how good they get at their craft.

Improving your editing abilities goes a long way toward improving the impact of every message you send, short or long. The following tools and tricks make you a more capable and confident self-editor.

Choosing a way to edit

You have three main ways to edit writing. Try each of the following and see which you prefer — but realize you can always switch your editing method to best suit a current writing task or timeline.

Option 1: Mark up print-outs

Before computers, both writers and editors worked with "hard copy" because it was the only choice. For about a century before computers, people wrote on typewriters, revised the results by hand, and then retyped the entire document. If you were reviewing *printer's proofs* — preliminary versions of material to be printed — you used a shorthand set of symbols to tell the typesetter what to change.

These symbols offered uniformity; every editor and printer knew what they meant. Typing and printing processes have changed radically, but the marks are still used today and remain a helpful way to communicate text changes among people.

TIP

Many professional writers still edit their work on hard copy print-outs because on-screen editing strains the eyes and makes us more error-prone. You may find physically editing your copy with universal marks to be more satisfying; you have something to show for your efforts when you're done. In addition, editing on paper can help you switch over to the editor's side of the table. Of course, you must then transfer the changes to your computer.

REMEMBER

Proof marks vary between the United States and the United Kingdom, and some organizations have their own special marks or special meanings.

Option 2: Edit on-screen

After you draft a document, you can simply read through it and make changes. Younger writers may never have considered any other system. You can substitute words and reorganize the material by cutting and pasting with a few mouse clicks or keystrokes. The down side to this method of editing is that you're left with no record of the change process. (See the next section for a useful alternative.)

When maintaining a copy of your original text matters, save your new version as a separate document. Amend its name to avoid hassle later, in case a series of revised versions develops.

TIP

Keep your renaming simple yet specific. If the document is titled "Gidget article," title the edited version "Gidget 2," for example, or date it "Gidget 11.13." When you edit someone else's document, tack on your initials: "Gidget.nc," for example. Be sure your titling allows for easy identification of the various versions to avoid time-wasting confusion later.

Option 3: Track your changes

Most word-processing software offers a handy feature to record every change you make to the text in a document. In Microsoft Word, for example, select the Review tab, and you'll see a tracking pane. Click Track Changes "On" and edit away. You can delete and add words, fix spelling and grammar, and move pieces around at will.

Changes will show up on the copy in a color other than black or in small text boxes off to the side (depending on your choice of screen view). Deletions appear as strikethrough text or off to the side. You can add "comments" to yourself, or if you're sharing the document, you can add comments to the other readers.

The system takes some personal trial and error but provides a useful tool for your editing experiments. It's easy to change your mind about a correction or substitution and revert the text back to the original.

However, when you're tracking changes on a heavily edited document, you can end up with something quite complicated. Spare yourself the confusion by selecting to view the document as "Final" with all your proposed changes incorporated, or opt not to view insertions and deletions, depending on your version of Word. You don't lose your edits; they're just hidden from immediate sight.

When you finish editing, save a version that shows the revisions, then go back to the Review tab and choose "Accept" or "Reject" changes. Accept all changes, or go through your document section by section or even sentence by sentence. You emerge with a clean copy; save this version separately from the original. Proof the new version carefully because new errors creep in when you edit. Always.

TIP

Word's Track Changes tool can help you improve your writing process and offers a way to share refinement stages with others when needed. (Numerous online tools, such as Google Docs, also help you share document development.) But when you ultimately send the message to your audience, be sure your final saved version does not reveal the change process: Turn Track Changes off and make sure all changes have been accepted.

Distancing yourself from what you write

REMEMBER

The first step for a self-editor is to consciously assume that role. A professional I know keeps a special hat to physically put on to help him switch roles. Forget how hard some of the material was to draft, or how attached you are to some of the ideas or language. Aim to judge as objectively as you can how well your message succeeds in the goals you set for, and find ways to strengthen it.

Your best tool to achieve this distance is the one that cures all ills: time. In Chapter 2, I suggest that you accord equal weight to the importance of planning, drafting, and editing. But ideally, that last part isn't done in the same seamless time frame as the first two stages.

TIP

Try to build in a pause between drafting and editing. Pausing overnight (or longer) is highly recommended for major business documents. If your document is really long or important, try to edit and re-edit in a series of stages over days or even weeks. Some copy, such as a website home page or marketing piece, may never be "finished." It evolves over time.

PRACTICING THE STRIPPER'S ART: IN WRITING, LESS IS USUALLY MORE

Your goal for every message and business document is "just enough." This applies both to substance and language:

- **Substance:** Aim to make your point and achieve your goal without overkill that loses your reader or damages your argument.

- **Language:** A windy presentation dilutes impact and may slow reading to the point of no return. Aim to state your case, make or respond to a request, present an argument, or accomplish any given purpose in the most concise way.

Build every message with complete words, sentences, and commonly accepted grammar. (Abbreviated messages do have their place, however. See "Putting emoji, texting, and instant messaging into perspective" later in this chapter for more on this.)

What is your ideal length? Many documents suggest their own answers. If you're responding to an RFP (request for proposal) that's ten pages long, a one-page response probably doesn't suffice. You must supply detail and backup. If you're applying for a job, even a well-done paragraph can't take the place of a résumé. Always take a document's purpose into account to judge appropriate length and depth.

For short and/or less consequential messages, an hour or two between drafting and editing helps. A top-of-your-head email or text message that doesn't seem important can still land you in a lot of trouble if you send it out without vetting. If an hour isn't possible, just a quick trip to the coffee maker or some time on another task can clear your mind and refresh your eyes.

So, put the message away and then revisit it after a deliberate delay. When you return, you see your words with fresh eyes — an editor's rather than the writer's.

Reviewing the Big and Small Pictures

Your job when self-editing is to review what you wrote on two levels:

>> **The macro level:** The thinking that underlies the message and the content decisions you made

>> **The micro level:** How well you use language to express your viewpoint and ask for what you want

Let's look at both.

Assessing content success

Start your edit with a big-picture review, leveraging the mental distance you gained by putting the piece aside for a while.

REMEMBER

Read through the entire document and ask yourself:

>> Is what I want clear from reading the message?

>> Does the content support that goal?

>> Is anything missing from my argument, my sequence of thoughts, or my explanations? Do I include all necessary backup?

>> Do I give the reader a reason to care?

>> Do I include any unnecessary ideas or statements that don't contribute to my central goal or that detract from it?

>> Does the tone feel right for the person or group I'm communicating with?

>> Does the whole message present "me" in the best possible light?

>> Are there any ways my reader can possibly misunderstand or misinterpret my words?

>> How will the reader *feel* when she reads this? How would *I* feel? What will the reader *do?*

REMEMBER

The initial editing challenge is to drill to the core of your message. If you followed the step-by-step process presented in Chapter 2 to create the document, check now that you met your own criteria and that every element works to accomplish your goal.

Your objective answers to these nine questions may lead you to partially or substantially revamp your content. That's fine — there's no point working to improve presentation until you have the right substance.

TIP

You may choose to do the big-picture revision right away, or plan for it and proceed to the second stage, the micro-level of editing: crafting the words. It's much easier to make the language more effective when you know exactly what message you want to deliver.

Assessing the effectiveness of your language

You have two ways to get instant, objective feedback on how well you used language.

>> **Use a readability index.** Most word-processing software can give you a good overview of the difficulty of any written piece. As Chapter 3 details, Microsoft Word's Readability Statistics box provides helpful information on word, sentence, and paragraph length; the number of passive constructions; and the degree of ease with which people can read and understand your message. Use these statistics to pinpoint how you can improve your sentences and word choices.

>> **Read it aloud.** Reading what you write aloud is a favored method for many writers. As you speak your writing quietly — even under your breath — you identify problems in flow, clarity, and word choice. Asking someone else to read your words aloud to you can put you even more fully in the listener role.

In addition to telling you whether you achieved a conversational tone, the read-aloud test alerts you to eight specific problems common to poor writing. I recommend solutions to four of these problems in Chapter 3.

>> **Problem 1:** A sentence is so long it takes you more than one breath to get through it.

Solution: Break it up or shorten it.

>> **Problem 2:** You hear a monotonous pattern with each sentence starting the same way.

Solution: Change some of the sentence structures so you alternate between long and short, simple and complex.

>> **Problem 3:** All or most sentences sound short and choppy, which creates an abrupt tone and dulls the content.

Solution: Combine some sentences to make the read smoother.

>> **Problem 4:** You stumble over words.

Solution: Replace those words with simpler ones, preferably words that are one or two syllables long.

The read-aloud method can reveal four additional challenges. We look at each problem in greater detail in following sections, but here's a quick overview.

>> **Problem 5:** You hear yourself using an up-and-down inflection to get through a sentence.

Solution: Make the sentence less complicated.

>> **Problem 6:** You hear repeated sounds produced by words ending in *-ize, -ion, -ing, -ous,* or another suffix.

Solution: Restructure the sentence.

>> **Problem 7:** You notice numerous prepositional phrases strung together — of, with, in, to, for.

Solution: Change your wording to make fewer prepositions necessary.

>> **Problem 8:** You hear words repeated in the same paragraph.

Solution: Find substitutes.

REMEMBER

If you read your copy aloud and practice the fix-it techniques discussed in Chapter 3 and the following sections, you give yourself a gift: the ability to bypass grammar lessons. After you know how to spot a problem, you can use shortcut tools to correct it. Even better, you can track your own patterns and prevent the problems from happening.

Everyone writes with his or her own personal patterns. The better handle you gain on your own patterns, the better your writing, and the faster you achieve results.

Now for some detail on handling problems 5, 6, 7, and 8.

Avoiding telltale up-down-up inflection

"Fancy" words, excess phrases, and awkward constructions force sentences into an unnatural pattern when read aloud. The effect is rather like the typical up-down-up-down inflection of the tattletale: I know who **DID** it.

For example, read the following sentence aloud and see what pattern you force on your voice:

> *All of the writing that is published is a representation of our company, so spelling and grammatical errors can make us look unprofessional and interfere with the public perception of us as competent businesspeople.*

Simply scanning the sentences tips you off to its wordiness. This single sentence contains two phrases using "of," two statements with the passive verb "is," and three words ending in "-ion." They produce an awkward, wordy construction. Plus, the sentence contains 34 words — far more than the average 18 I recommend — and more than five words have three or more syllables (see Chapter 3).

You don't need to be a linguistic rocket scientist to write a better sentence. Just go for simple and clear. Break up the long sentence. Get rid of the unnecessary words and phrases. Substitute shorter friendlier words. One way:

> All our company's writing represents us. Spelling and grammar errors make us look unprofessional and incompetent.

After you simplify, you can often find a third, even better way to write the sentence. A third pass might read:

> When we make spelling and grammar mistakes, we look unprofessional and incompetent.

Looking for repeat word endings

Big clues to wordy, ineffective sentences come with overused suffixes — words ending in *-ing, -ive, -ion, -ent, -ous,* and *-y.* Almost always, these words are three or more syllables and French or Latinate in origin, and signify abstractions. Several in a sentence make you sound pompous and outdated. They often force you into convoluted, passive constructions that weaken your writing and discourage readers. (See "Moving from Passive to Active" later in this chapter for more on activating passive construction.)

TIP

Sprinkle these words throughout your written vocabulary but never let them dominate. Try for one per sentence, two at most. Avoid using a string of these words in a single sentence. Find these stuffy words either visually, by scanning what you write, or orally — read the material out loud and you'll definitely notice when they clutter up your sentences.

The following sections demonstrate some examples of overly suffixed wording and how to fix it. If you are unenthusiastic about grammar lessons, proceed happily: My goal is to help you develop a *feel* for well-put-together sentences and how to build them. Once you notice problems, you can correct them without thinking about rules.

The -ing words

Consider this sentence:

You may not initially find the challenge of improving your writing to be inspiring, but the result will be gratifying.

One short sentence with four words ending in *-ing!* Read it aloud and you find yourself falling into that up–down–up inflection. You can fix it by trimming down to one *-ing* word:

The challenge of improving how you write may not inspire you at first, but the results will reward you well.

Here's a sentence I wrote for this chapter:

Besides, there's something more satisfying about physically editing your copy and using the universal markings.

I didn't spot the five words that end in *-ing* until my third round of editing! Once you see a problem like this, play with the words to eliminate it. Then check that it matches your original intent. I rewrote the sentence this way:

Besides, you may find it more satisfying to physically edit your copy with the universal marks.

REMEMBER

When you're both the writer and editor, you're doubly responsible for knowing what you want to say. Fuzzy, verbose writing often results from your own lack of clarity. So, when you spot a technical problem, think first about whether a simple word fix will work. But realize that you may need to rethink your content more thoroughly. After you know exactly what you want to say, a better way to write the sentence emerges, like magic. This is how writing helps you think better.

When you edit someone else's work, knowing the writer's intent is harder. You may not understand what she's going for, and then it's all too easy to shift her meaning when you try to clarify. You may need to ask the author how to interpret what she wrote. Or make the changes and as appropriate, check that they are okay with her. Don't be surprised if she objects. The writer/editor partnership is often a tense and complicated one.

The -ion words

The following is cluttered with *-ion* words and incredibly dull:

To attract the attention of the local population, with the intention of promoting new construction, we should mention recent inventions that reduce noise pollution.

Reading aloud makes this sentence's unfriendliness instantly clear. Also, note that piling up lots of *-ion* words leads to an awkward passive sentence structure.

The problem with too many *-ion* words can be way more subtle, as in this sentence from an otherwise careful writer:

> *Whether they are organizing large demonstrations, talking with pedestrians in the street, or gathering signatures for a petition, their involvement was motivated by the realization that as individuals within a larger group, they had the potential to influence and bring about change.*

In addition to four words with the *-ion* suffix, the sentence also contains three ending in *-ing*. The result is a rambling, hard to follow, overly long sentence that feels abstract and distant. This sentence is challenging to fix. One way:

> *They organized large demonstrations, talked with pedestrians, and gathered signatures. Their motivation: Knowing that as individuals, they could influence and bring about change.*

Does it say exactly the same thing as the original? Perhaps not, but it's close. And more likely to be read.

Notice that after I cut down the *-ion* and *-ing* words, some of the cluttered phrases become more obvious:

>> Of course, pedestrians are "in the street" — so why say it?

>> The phrases "for a petition" and "had the potential" are both overkill.

Always look for phrases that add nothing or offer unnecessary elaboration — and cut them. Your writing will improve noticeably.

The -ize words

Similar to *-ion* and *-ing* words, more than one *-ize* per sentence works against you.

> *He intended to utilize the equipment to maximize the profit and minimize the workforce.*

In fact, you rarely need these kinds of Latinate words at all. In line with the principle of using short, simple words as much as possible, shift *utilize* to *use* and *maximize* to *raise*. And you can more honestly state *minimize* as *cut*. Note how multi-syllable words are usually embedded in abstract statements that distance us from a feeling of reality.

Modern business language keeps inventing *-ize* words, essentially creating new verbs from nouns. Here's a sentence that contains two of my least favorite words:

He knew that incentivizing the agreement might not succeed in impacting trade in a positive manner.

"Incentivizing" and "impacting" are among the nouns that have recently morphed into verbs through common practice. I personally avoid their use but acknowledge that living language seeks to fill in its deficits and also serve our appetite for speed. Without "incentivize," we'd need to say "offering an incentive." "Impacting" is a stronger word than "affecting," and more compact than "has an impact on."

The -ment, -ly, and -ous words

Words with these suffixes are usually complicated versions of words available in simpler forms.

A silly example that combines all these forms shows how using long words forces you into that unnatural rhythm, passive structure, and wordy phrases full of unnecessary prepositional phrases:

Continuous investment in the anonymously conceived strategic plan recently proved to be an impediment to the actualization and inadvertently triggered the anomaly.

WARNING

Unfortunately, much modern business writing is filled with convoluted language, clichés, and hyperbole at the expense of substance. When you try to edit some of it — such as this absurd example — you're left with . . . nothing at all. The fact that no one is impressed with empty writing, or likes to read it, doesn't stop people from producing it by the virtual ton. This is a mystery I can't solve.

But I'm hopeful: Research is under way to correlate good writing and communication with the bottom line. Towers Watson, a global management consulting firm, conducts high-profile surveys on the financial impact of effective communication, and the American Management Association is interested in the ROI-writing connection. The *Harvard Business Review* issues a growing abundance of material on executive communication. Meanwhile, the lesson is clear: Don't write in empty business-speak — it won't reward you. Just hope that your competitors keep writing that way.

Pruning prepositions

TIP

Another way to reduce wordiness is to look for unnecessary prepositional phrases — that is, expressions that depend on words like *of, to, from, for,* and *in*. Here again a good general rule is to avoid repeating the same form of speech in a single sentence whenever possible. For example:

Original: Our mission is to bring awareness of the importance of good writing to the people of the business community.

Revised: Our mission is to build the business community's awareness that good writing matters.

A sentence with unnecessary prepositions is often clumsy:

Original. He invested 10 years in the development of a system to improve the performance of his organization.

Revised: He spent 10 years developing a system to improve his organization's performance.

Original: Can it possibly be interpreted as a mistake by a reader?

Revised: Can a reader possibly interpret it as a mistake?

And notice that when you cut prepositions, you discover additional ways to improve a sentence. Some examples of this progressive thinking:

Original: Here are some of the imperatives of becoming a good communicator.

Revised: Here are some imperatives of becoming a good communicator.

Better: Here is how to become a good communicator.

Original: Research is needed to evaluate the potential for each idea.

Revised: Research is needed to evaluate each idea's potential.

Better: We need to research each idea's potential.

Original: Writing the proposal is necessary for clarifying your goal.

Revised: Writing a proposal will clarify your goal.

Better: Writing a proposal clarifies your goal.

TIP

Notice how weak wording generates more weak wording — passive verbs and overuse of prepositions come in bundles. Fix one problem in a sentence and you are easily able to identify and fix others. This lets you take different routes toward improvement. You can consciously look for extra "little words" in a sentence, for example, especially when they repeat, and follow up the clues they provide to boring verbs and awkward construction. The read–aloud editing method works well for this.

Here are a few more ways to reduce your wordy phrases:

>> **Use an apostrophe.** Why say the *trick of the accountant,* when you can say *the accountant's trick?* Why write *the favorite product of our customers,* when you can write *our customers' favorite product? Each idea's potential* works better than *the potential for each idea."*

>> **Combine two words and remove an apostrophe.** The phrase *build the community's awareness* can also read well as *build community awareness.*

>> **Use a hyphen.** Rework the CEO's fixation on the bottom line to the CEO's bottom-line fixation.

Cutting all non-contributing words

Extra words that don't support your meaning dilute writing strength. Aim for concise. Use the set of clues I describe in the preceding sections and zero in on individual sentences for ways to tighten. Here's a case in point:

With the use of this new and unique idea, it will increase the profits for the magazine in one particular month, July.

Extra words hurt the sentence's readability and generate bad grammar. Even though the sentence is fairly short, it manages to jam in two prepositions (*of* and *for*), an altogether useless phrase (*with the use of*), and an unnecessary word repetition — *new* and *unique.* Of course, the sentence construction is confusing as a result. A better version:

This new idea will increase the magazine's profits, particularly in July.

An objective look at your sentences may reveal words and phrases that obviously repeat the same idea. Here's a sentence I wrote for this chapter, which talks about editing hard copy from a computer print-out:

Of course, you must then transfer your changes to the original on your computer.

In context, the original document was clearly on the computer, so I cut the unnecessary phrase:

Of course, you must then transfer the changes to your computer.

Consider this explanation of Track Changes that I wrote:

Now when you make a change, the alteration is indicated in a color and any deletion is shown on the right.

The rewrite:

Your changes then show up in color, and deletions appear outside the text on the far right.

The revision works better because it eliminates unnecessary words and with them, the passive construction of *alteration is indicated* and *deletion is shown.*

TIP

Take aim at common phrases that slow down reading. Substitute simple words. Often you can substitute single words for formal, space-wasting phrases. The words on the left are almost always non-contributors; choose those on the right. Try making a list of the phrases you often use and consciously minimize them. Your writing will move a big step forward.

Wordy	Better
at this time	now
for the purpose of	for, to
the reason for that	because
in accordance with	under
is able to	can
it is necessary that	must, should
in an effort to	to
in order to	to
in regard to	about
in the amount of	for
in the event of	if
in anticipation of	before
in the near future	soon
on the occasion of	when
is indicative of	indicates
is representative of	represents
regardless of the fact that	although
on a daily basis	daily

PUTTING EMOJI, TEXTING, AND INSTANT MESSAGING INTO PERSPECTIVE

First came pictographs — visual symbols that represent things and ideas. Early human beings drew their images on cave walls and other rocky surfaces, and the first writing — invented a mere 5,000 years ago — consisted of visual symbols. The alphabet was devised later because it's faster and more convenient than using thousands of different pictures. The Romans chipped their messages into stone tablets and monuments, but this was such hard going that they jammed in whole strings of abbreviations and acronyms that still make translation difficult. The ancient Egyptians also depended on word shortcuts and omissions to make their point. Later, mathematics developed as a language to communicate concepts about the physical world for the same reason, conciseness.

So, we humans have always looked for faster and easier ways to communicate both everyday transaction and big ideas — and we're still looking. In this context, instant messaging (IM) and texting, with abbreviation and word skipping, make perfect sense. Typing on the miniscule keyboards of our smartphones more or less demands it. Language experts point out a plus — it teaches conciseness. And emoji? We can view this phenomenon as bringing us back to the beginning: pictographs. Members of Generation Z (those folks born after 1995) use them in highly subtle ways to convey emotional content, a quality lacking in impersonal formats like email.

But IM, texting, and emoji pose a problem: You can't assume everyone understands the abbreviations and symbols or likes communicating with them. Generally speaking, older people tend to lag behind in adopting new communication trends. Even younger readers may not consider these forms appropriate for business use. Bottom line: Writing in a manner your readers may not understand or like doesn't make sense.

Readers who are comfortable with texting shortcuts may still expect a more formal style in other media, including email. So, don't risk your effectiveness by transferring informal texting strategies to other business writing. Limit it to appropriate media and audiences that you're sure will respond well. If you like to sprinkle smiley and frowny faces around your emails, visualize your reader and how he may react before doing so. Right now, intensive emoji enthusiasts use them as a private language not intended for outside consumption, so cross-generational communication is not yet an issue. But if you're part of an older generation, think twice about using trendy approaches to look cool!

Moving from Passive to Active

Most people write much too passively. They use far too many verbs that are forms of *to be*, which force sentences into convoluted shapes that are hard for readers to untangle. Worse, all those *to be* verbs make writing so dull that many readers don't even want to try. Let's look at passive verbs from the editing angle.

TIP

Active verbs say everything more directly, clearly, concisely, and colorfully. If you want to transform everything you write — quickly — pay attention to verbs and build your sentences around active ones.

Thinking "action"

TIP

Active voice and action verbs are not the same thing grammatically, but this isn't a grammar guide. For practical purposes, don't worry about the distinction. Just remember to cut back on the following word choices:

>> **Is + an -ed ending:** *Your attention is requested.*

>> **Are + an -ed ending:** *The best toys are created by scientists.*

>> **Were + an-ed ending:** *The company executives were worried about poor writers who were failing to build good customer relations.*

>> **Was + an-ed ending:** *The computer was delivered by Jenny.*

>> **Will be + have + an-ed ending:** *We will be happy to have finished studying grammar.*

>> **Would be + an-ed ending:** *The CEO said a new marketing plan would be launched next year.*

The solution in every case is the same: Figure out *who* does *what,* and rephrase the idea accordingly:

>> *We request your attention. Or, pay attention!*

>> *Scientists create the best toys.*

>> *Company executives worry that bad writers fail to build good relationships.*

>> *Jenny delivered the computer.*

>> *We're happy to finish studying grammar.*

>> *The CEO plans to launch a new marketing plan next year.*

Verbs endings with *-en* raise the same red flag as those ending in *-ed*. For example, *I will be taken to Washington by an India Airways plane* is better expressed as *An India Airways plane will fly me to Washington* or *I will fly to Washington on India Airways*.

When you rid a sentence of *to be* verbs, you win a chance to substitute active *present tense verbs* for boring, passive, past tense ones. Many professionals work this tactic out on their own through years of trial and error (trust me on this). Writing in the present tense takes a bit more thought at first but quickly becomes a habit. Use present tense everywhere you can and see your writing leap forward in one giant step.

Look closely at all your sentences that contain *is, are,* and the other *to be* verbs. See whether an action verb can bring your sentences to life. Often, you can use the present tense of the same verb:

> *He is still a pest to the whole office about correct grammar.*

is better stated as,

> *He still pesters the whole office about correct grammar.*

Other times, simplify your verb to the present or past tense to convey a sense of an actual happening:

> *Michael succeeded in breaking the pattern of expectancy.*

is more engaging as,

> *Michael broke the pattern of expectancy.*

Trimming "there is" and "there are"

Big-time culprits in the passive sweepstakes are the combinations *there is* and *there are*. This problem is easy to fix — just commit never to start a sentence with either. Keep away from *there will be, there have been,* and all the variations. Don't bury them inside your sentences, either.

Check out the following examples and improvements:

> **Original:** *There were 23 references to public relations in the report.*
>
> **Revised:** *The report cited public relations 23 times.*

Original: *There is a helpful section called "new entries" at the top of the page.*

Revised: *A helpful section called "new entries" appears at the top of the page.*

Original: *It's expected that in the future, there will be easier ways to communicate.*

Revised: *We expect easier ways to communicate in the future.*

In every case, using an active verb does the trick, and almost all reworked sentences are in the present tense.

Cutting the haves and have nots

Like the *to be* verbs, using the various forms of the verb *to have* signals lazy writing. Find substitute words and a faster way to say what you mean as often as possible. A few examples and possible rewrites:

Original: *I have not been able to revise the proposal in time to meet the deadline.*

Revised: *I didn't meet the proposal deadline.*

Original: *Here's what can be accomplished this year provided I have cooperation from the relevant people.*

Revised: *Here's what I can accomplish this year if the relevant people cooperate.*

Original: *We have to make use of the talents we have.*

Revised: *We must use our own talents.*

Using the passive deliberately

Despite all the reasons for minimizing passive sentences, passive verbs are not "bad." You need them on occasions when the "actor" is obvious, is unknown or unimportant, or is the punchline. For example:

The computer was developed in its modern form over a number of years.

After long trial and error, the culprit was finally identified as the Red Toad.

You can also make a case for using the passive voice when you need to frame a message in terms of *you* rather than *we* or *I*. When writing to a customer, for example, you may be more effective to begin,

Your satisfaction with the product is what we care about most.

Rather than,

We care most about your satisfaction with the product.

The second statement gives the impression that "it's all about us." Of course, don't write an *entire* letter like the first opening — just the first sentence.

The passive is also useful when you don't want to sound accusatory. *The bill has not been paid* is more neutral than *You failed to pay the bill.*

Sidestepping Jargon, Clichés, and Extra Modifiers

Relying on words that have little meaning wastes valuable message space and slows down reading. Overused expressions also dilute impact, and "insider" language can confuse "outside" readers. Jargon, clichés, and unhelpful adjectives are hallmarks of unsuccessful business writing.

Reining in jargon

Almost every specialized profession has its *jargon:* terminology and symbols that shortcut communication and in some cases, make group members feel more professional and "inside." If a physicist is writing to other physicists, she doesn't need to spell out the formulas, symbols, and technical language. Her audience shares a common knowledge base.

Similarly, a lawyer can write to colleagues in the peculiar language he and his peers mastered through education and practice. A musician can exchange performance notes with other musicians in a way that means little to non-musicians.

WARNING

The risk arises when people talk or write to anyone other than fellow-specialists and use inside jargon. They forget that the general public does not share their professional language. If, for example, you're a scientist who needs to explain your work to a journalist, report on progress to company executives, order supplies, negotiate employment, or chat at a party, it's best to skip the scientific jargon entirely.

REMEMBER

Outside of our own specialized fields, we are all generalists. We want to be addressed in clear, simple language we can immediately understand. Judging by their messages to clients, many attorneys and accountants are among those who forget this basic principle — or perhaps no longer remember how to communicate in plain English.

But business writers face an additional challenge. A specialized, jargon-laden language flourishes full of buzzwords that means little — even to those who use it. For example, a technology company states in a publication:

> *These visible IT capabilities along with IT participation in the project identification process can drive the infusion of IT leverage on revenue improvement in much the same way as IT has leveraged cost cutting and efficiency.*

What does it mean? Who knows? All too often, corporate executives and consultants string together sets of buzzwords and clichés that communicate little beyond a reluctance to think. I know many editors who make good money saving some of these people from their worst utterances, but they sure don't catch them all.

Have some fun generating your own meaningless business language with the *Wall Street Journal's* Business Buzzwords Generator (`http://projects.wsj.com/buzzwords2014`). A few that came up when I last checked it out:

> *People, in the coming year, we need to strategically unpack our alpha.*

> *As part of our review of brand, we have decided to move forward with epic passion. Skate to where the puck is going to be.*

> *At the end of the day, the marketplace has changed. Aggregate strategically or cross-pollinate.*

Of course, sometimes a writer or organization deliberately chooses to bury a fact or a truth behind carefully selected words and phrases. Then you might argue that a message built on empty business jargon works well. But I don't recommend deliberately distorting the truth, writing without substance, or masking either situation with bad writing. Doing so just doesn't work, and it may boomerang. This widely circulated 2012 Citigroup press release (`www.citigroup.com/citi/news/2012/121205a.htm`) made the bank look ridiculous:

> *Citigroup today announced a series of repositioning actions that will further reduce expenses and improve efficiency across the company while maintaining Citi's unique capabilities to serve clients, especially in the emerging markets. These actions will result in increased business efficiency, streamlined operations and an optimized consumer footprint across geographies.*

Translation: *We're firing a lot of people to improve our numbers.*

To avoid producing empty business-speak, steer clear of words and phrases such as the following — some are perennials, others come and go:

360-degree view	optimization
best practice	over the wall
bleeding edge	peel the onion
blue-sky thinking	robust
boots to the ground	scalable
burning platform	shift a paradigm
core competency	swim lane
from the helicopter view	take it to the next level
full service	value proposition
leverage	vertical
move the needle	world class
open the kimono	

TIP

If you're writing a press release, website, or other promotional copy, check it for buzz-wordiness by asking yourself: Could this copy be used by any company, in any industry, to describe any product or service? If I substitute down-to-earth words for the clichés, does the message have meaning? Will my 17-year-old nephew laugh when he reads it?

Cooling the clichés

Jargon can be seen as business-world clichés. English, like all languages, has an enormous trove of "general" clichés, expressions that are so overused they may lose their impact. A few random examples that can turn up in business communication: *All's well that ends well, think outside the box, barking up the wrong tree, beat around the bush, nice guys finish last, a stitch in time, read between the lines.*

Clichés are so numerous they often seem hard to avoid. Often, they're idioms, and are, found in every language. They're popular for a reason — they communicate a meaning in shorthand. And they can be used well in context. But it pays to stay on the lookout for any that don't carry your meaning, or trivialize it. Instead, say what you want more simply, or perhaps develop an original comparison, as I explain in Chapter 3. And never forget that idioms and clichés are rarely understood by non-native English speakers, so try to avoid them altogether when writing to these audiences.

Minimizing modifiers

The best advice on using descriptive words — adjectives and adverbs — came from the great nineteenth-century American novelist Mark Twain:

> *I notice that you use plain, simple language, short words and brief sentences. That is the way to write English — it is the modern way and the best way. Stick to it; don't let fluff and flowers and verbosity creep in.*

> *When you catch an adjective, kill it. No, I don't mean utterly, but kill most of them — then the rest will be valuable. They weaken when they are close together. They give strength when they are wide apart. An adjective habit, or a wordy, diffuse, flowery habit, once fastened upon a person, is as hard to get rid of as any other vice.*

Twain wrote this advice in 1880 to a 12-year-old boy who sent him a school essay, but he's right on target for today's business communicators.

If depending on buzzwords and clichés is Sin #1 of empty business-speak, overuse of adjectives is Sin #2. Consider, for example,

> *The newest, most innovative, cutting-edge solution to the ultimate twenty-first century challenges . . .*

What, another solution?

TIP

Adopt whenever possible the fiction writer's mantra: Show, don't tell. Adjectives generally communicate little. In fiction, and especially scriptwriting, writers must find ways to bring the audience into the experience so they draw their own conclusions about whether a character makes bad decisions, is unethical, feels ugly or pretty, is suffering pain, and so on.

In business writing, "show, don't tell" means giving your audience substance and detail: facts, ideas, statistics, examples — whatever it takes to prove they need your product or idea, or you. Stating that something is innovative proves nothing. Adding an adverb, such as "very" innovative, just multiplies the emptiness.

Welcome opportunities to replace empty rhetoric with substance! There's no substitute for good content. Use good writing techniques to make that content clear, straightforward, and lively.

In Chapter 5, I move from focusing on sentences to creating solid paragraphs, solving organization problems, using strong transitions, and fixing the technical problems that most often handicap many business writers.

UNCLEAR WRITING IS AGAINST THE LAW!

By long tradition, the worst examples of opaque, confusing, and hard to understand writing come from none other than government. "Plain language" movements have gathered steam in a number of countries, including the United States and Britain, since the 1970s. Advocates point out that clear writing is essential for people to access services, follow regulations, and understand the law.

In the United States, sustained work by several nonprofit groups led to passage of the Plain Writing Act of 2010, which requires federal agencies to write all new publications, forms, and publicly distributed documents in a "clear, concise, well-organized" manner that follows the best practices of plain language writing. Extending the law to government regulations is an ongoing effort. In England, the campaign against small-print, bureaucratic language is similarly vigorous but a corresponding law has not been passed.

In both countries, efforts to clarify legal writing are underway as well. And an organization called PLAIN — the Plain Language Association International (www.plainlanguage network.org) — serves as a central resource for the plain language movement globally.

A special point of interest: Some studies demonstrate that the guidelines for better writing are basically the same across different languages: Short words, short simple sentences, fewer descriptive words, and good graphic techniques work well for Swedish writing, for example, just as for English.

Other interesting U.S. sites include The Plain Language Association (www.plain–writing–association.org) and the Center for Plain Language (www.centerfor plainlanguage.org), which gives awards for both admirable and most outrageous government-speak examples.

These and related websites offer a wealth of useful information and good "before" and "after" writing examples from both the public and private sectors. Movement leaders hope that promoting clear language in government will trickle across to the corporate world and inspire a linguistic house cleaning there.

Chapter **5**

Fixing Common Writing Problems

As you explore in Chapter 4, good self-editing requires you to look at your writing on two levels: macro and micro. Chapter 4 focuses on how you assess your content and present your material effectively. This chapter drills down to even more specific editing issues: techniques for organizing material and improving sentences and words.

REMEMBER

Every one of us has our own writing demons, persistent problems that show up in everything we write. Happily, most of these issues fall into common categories that you can correct with common-sense approaches. Even better, you don't need to master hundreds of grammar rules. This chapter gives you a repertoire of practical techniques for recognizing and addressing your own weaknesses. After you absorb them and begin putting them into practice, they enable you to head off problems *before* they pull you off-message or undermine your success.

If you need more motivation than to dramatically improve all your written communication, remember that *the process of thoughtful writing sharpens your thinking*. When you trouble to distill your meaning into direct, concise, compelling language, you clarify it for yourself as well as your readers. In a number of examples I show you how this works. Starting with a poorly written sentence, I move it through three or four successive editing stages. All the versions may be "correct," but I think you may agree that the final one works best.

Notice as you edit your own material that each improvement opens the door to more improvement opportunities. They add up to increase the impact of your messages and documents. Editing is a powerful communication tool. Once you absorb this truth, you may find it worth your time — and more fun than you may expect.

Organizing Your Document

Many people, including a number of experienced writers, say that organization is their biggest challenge. If you follow the process outlined in Chapter 2, which shows you how to plan each message within the framework of your goal and audience, you may be able to sidestep the organization challenge substantially.

But this may not altogether solve your problems, especially when documents are lengthy or complicated, written by more than one person, or simply strike you as confusing or illogical once drafted. You may need to review organization at that point and reshuffle or recast material. The following techniques help. You can implement them at the writing stage — or at the editing stage.

Paragraphing for logic

You may remember being told in school to establish a "thesis sentence" and develop each paragraph from that. If you found this advice a little dumbfounding, you're not alone.

TIP

Here's a much easier way to look at paragraphs. Start with the idea that each chunk of text should contain no more than three to five sentences. If you write your document that way, you avoid falling into a morass of confusing thoughts and easily achieve a logical flow of self-contained units — otherwise known as paragraphs.

If you routinely produce uninterrupted strings of sentences, don't despair: You can make the fixes later, during the editing stage. Read over what you've written and look for logical places to make breaks.

Can't decide where to insert breaks? Use the following technique:

1. **Scan your text to find places where you introduce a new idea or fact or where you change direction.**

   Break the flow into paragraphs at these points.

2. **If your paragraphs are still more than three to five sentences long, go through the whole piece again and make decisions on an experimental basis.**

   You'll check later to see if they work. The three- to five-sentence guideline is a general one that applies to print material. But an occasional one-sentence paragraph is fine and adds variety. When you write for online reading, shorter paragraphs work better, as explained in Part 4.

3. **Look carefully at the first sentence of each newly created paragraph.**

   See whether the new first sentence makes sense in connecting with what follows or whether it connects better with the preceding paragraph. If the latter, move the sentence up a paragraph and then break to a new paragraph.

   If a sentence seems not to belong with either paragraph, it may need to stand on its own or be rephrased.

4. **Look at your paragraphs again in order and check whether any wording needs adjustment.**

   Pay particular attention to the first and last sentences of each paragraph. You want each paragraph to link to the next. Using transitions helps with this — read more about these in "Working with transitions" later in this chapter.

   If when you scan the whole message you don't like the sequence of paragraphs, fool around with shuffling them. Adjust the language as necessary so that your paragraphs still clearly relate to each other.

TIP

You often find repeat words or whole ideas during this step, so make the necessary cuts and smooth everything out.

REMEMBER

The point of paragraphing is clarity. You want to deliver information in absorbable or usable chunks that lead from one to the next, rather than a single, long, confusing word dump.

Sometimes the reason you have trouble organizing your material is because you don't yet understand it well enough to effectively present it to others. Ask yourself: What *is* my point? What are the components of my argument? Number or list them if you haven't yet done so — you can omit the numbers later if that's better for your purpose. Also ask, am I missing critical pieces and need to add information or ideas?

Building with subheads

TIP

Another strategy for organizing, useful on its own or to supplement the paragraphing strategy described in the preceding section, is to add a few simple subheads. I mention subheads as an excellent graphic technique in Chapter 3. They are also useful guideposts for planning what you write, and can also be used to help clarify your message as you edit.

Suppose you're a department manager writing to tell your staff that a new customer relationship management system will shortly be introduced and they are required to attend training workshops. You realize that this will meet with resistance because everyone is used to the old uncoordinated and uncooperative system.

Brainstorm the points to make (see Chapter 2) and write them as a series of rough subheads. Perhaps:

>> New CRM system changes how we work

>> Everyone must use it

>> System will save us time

>> System will encourage information sharing

>> Mandatory workshop training schedule to come

>> Rollout date: March 6

>> Department Q&A meeting: February 1

Arrange your subheads in a logical order. In line with the principles laid out in Chapter 2, you want to instantly engage readers by signaling that the message directly relates to them and that it's important. So, you'd shuffle "rollout date" and "everyone must use it" to the top, and probably cover both ideas in the subject line. Then just fill in the relevant information under each heading. As you do this, additional topics may emerge that you didn't think of initially — for example, that creating support subgroups would help people feel more comfortable about adapting to the new system. Also, you want to motivate readers by appealing to the what's-in-it-for-me (WIIFM) viewpoint, so you might add a subhead like "how you will benefit." Find a logical place in your sequence of subheads and add the new ones.

In your final message, discard the subheads if you wish — or leave them in. Subheads usually work well to pull your readers through a message and keep them organized as well. They'll pick up the main points even if they just scan or don't read all the way through. Moreover, there's a psychological effect in presenting a clearly organized message. Readers feel you've got the situation well in hand and have thoroughly thought everything out. This feeling alone inspires greater confidence in both you and the new system, making people more receptive to the change.

REMEMBER

Long, complex documents benefit from the subhead strategy, too. For a report or proposal, for example, identify the necessary sections and, rather than subheads, write a headline for each. Then write a set of subheads for each section.

Drafting headings and subheads is a great way to be sure that you cover all the right bases, identify missing pieces early on, and build in good organization from project start. You also break up the writing process into doable bits so it's far less formidable. Be sure to use a consistent style for all your headings. Your word-processing program offers built-in styles, so it just takes a click to apply one.

Working with transitions

Transitions, those low-key words and phrases, are like the connective tissue that holds your skeleton together and empowers you to move where you want. Transitions tell readers how all the ideas, facts, and information in a piece of writing connect to each other. They grease your writing and pull people along in the direction you want to take them.

TIP

Good transitions signal good writing and good thinking. They help you organize your own ideas as a writer. And for the reader, they promote the feeling that your argument is sensible and even unassailable. Transitions are important tools for all writing — and for persuasive copy, they're essential.

Transitions can consist of single words, phrases, or sentences. They can be put to work within a sentence, to link sentences, and to connect paragraphs. Think of them in the following categories.

To continue or shift a line of thought, or indicate agreement or addition:

additionally	on the other hand
also	but
and	however
consequently	alternatively
for example	originally
furthermore	nevertheless
mainly	despite
so	in other words
sometimes	conversely

To establish a sequence or time frame:

as soon as	ultimately
at the moment	finally

first, second, third	later
to begin with	next
to conclude	for now

To indicate examples or emphasis:

in other words	for this reason
namely	in this case
significantly	often overlooked
surprisingly	on the positive side

To reinforce a desired focus or tone:

disappointingly	it sounds good, but
equally important	provided that
I'm sorry to say	given that
invariably	counterintuitively
luckily	of particular interest
unfortunately	at the same time
unless	in the hope that

Notice that the last set of words and phrases are prejudicial — that is, they orient a reader or listener to feel a certain way about what follows. Use them consciously.

Transitions give you a good way to begin paragraphs or sections, while putting that information in context of the full message. The following are examples of whole sentences that serve as transitions:

Based on this data, we've made the following decisions.

We've considered all the information and have reached some conclusions.

We should pay special attention to the sales figures.

A number of issues need to be addressed. Our priorities:

Notice how these introductory statements set up a super-simple way to organize subsequent material, including within long, complicated documents.

As with all writing principles, there can be too much of a good thing. When you give your writing the read-aloud test and it sounds stilted and clumsy, review your transitions — you may need to remove some. Do so and you still have a well-organized, convincing message.

Working in lists: Numbers and bulleting

Lists offer an excellent way to present information in a compact, to-the-point manner. They suit readers' Internet-trained text-skimming habits, and most people like them. They also automatically promote graphic variation, another plus for your document (see Chapter 3).

Numbered lists

Use numbered lists to present sequences of events, procedures, and processes. For example, a numbered list can guide readers on how to do something:

Follow these steps to sign up for the online workshop.

1. Go to the November workshops section of the company Intranet.

2. Choose "November Options."

3. Check the workshop and start date you want.

Scout actively for opportunities to organize a sequence by dates or milestones:

1. Jan. 10, Deadline 1: Submit project proposals

2. Feb. 10, Deadline 2: Finalize working plan

3. March 10, Deadline 3: Submit final budget

Using numbered lists may sound simple-minded, but they bestow a clarity that is so unambiguous, few people can misinterpret your meaning — no matter how hard they try.

TIP

You can also use numbered lists in more sophisticated ways. Bloggers use them, for example, to present blog posts in a popular and reader-friendly style: a number-centered headline followed by each numbered point, spelled out. For example:

5 Insider Secrets of Tripling Your Conversions Overnight

As I discuss in Chapter 12, many experienced bloggers think up a headline like that first, brainstorm for related ideas, and then write the copy. The Part of Tens at the end of this book follows the same pattern. This format appeals to readers and channels your knowledge in a different way, helping you uncover ideas you didn't know you knew.

When I wrote "Ten Ways to Advance Your Career with Writing" (Chapter 15), for example, I committed to the topic because it seemed like a subject people would want to know about. Then I brainstormed a list of possibilities, angling in on my knowledge base from a new perspective. I ended up with almost 20 ideas and chose the best.

Numbering is also a staple for presenters:

> *I'm going to give you five reasons why using this strategy will transform your life.*

> *Here are 7 reasons why there will not be a war.*

The technique works every time because audiences like knowing how much is ahead of them, and love ticking off the speaker's progress. It gives them easier-to-remember takeaways, too.

You need to know when to stop, though. In a speech, going above more than five numbered items is usually more than listeners can handle. In print, as with bullets, I suggest limiting yourself to seven. However, there's something magnetic about "ten."

TIP

Make items in your lists parallel in structure — begin them with the same part of speech. And they work best visually when they're approximately the same length. Both points apply to bullets as well and are illustrated in the following section.

Bulleted lists

Between on-screen writing habits and PowerPoint-type presentations, reading has become a bullet-heavy experience.

Like numbering, bulleted lists convey information tightly and neatly. They're appropriate for summarizing, offering checklists, and providing information-at-a-glance. What's more, readers like them — but only up to a point. Used incorrectly, bullets can kill. Audience interest, that is.

TIP

To successfully use bulleting, take account of the guidelines outlined here.

Don't use too many. Research shows that people can't absorb more than about seven bullets at one go. They tune out after that because each bullet typically makes a separate point and gives little logical connection to hold onto. If you must present more than seven bullets, break them into more than one list and intersperse some narrative material.

Use **the same sentence structure for every bullet.** Start each item similarly. Sentence structure must be parallel so as not to confuse readers. You can begin bullet points with action verbs, for example, such as when you present accomplishments in a résumé:

- *Innovated . . .*
- *Generated . . .*
- *Streamlined . . .*
- *Transformed . . .*
- *Mentored . . .*

Or you can compose a bullet list that starts with nouns, such as:

When you weekend in Timbuktu, be sure to pack:

- *Tropical microfiber clothing*
- *Sunglasses with a good UV coating*
- *Sunhat with extra-long visor*

WARNING

Don't be lazy and create bulleted lists of unrelated mix-and-match thoughts, like this:

Here are goals to aim for in business writing:

- *You want a conversational but professional tone.*
- *When you quote numbers, check that your readers use those systems.*
- *Don't be emotional or make things up.*
- *Jane is trying to standardize a similar look on charts and graphs. Once she does so, use that standard.*

You can refine this list by rearranging points two through four to start like the first one:

- *You want to check that all numbers quoted are in line with systems your readers use.*
- *You want to avoid emotion or making things up.*

But that approach produces an annoying repetition of *you want.* The solution: Find an introductory sentence that covers the points you want to make. For example:

In business writing, try to use:

- *Conversational but professional style*
- *Non-emotional tone*
- *Number systems familiar to your readers*
- *Consistent style for charts and graphs*

Or, just issue orders:

In business writing:

- *Use a conversational style*
- *Avoid an emotional tone*
- *Adopt a familiar number system*
- *Include real facts and anecdotes*

Punctuate and format bullets consistently. In this book, the first phrase or a sentence is often bold, and I don't use periods at the ends of bullet points that aren't complete sentences. In some bulleted lists, each item begins with a capital letter (that's the *For Dummies* style). In others, they're all lowercase.

There are numerous variables in punctuation and formatting. The styles depend on the situation and organization. Figure out your preferred style, or your company's, and apply it consistently to all your lists and your writing in general. Many organizations issue style guides that cover most aspects of writing and graphic presentation because consistency is important to branding. If such a guide is not available where you work, you can achieve your own consistency with a commercial style guide. Most commonly used are the *AP Stylebook* (Associated Press) and the *Chicago Manual of Style. For Dummies* uses a combination of its own style guide and the *Chicago Manual of Style.*

WARNING

Give bullet points meaning. Don't depend on bullet points to convince people of something or expect readers to fill in the gaps between them. Bullets are only formatting. If you've seen as many poor presentations as I have, you know that when bullets are not given meaning, they possess very little.

Tell readers what your bullets mean with good narrative writing or a quick introduction that puts the bullets in context. In a bio or résumé, for example, using all bullets to describe your assets defies readability. Begin with a well-written overall description of your current job followed by a list of your accomplishments — but put the information in context. For example, a job description can say "Consistent performance beyond company goals for three years," followed by your bulleted evidence (but no more than five to seven, and stated in sentences with parallel construction).

Don't automatically take the easy way out and use bullets and numbered lists when you have information to share or want to present something persuasively — which applies to most material you write. These formats may be fast to draft, but if they don't present your message as clearly as possible, you undermine your success. Take a hard look during the editing stage to see if your material might present better and be more persuasive in narrative form, or by translating some portions into a visual, such as a table or graph.

Catching Common Mistakes

Unlike the common cold, common writing problems can be treated and even prevented. The prescription is simple: Be aware of your own mistakes, which are nearly always consistent.

Improving your grammar is somehow a personal thing, so if you want solid grounding, I recommend that you scout what's out there in books and on the Internet. Choose a resource compatible with your learning style and dig in.

My grammar-related goal in this book, more modestly, is to:

>> Raise your consciousness so that you can recognize some of your own problems.

>> Give you practical tips for fixing those problems that require little grammar know-how.

>> Relieve you of some of your worries. What you're doing may be perfectly okay for today's less formal communication.

Infinitely more can — and has — been written about writing it right. See the sidebar "The journalist's grammar guidelines" later in this chapter for what may be the most succinct rundown ever created.

TIP

In the following sections, I show you the problems I most often find in even solid writers — all are easily fixed to make your writing a whole lot more effective right away. One general guideline to help you relax: *When your own writing confronts you with a grammar problem that's hard to resolve, or you just can't figure out what's wrong, write the sentence differently to sidestep the challenge altogether.*

Using comma sense

Stop stressing about commas! If visual cues don't work for you, use oral ones. The reading-aloud trick I recommend in Chapter 4 works surefire to tell you when you need a comma. Note the difference:

> *Eat Grandpa!*
>
> *Eat, Grandpa!*

If you read the words aloud to say what you presumably intend — that Grandpa should eat — the first option sounds this way:

> *Eat* (pause and downward inflection) *Grandpa*

A long pause with a change in inflection signals the comma is needed. And definitely, this sentence needs the comma. Notice in the example that the downward tone can be voiced after "eat," or the first syllable of "Grandpa."

Too many commas can also be a problem:

> *Reliance on the Internet, as the source of all information, produces problems for the connected generation.*

Read this sentence and you hear that it works better without pauses where the two commas are placed. They interfere with smooth reading and should be cut.

Badly placed commas in cases like this often signal a wording problem. A better version could read:

> *Relying on the Internet for all information creates problems for the connected generation.*

TIP

Reading aloud can also cure runaway or run-on sentences that typically depend on misused commas. Here's one that emerged from a writing seminar:

> *Grammar is something that everyone can always touch up on, the writers should use simple punctuation, properly place the punctuation marks, things like too many commas and semicolons can confuse the reader.*

The read-aloud test shows that the long, sustained pause after *touch up on* calls for starting a new sentence. The comma between the two middle thoughts doesn't work either because an *and* should connect them. Insert that conjunction and it's then clear that you need a period after *marks*, because to read meaningfully demands another sustained pause. The result:

Grammar is something that everyone can always touch up on. Writers should use simple punctuation and properly place the punctuation marks. Things like too many commas and semicolons can confuse the reader.

Another way of fixing this paragraph is to connect the whole second part with a transition and cut some redundancy, as in:

Writers should use simple punctuation and properly place the punctuation marks, because too many commas and semicolons can confuse the reader.

Train your ear and with a little practice, you improve your punctuation quickly. I once argued with the best grammarian I know about the reading-aloud method, running through a whole list of examples. Finally, she said, "The problem is it only works 97 percent of the time!" I figure I'll take my chances with the 3 percent and you may also prefer to.

Using "however" correctly

As with commas, reading aloud gives you the clue about how to use *however* in your writing.

Many perfectly decent writers embarrass themselves with sentences like these:

I planned to write the report over the weekend, however, my dog ate it.

Expense filings are due on January 15, however, exceptions can be made.

Reading these sentences aloud shows that long pauses are necessary before each *however*. You can break up both statements into two sentences with periods after *weekend* and *January 15*. The second sentence in each case starts with *However*.

You can also separate the thoughts quite correctly by adding a semicolon before *however* in both sentences. But generally speaking, semicolons seem old-fashioned in business writing. They have a literary air and are falling out of favor.

TIP

Alternatively, you can sidestep the "however" problem and also refine your wording in one of these ways:

>> Replace the *however* with *but*. If this substitution works, go with the *but*. It's correct and less stuffy as well.

>> Use *however* only to begin sentences.

>> Move a *however* that falls in the middle of the sentence to the beginning and see whether the meaning holds. For example:

He agreed with Jane, however, she was wrong.

He wants to know, however, so he can plan his vacation.

Moving *however* to the front makes nonsense of the first sentence. With the second sentence, however, the move retains the basic meaning.

Matching nouns and pronouns

Using the wrong pronoun is incredibly common, even in the work of professionals. For most communication jobs today, candidates must take a writing test. All those I've seen include a disproportionate number of questions geared to reveal this failing.

Pronouns have a simple function — to stand in for nouns so you don't have to keep repeating them. One cause of confusion is when to use *me* instead of *I*, *he* rather than *him*, and so on. For example:

Just between you and I, Jean was correct.

Mark, Harold, and me will go to the conference.

Both sentences are wrong. One way to figure that out: Switch some of the wording so the correct pronoun becomes obvious. In the first sentence, if you substitute *us* for *you and I*, it works fine. But if you substitute *we* (the plural for *I*), the sentence sounds absurd and you're clearly wrong. *Me* is therefore correct.

In the second sentence, you can choose to say *We will go to the conference,* and because the singular for *we* is *I*, that pronoun is correct. Or, you can eliminate Mark and Harold from the scene altogether, in which case you obviously must say *I*, not *me*.

TIP

As a general rule, go with what seems natural; but check yourself out. Try adding or subtracting words, as in the preceding examples.

Another cause of confusion is when to use a plural pronoun (like *their*) as opposed to singular (*his, its*). In these situations, stay alert to the original noun.

A journalist must always be attuned to their readers' interests.

This sentence is wrong because *journalist* is singular, not plural. But the sentence raises other issues. If I correct it to:

A journalist must always be attuned to his readers' interests.

Will I be accused of sexism? Perhaps, but the jury is still out on how to avoid this. You can

>> Say *his or her readers,* but that repetition gets tiresome.

>> Switch back and forth between the masculine and feminine. This approach works in longer documents, and that's what I do often in this book.

>> Change the original noun to plural:

Journalists must always be attuned to their readers' interest.

>> Rework the sentence to avoid the problem entirely:

Journalists must always be attuned to reader interest.

When you've altered the sentence this far, if you take one more look, you'll see an option for shortening it further and making it more dynamic:

Journalists must always attune to reader interest.

That's the present tense trick referred to in Chapter 4. *Be attuned* sounds passive and like a state of being rather than action. *Must attune* feels like an imperative and an active process. It even provokes some curiosity: How *does* a journalist attune to his readers?

Here's another sentence. See if you can correct it before looking at my version:

Everyone should use their discount when ordering online.

This is a very common mistake because while *everyone* is obviously singular, correctness puts you into that awkward him-her territory. A few alternatives via the sidestepping technique:

Use your discount when ordering online.

Everyone should apply the discount when ordering online.

When you order online, use your discount.

All will work. They say marginally different things, so your choice depends on the message context and medium. If you're writing a print piece like a flyer or advertising circular, you'd probably use the first statement. If you're writing a blog about leveraging discounts, probably the second seems most natural. If the statement was destined for a website that sells the product, *ordering online* becomes extraneous — it is obvious people are ordering online — so you'd be better off with

Use your discount when you order.

Some pronoun issues reflect cultural differences. In the United States, an organization is considered singular, so you say:

The company is widely criticized for its actions.

But in the United Kingdom, the plural is used (and the spelling differs):

The company is widely criticised for their actions.

The words that cause the most trouble in the noun–pronoun matchup are:

Each, anyone, anybody, everyone, either, neither, nobody

All are singular. Pronouns to represent them must be singular, not plural. For example:

Everyone in the women's club must vote for her choice of president.

Nobody on the jury should ignore his or her instincts.

Of course, the second sentence puts us back in the annoying "his or her" territory. Do you see a way to sidestep the awkwardness?

Weighing "which" versus "that"

Almost always, choose *that* rather than *which*. The latter word refers to something specific. When you're not sure which to use, try using *that* and see whether the sentence has the same meaning. If it does, keep *that*. For example:

The report that I wrote at home is on John's desk now.

But if you find that *that* doesn't reflect your meaning, you may mean *which*.

Note that you can write the sentence this way:

The report, which I wrote at home, is on John's desk now.

The second version calls attention to *where* you wrote it. And observe that you need two commas to set the clause off. *Which* always requires two commas unless the phrase appears at the end of the sentence. Another instance:

We provide afternoon breaks which, we know, help reduce stress.

You're using *which* correctly if you can eliminate the phrase inside the commas (*we know*) without changing the sentence's basic meaning. If you remove the non-essential phrase, the sentence becomes:

We provide afternoon breaks that help reduce stress.

Does this sentence carry exactly the same meaning as the original? Basically yes, but if the "we know" is important, it doesn't. In order for a sentence to carry your meaning, you must know what you want to communicate. I find my word-processing program is a demon at catching the that-which mistake, so when it's highlighted on the page or in the spell-check stage, listen. Usually it's telling you to change *which* to *that*.

Considering "who" versus "that"

For reasons I can't understand or explain, contemporary writing is chock-full of *thats* and very few *whos*. People have become depersonalized into objects. Speaking for myself, I find this practice disrespectful. The following sentences are all incorrect:

The new office manager that started on Monday already called in sick.

New customers that want to use the discount must register.

I don't like a person that never changes her mind.

REMEMBER

As a favor to me, please use *who* when referring to people. Inanimate objects and ideas are *that*. You may choose to refer to animals as *who*, but some prefer *that*.

Choosing "who" versus "whom"

This is foggier territory. Grammar enthusiasts insist that you differentiate between the word used as a subject (*who*) and as an object (*whom*, as in *to whom*). But adhering to the rule can land you in some stuffy places.

To whom should I address the package?

With whom should I speak?

To whom it may concern . . .

In the first two sentences, the less correct version works better for general business writing — reflecting the natural conversational style you're aiming for:

Who should I address this package to?

Who should I speak to?

TIP

In the case of the last example, don't use an archaic phrase like *to whom it may concern* at all. Always find a specific person who may be concerned, and use her name. If that's impossible, use a title *(Dear Recruitment Chief)* or a generic address *(Dear Readers)*.

Beginning with "and" or "but"

Like other wording choices addressed in this section, grammatical standards have relaxed, and only the rare individual complains about sentences that begin with *and* or *but*. *The Wall Street Journal* does it, the *New York Times* does it. I do it, a lot. And so can you.

But not so often that it loses its effect. Starting sentences with these conjunctions adds to your rhythmic variety and gives you a way to add a little verve, especially to online writing. It works best with short sentences.

Because can be used the same way, although I still hear people repeating the schoolroom mantra against starting sentences with that word. And you can start an occasional sentence with *"yet," "or,"* and *"so."*

Using sentence fragments

You probably recall your grade school teachers drilling this idea home: "Every sentence must be complete! Noun, verb, object!" Technically this remains true, but as our pace of life speeds up, so must our written language. For example, it's fine — except when writing the most formal documents — to say:

> *Here's the summary. Pretty long, I know.*
>
> *Do I like following the rules of grammar? Not so much.*
>
> *Use good grammar in everything you write. Unless breaking the rules makes sense and doesn't look like a mistake.*

REMEMBER

Fragments carry the business-casual tone that works for most practical writing. They give you short punchy bits that speed up reading, help promotional copy sound breezy or even cheeky, and break up sentence rhythm neatly: "Never again!" "Maybe next time." "Yes, tomorrow." When you write online copy, unless the material is really formal, use fragments to keep people engaged. On-screen reading is more strenuous so speed readability is especially important. But keep fragments interspersed with "real" sentences and be sure your copy remains crystal clear. Notice in the three examples that the fragments wouldn't make sense without the preceding sentences.

Ending with prepositions

An often-quoted piece of wit attributed to Winston Churchill underscores the silliness of strictly obeying some rules:

This is the sort of bloody nonsense up with which I will not put.

Obviously, it's more natural to say,

This is the sort of bloody nonsense I won't put up with.

Similarly, sentences such as these that end with prepositions are fine:

Leave on the horse you rode in on.

See if the answers add up.

He's a man I can't get along with.

We didn't know where he came from.

Don't make fun of grammarians, just because some of their ideas don't go where you want to.

TIP

Many stock phrases end with prepositions and there's no reason not to use them wherever they fall in a sentence. This especially applies if writing "correctly" requires an unnatural-sounding manipulation of language. The general guideline for business writing is: Use what feels comfortable in conversation.

Fine-tuning punctuation

Commas, periods, question marks, and other punctuation signals matter a lot: They tell people how to read your writing. Often, they substitute for the tone of voice, inflection, gestures, and body language we naturally use when delivering a message in person. Some marks — like commas, periods, and question marks — are essential. The question mark always denotes a rising inflection. Did you know that every language in the world asks questions with this rise? Curiosity is built into our human brains.

But other punctuation indicators go in and out of style. Here are my personal opinions on current punctuation style for practical business writing. Take them to heart or not based on your own preferences and each writing situation. I have found that once I looked into it, punctuation is more interesting than I expected, so see if you think so, too.

The *semicolon* should be used sparingly in business writing, at best, because it usually accompanies complexity — long sentences that demand deciphering.

Parentheses are similarly unpopular because they're distracting and slow down reading. The modern slant is "stick to the point" and don't confuse people with more than they need to know. So generally speaking, decide whether what they contain is worth including in the message or else omit the statement altogether. An exception is when you refer to something specific, as in *(see Chapter 4)*, a phrase that appears often in this book. Parentheses remain useful to denote an aside, despite these caveats — just be sure they don't interfere with reading.

The *dash*, on the other hand, is quite popular and as you probably noticed, I'm partial to it myself. It carries a tight telegraphic feeling and saves space. But too many will kill the broth, so keep the number down and resist using them to save yourself from thoughtful writing. And remember that generally, you need two of them, one before and one after the comment.

Colons are helpful when used to precede lists and examples. They can also produce special effects when you want to emphasize something: *The CEO called for great new ideas that involve no risk to the company: The silence was deafening.* Depending on your style guide, the part following the colon should be capitalized if it is a complete sentence, or not.

Quote marks are a bit tricky and writing testers like to trip people up with them. The basic rule: In the United States, periods and commas always go inside the marks. Question marks and exclamation points only go inside if they are part of the actual quote. But in the United Kingdom, single quote marks are used, and periods and commas go on the outside.

Along with emoji, *exclamation points* illustrate the living language idea best of all. They were until recently identified with "girlish enthusiasm," and business writers scrupulously avoided them. But today, because we depend so much on written communication in our work lives, the emotional deficit of written language often makes itself felt. Exclamation points have risen to the occasion.

To equip our contemporary media with a little emotion on demand — enthusiasm, excitement, surprise, intensity — exclamation points have been called back into service.

Exclamation points can also communicate a higher level of importance — *Pay attention!* But just as with revealing emotion on the work scene, exclaim in writing with discretion. More than one or two per message and they rebound on you. Emoji potentially give you far more emotional content, but as I cover in Chapter 4, using more than a smiley face may be inappropriate for some of your important audiences.

The *serial comma* is the comma you use — or don't use — for the last item in a list. For example, you can write a sentence this way: *Nancy picked up parsley, sage, rosemary and thyme.* Or, *Nancy picked up parsley, sage, rosemary, and thyme.*

THE JOURNALIST'S GRAMMAR GUIDELINES

Business writers can learn a lot from journalists, whose full-time work is figuring out how to present ideas and information in the clearest, most succinct, and interesting way possible. Unfortunately, as the newspaper industry shrinks, it provides an ever-smaller training ground for writers.

This classic list of rules was originally taken from a bulletin board at Denver's *Rocky Mountain News* and has appeared, with different add-ons, in a number of journalism books. The *Rocky Mountain News* stopped publishing in 2009, but many a writer keeps this demonstration of grammar pitfalls on hand.

1. Don't use no double negatives.

2. Make each pronoun agree with their antecedent.

3. Join clauses good, like a conjunction should.

4. About them sentence fragments.

5. When dangling, watch your participles.

6. Verbs has to agree with their subjects.

7. Just between you and I, case is important too.

8. Don't write run-on sentences they are hard to read.

9. Don't use commas, which aren't necessary.

10. Try to not ever split infinitives.

11. It's important to use your apostrophe's correctly.

12. Proofread your writing to see if you any words out.

13. Correct speling is essential(!)

14. Avoid unnecessary redundancy.

15. Be more or less specific.

16. Avoid clichés like the plague.

If you use a style guide, it will give you a consistent approach to follow. *For Dummies* style is based on the *Chicago Manual of Style*, which requires the "extra" comma. Throughout this book, that's how sentences are written — except where my sharp-eyed editor or proofreader missed the omission or decided they didn't apply. The paradox is that while serial commas help book copy to be read thoughtfully and more memorably, and therefore support learning, they don't promote the speed-reading that is essential for business writing. If you have a style choice, I recommend not using the serial comma, except in cases where you find it clarifies your sentence. Consistency in this regard is not a big concern for everyday messaging.

Reviewing and Proofreading: The Final Check

Before sending out your message or document into the world or to its target audience of one, review it at both the big-picture macro level and the close-in micro level.

WARNING

Editing is essential, but almost always, the process can unintentionally shift meaning and introduce new mistakes. Plan to review any passages you reworked at least one extra time.

Checking the big picture

Once you've edited your message or document and are satisfied with the writing, it's time to return to the big picture and assess your overall message in terms of content, impact, and tone. It's not sufficient to send a technically perfect message that isn't ready to accomplish what you want!

DOESN'T MY COMPUTER CATCH GRAMMAR GOOFS?

I said this before, but it's worth repeating: Microsoft Word and other word-processing programs have grammar- and spell-checking features that identify possible mistakes and indicate potential fixes. While these tools can help, accepting the corrections unquestioningly is like trusting a smartphone's word-guessing function. The more sophisticated this gets, the more potential for mayhem. Just in the past hour my own computer translated "They had a passion for sharing their ideas" into "They had a passion for sharing their disease." Pay attention to the corrections and changes your word-processing program wants to make, in both spelling and grammar, and evaluate them thoroughly. Always reread after the check.

Forgetting all the work and the decisions that went into what you've written and edited, look at your text as a self-contained piece and consider:

>> Is my *purpose* — what I want to accomplish — absolutely clear?

>> Does the piece support my personal agenda? For example, does it promote the relationships I want to build, represent me in the best professional light, and contribute toward my larger goals?

>> Do I get to the point quickly and stay on message? Does every element of the message support the result I want?

>> Does the message move well and smoothly from section to section, paragraph to paragraph?

>> Is the level of detail correct? Not too much, not too little, just enough to make my case?

Step even further back and read your document from your recipient's viewpoint.

>> Will the reader know what I want and exactly how to respond?

>> Is the message a good match in terms of tone, communication style, and audience characteristics? Does it focus on what's important to the reader?

>> If I were the recipient, would I care about this message enough to read it — and respond?

>> Did I provide appropriate evidence to support the case I'm making? What unanswered questions could the reader possibly have?

>> If I were the reader, would I give the writer what he wants?

>> Can anything in the message possibly be misinterpreted or misunderstood? Could it embarrass anyone?

>> How does it look: Accessible? Easy to read? Plenty of white space? Good graphic devices? Visuals as called for?

And finally,

>> Will I feel perfectly fine if this document is forwarded to the CEO, tweeted to thousands of strangers, mailed to my grandmother, or printed in a daily newspaper?

Correct any problems using ideas and tips in this book, plus your own common sense. Chapter 2 tells you how to understand your goals and your audience and build messages that draw the response you want. Choosing appropriate graphic options is covered in Chapter 3, and the preceding sections of this chapter.

Proofreading your work

In professional communication circles, proofreading is seen as separate from writing and editing. But in these economically tight times, copywriters, journalists, and even book authors often wear all three hats. Many publications now outsource their proofing services, or eliminate them altogether. If you've noticed a growing number of mistakes in what you read, that's the reason.

TIP

On a daily basis, obviously proofreading is all up to you. But you can still reach out for help. Many writers use a buddy system to back them up on important material, and you can, too. A colleague, friend, or partner may be happy to supply editing advice with you in exchange for the same help. As the saying goes, two sets of eyes are better than one.

SUREFIRE PROOFREADING TIPS

Try This: Here are some ways to do the best job proofing your own work, or someone else's. They're based on my own hard-won experience and I share them, like everything in this book, to save you all that trial and error.

1. Use one of the systems I explain at the beginning of Chapter 4 so your proofreading is systematic and clear.

2. Make sure in the case of a major document to keep an original unedited version.

3. Try to proofread when your eyes and mind are fresh, and take frequent breaks.

4. Proofread more than once — ideally three times — and allow some time between sessions.

5. Carefully check sentences before and after every change you make, because editing usually generates new errors.

6. Pay special attention to the places where you find an error, because errors often clump together (perhaps you were tired when you wrote that part).

7. Look for words that are often misspelled. Every grammar book has these lists or you can easily find one online; keep a copy on your desk.

8. Examine all the "little words," including *on, in, at, the, for, to*. They may repeat or go missing without your noticing if you don't pay attention.

9. Look up all words you aren't sure about. Choose a dictionary you like, or just Google the word.

10. Triple-check names, titles, numbers, subheads, and headlines.

11. Rest your eyes regularly, especially if you're proofreading on-screen. Looking out a window into the distance helps. So does setting your computer screen to a comfortable brightness.

12. Try enlarging the on-screen type for easier viewing — but not so much that you don't see the whole sentence, paragraph, or section.

13. Read challenging portions of text backwards. This approach helps a lot with material that is highly technical or contains numbers.

14. Resist relying solely on your computer's or smartphone's auto-correct feature. The more aggressive these systems get, the more big mistakes and potential disasters they introduce.

15. Recheck all the places where a mistake would prove most embarrassing: headlines, lead sentences, quotes.

Creating your personal writing improvement guide

Most writers are highly consistent in the errors they make, so creating a list of your writing shortfalls helps you sharpen up — and ultimately speed up — your writing.

Try This: Treat yourself to an in-depth session to review either a major document or a batch of smaller messages. Or gather information and insights over time. Better yet, do both. Start by thoroughly editing your selected work using the various criteria I explain in this book. Look for patterns of errors and less-than-wonderful writing. Addressing these particular problems will really benefit you.

Record the challenges — and the solutions — systematically. For example, in editing the chapter you're reading now, I made notes about what I found to need improvement. That list appears on the left. Then I wrote down the solutions on the right.

My Problems	Solutions
Too many words ending in -ing	Find substitutes for most and rewrite as necessary.
Too many long sentences	Break them up or tighten by cutting.
Need to fix sentence rhythm often	Read the sentences aloud and add or cut words so they move better.
Too many sentences per paragraph	Break them up.

My Problems	Solutions
Too many long words	Replace with short ones, mostly.
Too much passive voice	Substitute active more interesting verbs.
Repeated and boring words	Replace them. To do this quickly, look up the word up to find synonyms in an online the-saurus (for example, search for *"boring" syn*).
General wordiness	Keep an eye on Microsoft Word's Readability Statistics, and find more interesting verbs that promote an action feel.
Too many qualifiers (such as *you might, you can, you should*) and extra phrases	Cut, tighten, and/or rewrite. Cut the hedge words and write in present tense!

This analysis produces a road map I can use to review everything I write, from an email to a home page to a proposal.

Get even more specific and add categories, like words you often misspell or incor-rect use of possessives. Scout for solutions in this book and other sources, and equip yourself with tools to lick the problem.

To care about what you write is a different way of thinking. Do you really need to plan, draft, edit, cut, rewrite, add, subtract, edit, and proofread everything you write? You be the judge. But before you decide most of the process isn't necessary, consider whether or not your reputation and effectiveness are on the line nearly every time you write. I bet they are.

HOW DO I KNOW WHEN IT'S OKAY TO BEND THE GRAMMAR RULES AND WHEN IT'S NOT?

A good rule of thumb: Does it look like an unintentional mistake? Or can a reader possi-bly interpret it as a mistake? If either is possible, it's not okay to bend the rules. You don't want to look careless or like you're trying to be cute or clever. It's just too expen-sive in terms of credibility and authority. And errors disrespect the reader. In such cases, even if it hurts to be more formal, bite the bullet and rewrite more sedately. This princi-ple applies to general tone as well as language. Irony and sarcasm can be downright dangerous in written communication, where there's no inflection or smile to deflect the edge. Don't assume a smiley face will do the trick.

Try This: Use the plan-draft-edit process for everyday messages and see if you start getting what you want more often. I believe you will. The good — no, great news — is that when you practice the plan-draft-edit process on the small stuff, you're ready to use it for the big stuff: proposals, reports, articles, websites, blogs, and marketing materials. You'll ultimately save time and plenty of headaches.

Now that you're ready to apply all these ideas to your workday writing life, in the next chapter I focus most immediately on email messaging. This short-form communication is the lifeblood of most organizations and has become a central staple for marketing, overshadowing its more glamorous cousin, social media. Don't overlook its value or pass up honing your skills with email.

2

Applying Your Skills to Business Messages and Documents

Understand why email matters in the business world and how to make the most of this everyday communication tool.

Learn strategies to fast-forward your agenda with email without overwhelming or turning away your audience.

See why long-form business documents are more important than ever and how adopting an entre-preneurial mind-set can help you develop valued reports and write winning proposals.

Learn how to create strong and interesting executive summaries by giving perspective to complex material, determining what matters, and putting headlines to work.

Chapter **6**

Writing Messages That Get Results

L ove it or hate it, you can't leave it — email is the central nervous system of business life all over the world. Companies may declare "e-free Fridays" or add newer media like instant messaging or social networks to communicate, but you probably still find that your work life centers on managing your email inbox.

The volume and omnipresence of email in your life gives you the opportunity to accomplish your immediate and long-range goals, or screw up both. This chapter shows you how to make the most of this powerful medium and sidestep the traps.

REMEMBER

People have been talking for a long time — in some cases hopefully — of email's imminent demise. But it hasn't been replaced yet, and in fact, it's more important than ever. It's the basic tool of global communication, of growing interest to more and more businesses, and has become a major marketing tool. Recent research by the consulting firm McKinsey & Company found email to be 40 times as effective as Facebook and Twitter for acquiring new customers. So don't minimize its value to your work life. I cover email for marketing in Chapter 7, and concentrate here on using it for general business communication.

Fast-Forwarding Your Agenda with Email

If you're wishing for a way to show off your skills, judgment, competence, and resourcefulness and have decision-makers pay attention, *shazam* — email is *the* opportunity.

Yes, everyone is overwhelmed with too much email and wants most of it to go away. Consider your own inbox and see if you agree: Most of the email you receive is unrelated to your interests and needs, and most of it is badly thought out and poorly written.

Then take a look at your outbox. Ask yourself (and why not be honest?) how many messages you carelessly tossed off without planning or editing. You may feel that this is the nature of the medium — here one minute, gone the next, so not worth investing time and energy. But email is the tool you depend on to get things done, day in and day out.

Moreover, email has become the delivery system for many forms of communication. In earlier times, you'd write a cover letter to accompany a résumé, for example, and today you deliver it electronically. But a cover letter for a job application is still a cover letter — no matter how it's delivered. A short business proposal may also be sent by email, but like a cover letter, needs to be better written than ever. Competition only grows. Resist the temptation to write such material in an off-the-top-of-your-head fashion.

REMEMBER

Good email messages bring you the results you want more often. Even more, writing good messages every time — no exceptions — brings you amazing opportunities to reach the people you want to reach with a message *about you:* how intelligent, resourceful, and reliable you are, for example, and how well you communicate. Even those humdrum in-house email messages contribute incrementally to your positive image as an efficient professional, and give you a long-range advantage way past accomplishing your immediate goal.

Send relevant, direct, concise email that has a clear purpose and respects people's time, and you get respect back. People notice and respond to well-written messages, though admittedly, most do so unconsciously.

The higher you go in an organization's hierarchy, the more people tend to recognize good writing and value it because they see so little of it these days. Executives are acutely aware of how badly written email, even on mundane matters, can create

>> Misunderstandings that generate mistakes

>> Needless dissent among employees and departments

>> Inefficiency, because countering unclear messages demands much more communication

>> A staggering waste of collective time and productivity

Smart leaders are even more aware of how poor email messaging can affect an organization's interface with the world at large, resulting in

>> Weakened company image and reputation

>> Disaffected customers

>> Missed opportunities to connect with new customers

>> Long-term damage to relationships with the public, investors, suppliers, lenders, partners, media, regulators, and donors — all of which directly affect the company's bottom line

Take email seriously and it will give you many happy returns. Decision-makers in your workplace who value clear communication will value you all the more. In addition,

>> **Email offers huge opportunities to develop relationships in the course of doing business.** To build and sustain a network of trusted colleagues and contacts in-house and out can only benefit you over the long term.

>> **Email gives you access to the loftiest heights.** Fifteen years ago, the idea that you could directly write to your CEO, or the hiring manager of your dream employer, was unthinkable. Now you can, and she may read it and even respond — if you make your message good.

>> **Email is your ticket to connecting with people all over the world.** Without it, international trade would depend on mail systems and faxes for making initial contact. Surely email is the unsung hero of globalization.

TIP

If you're an independent entrepreneur, consultant, freelancer, or outside contractor, recognize that email can make or break your enterprise. Written well, email can help generate what you need: in-person meetings, opportunities to compete for business, new agreements, relationships of trust, and ways to promote what you do.

The guidelines for writing email apply to every type of memo, if your organization has its own in-house communication system, and also to letters. Letters have their own special characteristics as well and I talk about those adaptations later in this chapter. So keep in mind that email is a kind of writing microcosm. Practice your skills here and you know most of what you need for every business writing medium. And — a promise that may sound rash but really isn't — whatever does replace email someday, these same ideas will make it work.

Starting Strong

Your first imperative in drafting an email: Draw your reader to open it and read it. Sound easy? Not at all, given the sheer volume of messages that motivates most people to press the Delete key for any excuse they can come up with. That's another reason why every email you send must be good: You don't want a reputation for sending pointless, hard-to-decipher messages that lead people to ignore the important ones that you craft carefully.

With email, the lead has two parts: the subject line and the opening sentence or paragraph. I explore each in detail in the following sections.

Writing subject lines that pull people in

Take another look at your inbox and scan the subject lines. Note which ones you opened and why. Most of them probably fall into one of these categories:

>> Must-read because of essential information

Subject: New location, May 3rd meeting

>> Want-to-read because I like the writer (in which case, the "From" matters, too)

From: Chris Brogan

Subject: This One Change Improved my Life

>> Want-to-read because you need the information or it may be valuable

Subject: Free tools to recover deleted files

>> Want-to-read because it looks like a good deal

Subject: Lowest iPhone price in history

>> Want-to-read because it sounds interesting or fun

Subject: Our baby panda isn't camera shy!

>> Want-to-read because it makes me curious

Subject: Spacesuit Diapers

>> Want to read because I'm in the market for new furniture

All chairs: 20% off and free shipping

REMEMBER

Few messages are required reading. In the preceding list, only one subject was a must-read for me. Your challenge in writing email subject lines is to zero in on what's most likely to concern or interest your reader: not all readers — the readers you want. But you must always be fair. Don't promise something in the package that isn't actually there upon opening.

To create a good subject line that keeps fingers off that Delete key, follow these steps:

1. **Figure out what's most relevant to your reader in the message — why the person should care.**

2. **Think of the absolutely most concise way of saying it.**

3. **Put the key words as far to the left as possible so your recipient understands the core of your message instantly.**

Subject lines work best when they're as specific as possible. Here are two examples of email messages I didn't open because the subject lines were too vague and general to capture my interest, along with ways the message could work better.

> Poor: *Important question*
>
> Better: *Where is tomorrow's workshop?*
>
> Poor: *June newsletter*
>
> Better: *New Twitter techniques in June issue*

Ensuring that the most important words appear in your recipient's inbox window and aren't cut off for lack of space — or because they're reading on smartphones and other hand-held devices — is worth thinking about every time. Few people pay attention to this simple principle, so build this habit to reap a real advantage.

Investing in good, accurate subject lines always rewards you. You may not be able to deliver the whole of your subject in the limited amount of characters your recipient's inbox allows, but try to get the main point across. Unless it's a marketing message, you needn't aim to be clever; but if your message is important, spend some time to make the first few words intriguing.

WARNING

If you can't come up with a tight subject line that communicates the core of your message, consider the possibility that your message may not have a core — or any relevance at all — to your reader. Review both the subject line and the entire message to see whether you're perfectly clear on why you're writing and what outcome you want.

Be sure to review your subject line after you write the whole message. You may shift tack in the course of writing. In fact, the writing process can nudge you to think through your reason for creating the message and how to best make your case. Drafting the message first and then distilling the subject line is often easier.

TIP

Don't be lazy about changing the subject lines of long message threads. If you don't, people may overlook your new input. Later on, both you and the recipient may be frustrated when looking for a specific message. Try for some continuity, however, so it doesn't look like a whole different topic. If the first email of a series is identified as "Ideas for Farber proposal," for example, a new subject line might say "Farber proposal Nov. 3 update." Keep the subject lines obviously relevant to everyone concerned.

Many people use email as their personal database to draw on as needed, so always use the subject line to make messages findable.

Using appropriate salutations

The greeting you use is also part of the lead. Draw on a limited repertoire developed for letters:

> *Dear . . .*
>
> *Hi . . .*
>
> *Hello . . .*

You can use "Greetings" or something else, but be sure it doesn't feel pretentious.

Follow with first name or last as appropriate, using the necessary title (Miss, Ms., Mrs., Mr.). For the plural, Mesdames and Messieurs definitely feel over the top for English speakers. For groups, you can sometimes come up with an aggregate title, such as "Dear Software X Users," "Dear Subscribers," "Hi Team," and so on. Don't be homey or quirky. Using "Folks," for example, can grate on people sooner or later. Avoid generalizations like "Dear Customer" if you're writing to an individual. These days, people expect to be addressed by name.

TIP

Often, people who know each other well or are transacting business in a series of email dispense with the title, and simply start the message with the person's name — for example, "John." That's fine if doing so feels comfortable. Generally speaking, don't omit a name altogether and plunge right into your message. You miss an important chance to personalize. You can, however, build a name into the opening line, as in: "I haven't heard from you in a while, Jerry, so thought I'd check where things stand."

Drafting a strong email lead

REMEMBER

The first sentence or two of your message should accomplish the same goal as the lead of a newspaper article: Maintain your readers' attention, present the heart of what you want to say, and give them a reason to care. You must also tell readers the reason you're writing: what you want.

Because email leads usually include the same information that appears in the subject line, try not to repeat the same wording or exactly the same information. Email copy occupies valuable real estate. Your best chance of enticing people to read the whole message is to make the lead and everything that follows read fast and tight and not be repetitive.

Your email lead can consist of one sentence, two sentences, or a paragraph, as needed. When the subject line clearly suggests your focus, you can pick up the thread. For example:

Subject: Preparing for the August meeting

Hi Jenn,

Since we need the materials for the Willow conference in less than a week, I'd like to review their status with you ASAP.

Often you need a context or clarifying sentence before you get to your request:

Subject: Timing on design hire

Hilary, you mentioned that you'd like to bring in a graphic designer to work on the stockholder report ASAP. However, I won't be able to supply finished copy until April 3rd.

TIP

Note how quickly both of the preceding messages get to the point. Your everyday in-house messages should nearly always do so, whether addressed to peers, subordinates, or immediate supervisors. But never sacrifice courtesy. The right tone is essential to make your message work. For more on this, see the sidebar "Finding the right tone for email" later in this chapter.

When you write to people who are outside your own department or company, you often need to frame carefully. Suppose you're responsible for fielding customer complaints and must write to an irate woman who claims your company sold her a damaged pair of boots.

Dear Ms. Black,

Your letter explaining that your Magnifique Boots arrived badly damaged has come to my attention. I'm so sorry you had this problem and am happy to resolve it.

REMEMBER

Good subject lines and leads rarely just happen: You achieve them by thoughtful planning. If you prefer to figure out the main point through the writing process itself, be sure you leave time to edit your opening and subject line before sending.

Building Messages That Achieve Your Goals

You build a successful email message at the intersection of goal and audience. Intuition can take you part of the way, but analyzing both factors in a methodical way improves all your results. Knowing your goal and your audience is especially critical when you're handling a difficult situation, trying to solve a problem, or writing a message that's really important to you.

Clarifying what you want

Email often seems like a practical tool for getting things done. You write to arrange a meeting, receive or deliver information, change an appointment, request help, ask or answer a question, and so on. But even simple messages call for some delving into what you really want.

Consider Amy, a new junior member of the department, who hears that an important staff meeting was held and she wasn't invited. She could write the following:

> *Tom, I am so distressed to know I was excluded from the staff meeting last Thursday. Was it an oversight? It makes me feel like you don't value my contribution! Can we talk about this?*

Bad move! Presenting herself as an easily offended childish whiner with presumptions undermines what she really wants — to improve her positioning in the department. Instead of using the opportunity to vent, Amy can take a dispassionate look at the situation and build a message that serves her true goal:

> *Tom, I'd like to ask if I can be included in future department meetings. I am eager to learn everything I can about how we operate so I can do my work more efficiently and contribute more. I'll very much appreciate the opportunity to better understand department thinking and initiatives.*

With external communication, knowing your goal is just as important. For example, if you're responsible for answering customer complaints about defective appliances and believe your goal is to make an unhappy customer go away, you can write:

> *We regret your dissatisfaction, but yours is the only complaint we have ever received. We suggest you review the operating manual.*

If you assume your job is to mollify the customer on a just-enough level, you may say:

> *We're sorry it doesn't work. Use the enclosed label to ship it back to us, and we'll repair it within six months.*

But if your acknowledged goal is to retain this customer as a future buyer of company products, and generate good word of mouth, and maybe even positive rather than negative tweets, you're best off writing:

We're so sorry to hear the product didn't work as you hoped. We're shipping you a brand new one today. I'm sure you'll be happy with it, but if not, please call me right away at my personal phone number . . .

For both Amy's and the customer service scenarios, keeping your true, higher goals in mind often leads you to create entirely different messages. The thinking is big picture and future-oriented. In Amy's case, the higher purpose is to build a relationship of trust and value with a supervisor and gain opportunities. In the unhappy customer case, you want to reverse a negative situation and cultivate a loyal long-term customer.

TIP

Be the best person you can in every message you send. Every email is a building block for your reputation and future. And email is never private: Electronic magic means your message can go anywhere anyone wants to send it — and you can't count on erasing it, as so many public figures are shocked to discover.

Assessing what matters to your audience

After you're clear on what you want to accomplish with your email, think about your audience — the person or group you're writing to. One message, one style does not fit all occasions and individuals. As Chapter 2 details, when you ask someone to do something for you in person, you instinctively choose the best arguments to make your case. You adapt your message as you go along according to the other person's reactions — his words, body language, expression, tone of voice, inflection, and all the other tiny clues that tell you how the other person is receiving your message in the moment you're delivering it.

An email message, of course, provides no visual or oral feedback. Your words are on their own. So your job is to think through, in advance, how your reader is most likely to respond and base what you write on that.

Anticipating a reader's reaction can take a little imagination. You may find you're good at it. Try holding a two-way conversation with the person in your head. Observe what she says and how she says it. Note any areas of resistance and other clues.

TIP

You also have another surefire way to predict your reader's reaction: Systematically consider the most relevant factors about that person or group. Chapter 2 gives you a comprehensive list of factors that may relate to what you want to accomplish.

Do you need to consider so many aspects when you're drafting every email? No, if your goal is really simple, like a request to meet. But even then, you're better off knowing whether this particular recipient needs a clear reason to spend time with you, how much notice she prefers, if she already has set feelings about the subject you want to discuss, and so on. It makes a difference if you're writing to someone higher up the ladder with a crushing schedule or your colleague next door. You can tilt the result in your favor — even for a seemingly minor request — by taking account of such things.

The more important your message is to you, the more carefully you must think it out and consider your reader's framework. Sometimes just one facet of the person's situation or personality may matter, like his attitude toward new technology. The person's age may be relevant to shaping both content and tone. Politically incorrect as it may sound, different generations have different attitudes toward work, communications, rewards, authority, career development, and much more. If you're a Millennial (born after 1980) or Gen X'er (born between 1965 and 1980), you need to understand the Boomer's (born between 1946 and 1964) need for respect, hierarchical thinking, correct grammar, courtesy, in-person communication, and more. "Goal" and "audience" are the planning guideposts that never fail you.

Try This: I often ask participants in writing workshops to create detailed profiles of their immediate supervisors. Pretend that you're an undercover secret agent and you're asked to file a report on the person you report to. Take 10 minutes and see what you can put together. First scan the demographic, psychographic, positioning, and personality traits outlined in Chapter 2 and list those you think relevant to defining that person (for example, age, position, information preferences, hot buttons, decision-making style). Then fill in what you know or intuit about the person under each category. I promise you'll find you understand far more about your boss than you think.

Read through the completed profile and I bet you'll see major clues on how to communicate better with that important person, as well as how to work with him successfully in general and make yourself more highly valued. You may uncover ways to strengthen your relationship or even turn it around.

Suppose you're inviting your immediate supervisor, Jane, to a staff meeting where you plan to present an idea for a new project. You hope to persuade her that your project is worth the resources to make it happen. First clarify your goal, or set of goals. Perhaps, in no particular order, you aim to

>> Obtain Jane's buy-in and endorsement.

>> Get input on project tweaks sooner rather than later.

>> Gain the resources you need for the project.

>> Demonstrate what a terrific asset you are (always, always a constant).

You know Jane is heavily scheduled and the invite must convince her to commit the time. What factors about her should you consider? Your analysis may suggest the following:

>> **Demographics:** Jane is young for her position, and the first woman to hold that job. Observation supports the idea that she feels pressured to prove herself. She drives herself hard and works 60-hour weeks.

>> **Personality/communication style:** She likes statistics. She likes evidence. She's an impatient listener who makes decisions when she feels she has just enough information. Her hottest button is being able to show her own manager that she's boosted her department's numbers. How to do that probably keeps her up at night, along with how generally to impress her boss toward her next promotion. She takes risks if she feels reasonably sheltered from bad consequences.

>> **Positioning:** She has the authority to approve a pilot program, but probably not more. She's probably being groomed for higher positions and is closely monitored.

>> **Psychographics:** She is famously pro-technology, a true believer and early adaptor.

Presto! With these four points, you have a reader profile to help you write Jane a must-come email — and even more important, a guide that enables you to structure an actual meeting that accomplishes exactly what you want.

Determining the best content

After you know your goal and audience, you have the groundwork in place for good content decisions. You know how to judge what information is likely to lead the person or group to respond the way you want. (See Chapter 2 for guidance on how to address groups and construct a reader who epitomizes that group.)

TIP

To figure out what you need to say, play a matching game: What information, facts, ideas, statistics, and so on will engage the person and dispose him to say "yes"?

Think about audience *benefits*. This important marketing concept applies to all persuasive pitches. Benefits speak to the underlying reasons you want something. A dress, for example, possesses features like color, style, and craftsmanship, but the benefit is that it makes the wearer feel beautiful. When you're planning a message and want it to succeed, think about the audience and goal, and write down your first ideas about matching points and benefits.

For example, to draw Jane from the preceding section to that meeting, based on your analysis, the list may include

>> Evidence that the idea works well somewhere else

>> Information on how cutting-edge technology will be used

>> Potential for the idea to solve a major problem for the department

>> Suggestion that other parts of the company will also be interested and impressed

Many other ideas may be relevant — it's great for the environment, it gives people more free time — but probably not to Jane.

FINDING THE RIGHT TONE FOR EMAIL

In everyday email, your tone contributes heavily to coming across as empathetic, so never overlook it. Tone is discussed as it applies to all writing in Chapter 2, but here is how to look at it for email in particular.

It's useful to think in terms of "business casual" in general, with variations according to your subject and audience. When you know the person, you can key in more closely by visualizing him for a moment. Imagine yourself in conversation with him and determine where his work life personality falls along the spectrum of formal and reserved to casual and friendly, and also, the atmosphere and professional relationship you have with him. Your email tone can correspond.

If you're writing to someone you don't know, or to a group, edge toward the more formal, but avoid sounding stilted or indifferent. Conveying a degree of warmth and caring is nearly always appropriate because who doesn't like that? We all want to feel we matter and that we're respected.

Strive for positive energy in all your email unless for some reason it feels inappropriate to the subject. Granted, you have limited ways to express enthusiasm and must balance word choice and content to achieve a positive tone. You can use an occasional exclamation point to communicate excitement, but don't scatter them everywhere and make yourself look childish. And unless you know your reader well, do not use emoticons, except for possibly a smiley face, to indicate a shared joke, for example. Keep in mind that older people especially may regard you as lightweight if you do this a lot. And some graphic emoticons don't translate between various technologies and may be auto-replaced with . . . who knows?

Structuring Your Middle Ground

Think of your email message like a sandwich: The opening and closing hold your content together and the rest is the filling. Viewed in this way, most email is easy to organize. Complicated messages full of subtle ideas and in-depth instructions or pronouncements are inappropriate to the medium anyway.

Email's typical orientation toward the practical means that how you set up and how you close count heavily — but the middle still matters. Typically, the in-between content explains why — why a particular decision should be made, why you deserve an opportunity, or why the reader should respond positively. The middle portion can also explain in greater detail why a request is denied, or provide details and technical backup, or a series of steps to accomplish something.

Try This: Here's a recap of how to plan a message demonstrating how the middle works. Take a message you wrote recently or are in progress of writing. Figure out the basic content by brainstorming what points will accomplish your goal in terms of your target audience, as outlined in the preceding sections. Then do the following:

1. **Write out a neat, simple list of the points to make.**

   One example is the list I created to convince Jane to come to a meeting with a positive mind-set in the "Determining the best content" section.

2. **Scan your list and frame your lead.**

   Your lead is the sentence or paragraph that clearly tells readers why you're writing and what you want in a way most likely to engage their interest.

   TIP

   Starting with the bottom line is almost always your best approach for organizing a message. Remember the reporter's mantra: "Don't bury the lead."

Skipping the subject line for now, a get-Jane-to-the-meeting message can begin like this:

> *Hi Jane,*
>
> *I'm ready to show you how using new social media can help us increase market share for our entire XL line. After checking the online calendar for your availability, I scheduled the demo for March 5 at 2 p.m. Can you meet with me and my team then?*

To structure the middle, consider the previously identified points that are most important to Jane:

>> Evidence that the idea works well somewhere else

>> Opportunity to use cutting-edge technology

>> Potential to solve a major problem

>> Potential for wide company interest

You then simply march through these points to build the body of the message. For example:

> My research shows that two companies in related industries have reaped 15 to 20 percent increases in market share in just a few months. For us, the new media I've identified can potentially move XL out of the sales doldrums of the past two quarters.
>
> Further, we'll be positioning our department at the cutting edge of strategic social media marketing. If we succeed as I anticipate, I see the whole company taking notice of our creative leadership.

The thinking you did before you started to write now pays handsome dividends. With a little reshuffling of the four points, you have a persuasive memo that feels naturally organized and logical. You not only know your content, but also how it fits together. Moreover, your simple invitation has an excellent chance of bringing Jane to the demonstration with an interested and positive attitude.

This process may sound easy to do with an invented example, but actually, working with real ideas, readers, and facts is even easier.

REMEMBER

Your biggest strength in building a successful message in any format — even "big" material like a website, proposal, or book — is to know your story. Organizing a clear email message is rarely a problem after you determine your content. You simply need to spell out for yourself such factors as:

>> How the person you want to meet with may benefit by seeing you

>> Why your recipient will find your report or proposal of interest

>> Why the employment manager should read *your* résumé

Review the list you assemble, decide which points best serve your purpose, and put them in a logical order. Your list may include more thoughts than you need for a convincing message, and you can be selective. That's fine. Cross them out. "Just enough" is better than too much.

Closing Strong

After you write your lead and the middle, you need to close. When you use the guidelines in the preceding sections to begin messages and develop the middle, your close only needs to reinforce what you want. An email doesn't need to end dramatically. Often, it works to circle back to the beginning and add any necessary information to the "ask."

>> If requesting a decision, saying something like, "I look forward to knowing your decision by October 21st."

>> If you're delivering a report, your close may be, "I appreciate your review. Please let me know if you have any questions or if you'd like additional information."

>> In the case of the memo to Jane, the closing might be simply, "Please let me know if March 5th at 2 p.m. works for you. If not, I'm happy to reschedule."

Sign off with courtesy and tailor the degree of formality to the occasion and relationship. If you're writing to a very conservative person or a businessman in another culture, a formal closing like "Sincerely" is often best. The same is true for a résumé cover letter, which is essentially a letter in email form and should look like a letter.

But in most situations, less formal end-signals are better: "Thanks!" "I look forward to your response." "Best regards," or a variant. Generally, avoid cute signoffs like "Cheers." I recommend always ending with your name — first name if you know the person or are comfortable establishing informality. Even if your reader is someone who hears from you all the time, using your name personalizes the message and alerts her that the communication is truly finished.

Actually, your finished message needs one more thing — finalizing the subject line. Consider at this point the total thrust of your content. Then decide what words and phrases work best to engage your audience's interest. The "Jane" subject line, for example, needs to get across that your message is a meeting invitation, suggest what it's about, and emphasize that it is worth her time. Perhaps:

Can you come: May 3rd Demo, Social Media Project

Polishing Your Email

Email deserves your best writing, editing, and proofreading skills. Often the message is *who you are* to your audience. You may be communicating with someone you'll never meet, in which case the virtual interaction determines the relationship and the success of the message. At other times, crafting good email wins you the opportunity to present your case in person or progress to the next stage of doing business.

REMEMBER

People look for clues about you and draw conclusions from what you write and how you write it. Even if your ideas are good, incorrect grammar and spelling lose you more points than you may suspect no matter how informal your relationship with the recipient seems.

The following sections run through some of my top tips for crafting copy that perfectly suits email.

Monitoring length and breadth

Generally speaking, keep email to fewer than 300 words and stick to one idea or question. Three hundred words can go a long way (the memo I wrote to draw Jane to the meeting in the preceding section ended up only 145 words total).

WARNING

Such limits are hard to consistently observe, but you're wise to remember how short people's attention spans are, especially for online reading. That's why you benefit from knowing your central point or request, and opening with it. Don't bury it as a grand conclusion. Nor should you bury any important secondary questions at the end.

TIP

Aim to make email as brief and as tight as you can. If your message starts to grow too much, reconsider whether email is the appropriate format. You may choose to use the message as a cover note and attach the full document. Or you may want to break the message up into components to send separately over a reasonable space of time.

Simplify style

Choose words and phrases that are conversational, friendly, businesslike, and unequivocally clear. Email is not the place for fanciful language and invention. You want readers to understand the message the first time they read it. If they are left to figure out your meaning, they will either stop reading or fill the lines in themselves and may end up with a different idea than you intended. This is where a lot of that expensive confusion comes from in every organization. Put your energy into the content and structure of your message, and express what you want to communicate in unambiguous and straightforward language.

Try to make your writing transparent, eliminating all barriers to understanding. Your messages may end up less colorful than they could be, and that's okay. Clear, concise language is especially relevant to messages directed at overseas audiences, because they may come to them with limited English language skills.

Going short: Words, sentences, paragraphs

The business writing guidelines in Chapter 3 apply even more intensely to email. You want your message to be readable and completely understood in the smallest possible amount of time. Draw on the plain old Anglo-Saxon word-stock and use mostly one- and two-syllable words. Use longer words when they're the best choice and serve a real purpose.

Short sentences work for the same reason. Aim for 10 to 15 words long on average. Paragraphs should be one to three sentences long to support comprehension and build in lots of air.

Using graphic techniques to promote clarity

These graphic techniques don't require special software or a degree in fine arts. They're simply ways to visually present information and make your writing more organized and accessible.

TIP

Do everything you can to incorporate generous *white space* (areas with no text or graphics) into your writing. Don't crowd your messages and leave them gasping for air. White space allows the eye to rest and focuses emphasis where you want it. Short paragraphs with double returns between them instantly create white space.

Add subheads

Subheads are great for longer email. You can make the type bold and add a line of space above it. Subheads for email can be matter of fact:

Decision point close

Step 1 (followed by Step 2 and so on)

Special considerations

Pros and cons

Background

This technique neatly guides the reader through the information and also enables you as a writer to organize your thinking and delivery with ease.

Try This: Drafting all your subheads *before* you write can be a terrific way to organize an email. Pick a message that you already wrote and found challenging. Think the subject through to come up with the major points or steps to cover and write a simple, suitable subhead for each. Put the subheads in logical order and add the relevant content under each. Now check if all the necessary information to make your point is there — if not, add it. Your message is sure to become clearer, more cohesive, and more persuasive.

Here's an extra trick. If you feel that you have too many subheads after drafting the entire message, just cut some or all of them out. You still have a solid, logically organized email message. Just be sure to check that the connections between sections are clear without the subheads.

Bring in bulleted and numbered lists

Bullets offer another excellent option for presenting your information. They are:

» Readily absorbed

» Fast to read

» Easy to write

» Useful for equipment lists, examples, considerations, and other groupings

However, observe a few cautions:

» Don't use more than six or seven bullets in a list. A long stretch of bullets loses all impact; they become mind-numbing and hard to absorb.

» Don't use them to present ideas that need context or connection.

» Don't mix and match. The items on your list must be *parallel,* so that they begin with the same kind of word — a verb, a noun, or an adverb.

Never use bullet lists as a dumping ground for thoughts that you're too lazy to organize or connect. If you doubt this advice, think of all the bad PowerPoint shows you've seen — screens rife with random-seeming bullets.

Numbered lists are also helpful, particularly if you're presenting a sequence or step-by-step process. Instructions work well in numbered form. Give numbered lists some air so that they don't look intimidating — skip a space between each item.

Consider boldface

Making your type bold gives you a good option for calling attention to key topics, ideas, or subsections of your message. You can use bold for lead-ins:

Holiday party coming up. *Please see the task list and choose your way of contributing.*

You may also use bold to highlight something in the body of the text:

*Please see the task list and choose your way of contributing **by December 10.***

Of course, don't overload your message with boldface or it undermines its reason for being. Keep in mind that boldface doesn't always transfer across different email systems and software, so don't depend on it too much for making your point.

Underlining important words or phrases is another option, but it tends to look outdated.

Respect overall graphic impact

REMEMBER

Avoid undercutting your content through bad graphic presentation. Plain and simple is the way to go. Use plain text or the simplest HTML — no tricky, cute, or hard-to-read fonts. Don't write whole messages in capitals or italics and don't use a rainbow of color — that's distracting rather than fun for readers. Don't vary the font size: Use one that's readable for most people, in the 12-point range. It's a good idea to check how your messages look once in a while by sending one to yourself — it may morph during its trip through cyberspace. Avoid a crammed-in feeling. People simply do not read messages that look dense and difficult. Or they read as little of them as possible. Like everything else you write, an email must look inviting and accessible.

Using the signature block

Contact information these days can be quite complex. Typically you want people to find you by email or telephone. Plus, there's your tagline. Your company name. Your website. Your blog. The book you wrote. The article you got published. Twitter. Facebook. LinkedIn. Professional affiliations and offices. And potentially much more.

Decide on a few things you most want to call attention to and refrain from adding the rest. Better yet, create several signature blocks for different audiences. Then you can select the most appropriate one for the people you're writing to. Don't include your full signature block every time you respond to a message, especially if you incorporate a logo, which arrives as an attachment. Check your email program's settings so the automatic signature is minimal, or altogether absent.

PRACTICING EMAIL SMARTS

Email is a great facilitator in many ways, but definitely has limits. Email's "easiness" can lead you to inappropriate use. Do not:

- **Present complicated issues or subjects.** Of course, you can attach a report, proposal, or other long document to an email, but don't expect an email in itself to produce an investment, donation, or other high-stakes buy-in.

- **Wax philosophical or poetic.** Readers look to email for practical communication and are annoyed by windy meanderings — even (or especially) if you're the boss.

- **Amuse.** Generally avoid sarcasm and irony, and most humor unfortunately, because it can be misinterpreted against your interests.

- **Spam.** Send email only to people directly concerned with the subject and don't send unnecessary replies. Don't forward cute anecdotes or jokes unless you're absolutely sure the particular person welcomes that. And don't forward chain letters: They can upset recipients. Don't forward anything without reading it. Thoroughly and carefully.

  Is it considered spamming to respond to a message chain with a minimalist confirmation, like "Yes, the meeting is at 3," or "I received your input?" Not when it feels necessary to close the communication circle. If your reader may feel left hanging, or any uncertainty can linger, then by all means follow up with the last word. Better safe than . . . you know what.

- **Respond to poorly considered and written email with poor email of your own.** You don't know who else may see them, and even those who write badly — perhaps through a feeling of executive privilege — may disrespect you for doing the same. Enjoy feeling superior (without expressing it, of course)! Your classy excellent email rewards you over the long run as almost nothing else can.

Good Letter Writing Techniques

You may be under the impression that you don't write business letters and never need to in today's fast-paced world. Think again. You are probably writing letters without realizing it. Don't be fooled by the fact that you're using an electronic delivery system and don't need a stamp. Acknowledge that your missive is a letter, and you do a much better job of achieving your goal.

When something important is at stake, recognize that what you produce merits extra care in terms of its content, language, and visual impression. This doesn't necessarily mean you need to find your old stationery. In many cases, it's perfectly fine to send your letter as an email. In other instances a physical letter serves you better. If you're a nonprofit manager writing to elderly donors, for example, relying on email is questionable. As always, consider your goal and audience in deciding on the best mode of delivery.

Here are some of the business-world occasions when you should think "Aha! This calls for a letter!"

>> **Introducing yourself:** If you're the new veterinarian in town writing to the patient list, or need to explain why a VIP should give you 10 minutes of her time, or why people should vote for you, you're courting the reader and must make the best possible first impression in order to secure what you want.

>> **Making a request:** If you want a referral, a recommendation, an invitation, an informational interview, a special assignment, a corner office, a favor of any kind, write a letter.

>> **Pitching something:** If you sell a product or service, one effective way is with a sales letter, either via the post office or email. When you market anything, you must apply your best strategizing and writing.

>> **Presenting formal applications:** When you apply for a job, submit a proposal, or compete for an educational opportunity, nine times out of ten, you need a cover letter. If it's optional, leaving it out is a mistake. Sometimes the letter must accomplish the goal on its own — when a job posting specifies a letter and no résumé, for example.

>> **Saying thank you, I'm sorry, or expressing sympathy:** Such messages are important and should be carefully personalized and meticulously written and presented. If they don't look as if you have given thought to such a message and taken trouble, they don't communicate that you care. A personal letter is much more effective than a greeting card.

>> **Expressing appreciation:** If someone gives you a wonderful break, takes a chance on you, offers significant advice, or makes an introduction for you, a letter from you to that person will be treasured — trust me. People so rarely do this. And it's worth considering a retrospective thank you to anyone in the past who inspired or helped you, too.

>> **Congratulating someone:** Supervisors, coworkers, subordinates, colleagues, suppliers — everyone welcomes a graceful congratulatory note when reaching a milestone, or achieving something significant.

>> **Documenting for legal purposes:** Letters can be called for as official records in relation to job offers, agreements, performance reviews, and warnings. These formal records may have legal implications now or in future. A binding contract can take the form of a simple-looking letter, so must be scrupulously

written if you want them to protect you. And know what you're agreeing to when sign those written by other people!

>> **Seeking redress:** If you have a complaint about a product or service, or how you've been treated, or how a print or digital publication has misrepresented you or your organization, to be taken seriously, write a letter.

>> **Expressing opinions and concerns:** Yes, Virginia, newspapers and other publications still run Letters to the Editor — and those editors know that this section is usually the most read feature of all. But it takes a good letter to be heard. Letters to local government and legislative offices reap a lot of attention, too.

>> **Inspiring people to care:** If you want friends and colleagues to actively support a cause you believe in, with money or time or connections, a letter bears much better testimony to the depth of your own commitment.

>> **Valuing privacy:** Letters carried by the postal system are privileged documents protected by the "secrecy of correspondence" principle. In many countries, it is illegal to open letters in transit. The privacy of digital communication remains murky, so printed-and-delivered physical letters offer a last bastion of privacy.

If you search online, you'll find a ton of prewritten and preformatted letters for every occasion. You may get some ideas from them, but almost never will a cookie-cutter template work as well as your own well-crafted letter. Often the tone is wrong and the content is bland and impersonal, which totally undercuts the reason you're writing a letter. So, I won't give you formulas. However, specific types of letters, such as marketing messages, job application letters, and networking notes, are covered in the relevant chapters ahead.

What letters have in common is the need to look good. They may be delivered electronically and can even be signed online in most legal situations today. But in many cases they should look like a letter, not an email. Check out the sidebar "Formatting your letters" for a basic format to customize to each occasion.

TIP

Consider at times the value of a real letter — the kind that you can hold in your hands, reread at will, and keep with your important or treasured documents. Do you have a shoebox of letters that connect you with important events or people of your past personal life? Many people do. Letters relating to our professional lives can have different but nevertheless strong associations for us, especially if they make us feel good. A physical letter is real and tangible and permanent in a way that an email is not.

We've gotten accustomed to the fact a digital message is fleeting, that most photographs viewed on our smartphones are rarely printed, and that social messages that take a lot of time to create are meant to disappear forever in a few minutes. This makes a meaningful communication we can hold onto even more valued.

I know several professional colleagues who make a habit of handwriting their messages to clients and other important connections on notepaper: thank you for the help or referral, happy holidays, happy birthday, congratulations on your award or your son's graduation. These savvy professionals look for opportunities to write notes like these. Don't laugh. When they visit these recipients' offices and see these notes prominently displayed on the contact's bulletin boards, the strategic value of this small effort is reinforced. I should tell you that these friends are all very successful.

Chapter 7 explains how to apply the basic writing principles to the big make–or–break business documents: proposals, reports, and more.

FORMATTING YOUR LETTERS

If your letter is being delivered by post, use a standard business format. If delivery is electronic, take pains to make the message look as much like a letter as possible so readers take it more seriously. Lots of books and websites present letter-formatting details, but here are the essentials:

- **Use block style.** Start every element flush left, but run it rag right (uneven rather than a straight line).

- **Eliminate indents.** Instead, skip a line space between paragraphs.

- **Choose clear, simple fonts.** Try Times Roman in 11 or 12 point or a sans-serif face like Helvetica if the message is short and need not look conservative.

- **Add graphic elements judiciously.** A headline, subheads, and color and type variations can be appropriate for sales letters; include just a few or none for other letters unless helpful for clarity.

- **Use letterhead with your logo if you have one.** You can create the look of letterhead on your computer. Incorporate a small digital file of your logo in messages you send electronically.

- **Supply contact information.** Make it full and complete, using the letterhead and signature block.

- **Pick proper paper.** Stick with white, or a light color paper, that doesn't interfere with reading.

- **Sign your name,** preferably in blue, which looks formal, but also makes your signature stand out rather than appearing to be mass-produced as part of the letter.

Chapter 7

Creating High-Impact Business Materials

Today, we all need to think like entrepreneurs. More and more people are starting full- and part-time businesses, and many earn their living as "independents" — professional specialists, consultants, and freelancers. Others, especially those new to the job market, supplement their incomes with freelance gigs and hope this work will grow into a future business. Even established employees benefit from an entrepreneurial mindset because they need to keep proving their value, pitch their own ideas, and compete for good opportunities on the job. A growing number of people find themselves contributing to their organizations' marketing in some way, too.

The comfortable jobs that allow the holder to subsist as just another cog in the machinery are fast disappearing. But who wants to be a cog anyway? If you prefer to be an active, successful, and happy member of your work community, good communication can be your key. The preceding chapter looks at how everyday messaging can further your career, whatever the enterprise and your role in it. At the same time, major business documents like reports and proposals are more important than ever — they can make or break an opportunity. I find that a surprising number of people are shortsighted about the value of them, however. This chapter gives you a wealth of tools and techniques to create reports that get attention, write proposals that get you what you want, and draft first-rate executive summaries.

Creating Valued Reports

Many situations call for reports that must be shaped to specific needs and goals. In general, there are two basic types of reports: activity reports and project reports.

Activity, or status reports, describe what was accomplished during a set period, whether weekly, monthly, quarterly, or annually. They include personal reports on how you spent your time and what you achieved, and consultants' reports to clients.

Project reports explain how something was carried out, results, and perhaps recommendations. Scientists report on their findings this way and so do people responsible for overseeing a new initiative or rollout. Such reports may contain complex information, for example, an actuarial report on likely outcomes of different decisions, or some white papers.

Many reports fall somewhere between these two basic types or blend both sets of characteristics. One constant is a strong executive summary, which I discuss how to write later in this chapter.

Writing activity reports

These reports typically occasion the biggest groans. Whether a weekly, monthly, or annual review of their activity is required, many people begrudge the time to write them as a distraction from their "real" work and treat them as busy-work imposed by inconsiderate managers.

Resist that feeling! If you think writing reports is boring, you're bound to produce dishwater documents that serve you badly. Consider *why* someone wants the information involved. If it's your supervisor, she may want to know:

>> Your progress (and everyone else's) in carrying out department initiatives

>> The need for course correction to meet goals and deadlines

>> Problems looming on the horizon — and opportunities

>> How well the staff is coordinating tasks and whether things are humming along smoothly

Especially when a staff consists of more than a few people, it's hard for the bigger-picture decision-makers to keep track of what's happening under their watch. Group meetings and written reports become important. Keep in mind, too, that your boss needs grist for his own report mill. He must in turn report to his superiors, and needs information from team members to do so. Good material enables him to write better reports. And some of your input may rise all the way up the line, perhaps to the top.

Managers base decisions on staff reports more often than you may suspect. Ideally, activity reports collectively add up to the larger perspective their roles demand and provide clues to help them deploy their resources more successfully. When you contribute informed observations and ideas, they're valued because you're closer to the action, whatever that is, and speak for that piece of reality. Reports keep those further from the ground in touch.

Accordingly, recognize that activity reports offer excellent chances to show off your capabilities and prove your value. Take the trouble to make them well-organized, well-strategized, informative, and concrete. And use good writing to make them as interesting as you can. If you suggest your own boredom through a rote delivery, what does that say about how you feel about your job and how you do it?

Just as with writing email, which is covered in Chapter 6, start with the perennials: goal and audience. Your *goal* is to provide useful information and perspective to the reader, and no less important, to present yourself as the thoughtful, skilled, resourceful, creative professional you are. Your *audience* is the manager who asks for the report as well as the whole ladder of managers above him or her.

Look at your report from your supervisor's viewpoint to gauge the appropriate content, level of detail, and style of writing. Take his informational preferences and decision-making style into account (see Chapter 2 on how to do this). A report's orientation also varies according to company culture and your role. If you manage a unit or department, you're responsible for reporting on the team's performance as well as your own.

Focusing reader attention

You can easily get lost in detail when reporting on an activity period or project. Remember that the reader doesn't care much about how you spent every second, but she does care about what you accomplished, any problems you encountered, and in some cases, your suggestions. The boss depends on you to analyze what occurred and filter out what matters.

Try This: If reports are a regular part of your work, take the time to develop a set of questions based on what you seek to accomplish and the nature of your work. Start with the following list. Cross out those that don't relate to your situation, adapt others as necessary, and add more questions so you end up with a customized list that leads you to know your story and helps you present it.

>> The most important thing that happened this month was _____.

>> The most important thing I accomplished was ____.

>> What progress did I make toward my goals?

>> What initiatives did I take or what new approaches did I use? What resulted?

>> What my bosses and colleagues should know about is _____.

>> My core message about the ups and downs of the last month is _____.

>> The problem I really need help with or support for is _____.

>> The good news is _____. The not-so-good news is _____.

>> After reading this report, the resulting decision, action, or feeling I want from readers is _____.

>> What I want most for myself is _____.

TIP

A report's substance should not center on what you did ("I spent five hours scouting for new clients and wrote email to three prospects"), but rather on what your efforts accomplished ("I secured two new agreements and I'm currently working with three interested prospects"). Writing a good report requires you to clearly know your work goals and how they relate to your audience.

Align your perspective with the bigger picture with additional questions such as:

>> What did I contribute to big picture goals? Long-term goals?

>> What's changed from the previous month(s)? The impact?

>> What has progressed, held steady, or regressed?

>> What comparisons are relevant — last month, last year, or another time frame?

>> Did I see any opportunities? Did I act on them or refer them to someone else? Any results?

If you want to go one step further, offer insights and data-based opinions. This is often expected from managers. Some questions to help with this:

>> What surprised me?

>> What occurred that should be taken into account in the future or bears watching?

>> Did the general climate of the past period offer challenges or advantages?

>> Is the team moving in the right direction? How or what would I change if I could?

>> What would be fun or thought-provoking to share?

>> What do I recommend based on the information in this report?

>> Do I see opportunities for collaborative action?

WARNING

Of course, decide on content judiciously. Consider company culture, your own role, and your relationship with superiors before making broad recommendations and sharing personal viewpoints. Keep this in mind when assembling your own list of questions. They should be appropriate but also give you scope to more proactively present yourself as a thinker and problem-solver.

Knowing your story

An activity report may have a prescribed format or you may have some degree of leeway in how you present your information. Either way, first figure out your story by answering the questions you developed in the previous section. If you have a prescribed format use that as a guide, but don't get lost in the format: Know what you want to say and figure out how to do so in the required configuration. Often you can set the perspective you want by beginning with a brief executive summary, which can be as short as a single introductory paragraph.

TIP

Even with guidance from a series of questions, it can be hard to distill your experience to find a perspective for a report. Here's a shortcut: Imagine a good friend asks you, "What did you do the past month (or the past three months or year)? What happened?" Think of how you would verbally answer your friend, and you may find your summary crystallizing nicely for you. Then use this perspective to frame the report and write the opening. In transferring your ideas from the oral to written medium, adapt as called for, but don't overly complicate the storyline and language.

Try This: If you're creating your own format for a report, use the subhead method I describe in Chapter 5. For example, if you're a department or unit head, you might structure your report this way:

Executive summary

Old initiatives, progress, and results

New initiatives, progress

Staffing changes

Unexpected challenges

Environment scan — big-picture situation that's relevant

Bottom line: Profits/losses

Projections

Resource or assistance needs

WARNING

If the categories for your reports are predetermined, or you inherited them through long company traditions, honor them. But don't turn into an automaton. Even though the powers-that-be may insist on a given format, their eyes tend to glaze over the fastest. Nothing makes for a duller report or application than filling out each section of required information as a rote task, in the number of words that seem called for. Doing so produces a lifeless litany that makes you look like a hack.

After you have a reasonably organized set of categories and spend some time thinking about your overall message, start working with one category or section at a time. Do this in sequence or not, according to your personal preference. Some people like to start with what's easiest for them. The beauty of sectionalizing the document is that you can choose your working method while knowing in advance how the pieces fit together.

Drafting the report

When you're ready to pull the whole report together, start at the beginning with the first section after the executive summary. For each section, open with a good summary statement — the *lead.* As with the lead for many kinds of writing, aim to capture attention and explain what information is coming. For reports and other business documents, a good generalization that puts the information in perspective works well. A section on staffing changes in a manager's quarterly report, for example, might begin:

> *The department successfully added three new highly qualified specialists in high-need technical areas this period, while losing two mid-managers by attrition. This improves our positioning and enables us to better accomplish our goal of upselling technical services to current clients. Only one of the managerial jobs needs to be filled.*

Then go on to fill in the details on the level you deem appropriate. Stay organized painlessly by identifying subsections for each major part. To follow up the preceding lead, your subsections might be:

New technical hires

Expanding service capacities

Manager attrition

Overall staff situation/outlook

Stay conscious of how each section contributes to your overall message, as well as how you're relating to the company's problems and priorities. Know thoroughly how things fit together and make sure you clearly communicate that to your readers.

Stick to your storyline — the big perspective — and use everything in the report to back that up. Don't bury what matters. To avoid overwhelming people with information, analyze what you can leave out. Providing too much detail may trivialize the important things you want people to absorb. If you don't provide a strong perspective, you leave readers to draw their own conclusions. Lawyers routinely confound the other side by dumping tons of unsorted documents on them that they are forced to wade through. Don't information-dump your readers, especially if you work for them. If necessary, you can put the data into an appendix.

Reporting project results

While the process for writing project reports is similar to writing activity reports, a project report may call for a different structure according to the subject. Here, too, aim to tell a story with a logical beginning, middle, and end.

Often the challenge of a project report is how to present an abundance of data and concepts in a way that holds together for readers. Faced with masses of poorly sorted information, most people will either stop reading or draw their own conclusions. Neither outcome is good for you. Take the time to determine your central message — and how you want your reader to react. Use the questions you draft in "Focusing reader attention" earlier in this chapter to guide you, but start with these:

> What was the reason for undertaking this work?
>
> What did I want to find out and why?

Identify the project's goal as closely as you can. For example, did you want to supply a basis for decision-making? Provide support? Question a current position? Predict outcomes from various scenarios? Justify an action? Or just keep specific audiences updated? A basic reporting sequence like this one suits many purposes:

> What we wanted to know and why (the problem or mission)
>
> What we did and how (abbreviated; this may not interest most readers)
>
> What happened
>
> What we learned and the evidence (as appropriate)
>
> Our conclusions (what we recommend, problems, next steps)

Section by section, create an engaging lead based on your most important result from the reader's perspective. When you have good news, flaunt it, don't bury it. On the other hand, don't obscure any bad news so it's overlooked or comes as a shock.

REMEMBER

A good report, like any major document, doesn't happen overnight. Don't position yourself to start from scratch when the deadline is tomorrow. Consider collecting information for the report gradually in a folder or on your computer or desk (or both), for each section. Add to the folders over time so you're not overwhelmed at the last minute desperately trying to remember what happened, where the figures are, and what it all means. Before you draft, give yourself time to read through all the material you gathered and decide on your message.

TIP

Here's a good way to cut through complex masses of information to the bottom line: After scanning your material, put it away for a few hours or days. Then without referring to it, summarize it orally or in writing. You may find that your brain filters out what matters, given a little distance.

For more help, see the sections later in this chapter on writing executive summaries and using editorial and graphic devices to energize your material.

Fast-Tracking Your Proposals

If the futurists are correct, you may have more proposal writing ahead of you than you suspect. Every year, many companies and not-for-profit organizations maintain smaller staffs and hire more consultants and independent contractors. Even if you stay in-house, you may find a growing need to pitch for new assignments or responsibilities in writing.

Sometimes you may need to prepare formal proposals in a format either prescribed by an organization or the occasion. For example, if you're aiming for investment capital, you need to meet your audience's expectations of content and style. In many cases, however, a far less formal proposal can succeed and may even be preferred by your target reader. More and more consultants I know use brief proposals to sell their services. Here, I show you how to write both varieties.

Writing formal proposals

Most RFPs (request for proposals) require formal, standardized responses. This is true in most big-business situations, and also for many grant applications. You may have a list of specifications to meet and a prescribed format. If you do, follow those specifications to the letter, especially if you're bidding for a government contract. At other times, you may have more leeway to organize your document as you like, or to interpret a set of guidelines.

TIP

For help with preparing a long-form, high stakes proposal, check out Internet resources and business management books. You can find abundant good advice on formatting and specific buzzwords to use, but you probably can't find much about the process of writing the proposal itself. Not to worry. Here are several tips for answering RFPs that can make the difference between winning a bid and losing out:

>> **Tell a story.** Even if the prescribed format makes storytelling tough, use the space to communicate a cohesive picture of what you recommend, what you'll do, and why you're the best person or company to do the job. True, specialists may scrutinize only a few sections, but key readers review the whole document and want it to make sense cumulatively — with as little repetition as possible. (See Chapter 9 for storytelling tips.)

>> **Know your audience's goal.** If you're pitching for a complex contract, take the time to understand the company and the problem it's trying to solve — it's always there. Read the RFP exhaustively between the lines and research the organization to see how the requested work fits into the company's overall needs — and by extension, how you can fit in. In doing this, you'll pick up keywords to incorporate and better understand the company's "voice" so you can respond in kind and show you're on the same wavelength.

>> **Give your audiences what they need.** Include content and details that specifically match audience expectations. Remember that most businesspeople want to increase profitability or efficiency. All reviewers want to know a project's timetable, how you measure success, the budget, who will do the work and their credentials, and your track record and specific qualifications for the job.

>> **Write simply and conversationally.** Use a slightly more formal tone than you'd use for everyday communication — fewer contractions, for example — but don't sound overly academic and stuffy. It's best to write in the third person, with the company as an entity, unless you are the central or the only person involved. A two-person organization can use "we," and if you have a virtual team to call on, "we" is also okay. Make your language lively but jargon-free. See Chapter 4 for more tips about how to do this.

>> **Speak their language.** Notice any statements that are emphasized or repeated. These are clues to the organization's hot buttons and perhaps sensitivities honed by experience. Incorporate key phrases and ideas in your responses, but don't come across as if you're parroting back their words rather than providing the answers they hope for. And be sure to explain how you'll measure outcomes!

>> **Remember the decision is about you.** Whatever you're proposing, you're asking someone to choose you and your team. Never skimp the biographical section. Show why each team member is right for the role, how the team works together, its accomplishments, and why you in particular can be trusted to deliver on time, within budget, and to specification.

>> **Go for the proof.** Don't say "the team is creative, reliable, and efficient." Cite examples, case histories, statistics, and testimonials that demonstrate these points, as appropriate. Impress with substance rather than empty claims. "Tests show that our concrete lasts 16 percent longer than other varieties" is better than "our concrete lasts forever."

>> **Edit and proof your work.** After writing, review and correct your document in several stages. (See Chapters 4 and 5 for more about this process.) One error costs you your credibility. Ask a friend with sharp eyes to proof for you, too. If you fail to showcase your ability to communicate well and correctly within the document itself, you lose ground regardless of what you're trying to win.

>> **Make it look good.** Your competitors will. Use all the graphic options to help your proposal read well and easily. Give your readers opportunities to rest their eyes. (See Chapter 3 for advice on using graphic tools.) Include relevant graphics — images, graphs, charts, infographics — but they must never be extraneous. If a lot rests on this document, ask a friend with design ability for guidance. Or find a good model and adapt elements of its design or the whole layout.

TIP

Often, those issuing the RFP provide a route for asking questions. Don't be too proud to do take advantage of this! If you're not sure whether you're eligible, better to find out first. If you don't understand a requirement, say so. If you don't know what supporting materials are welcome, ask. Take care to sound intelligent, listen, and follow up on the clues. The process is necessarily impersonal, but like all business, relationships matter — a lot. Use available opportunities to build those relationships as well as pinpoint helpful information.

REMEMBER

Always do a big-picture review of your document before sending out a proposal. Ask yourself (or a colleague) the following questions:

>> Did I demonstrate my understanding of the problem or goal?

>> Did I explain who we are and why we're the best choice?

>> Did I clearly state what I will do to address the problem and the expected outcomes?

>> Did I clearly spell out what "success" will look like and how it will be measured?

>> If different people worked on the proposal, has the whole piece been edited to read consistently and well?

TIP

Many candidates focus proposals on *process* and short-sell *results.* For example, a training proposal to update staff technology skills should talk less about how many workshops the program includes and more about the gains that result in efficiency, problem-solving, and error-reduction after the training. When possible, give the client a vision of how much better his people will function, or how his processes will improve, or how life and the world will be better if you are awarded the opportunity. But the vision must have "feet" — a solid grounding in actual possibility, not pie in the sky.

And, remember the professional proposal writer's mantra: Be SMART — Specific, Measurable, Achievable, Realistic, and Time-sensitive.

Writing informal proposals

In fast-moving times, few consultants or contractors want to do more than necessary to win the job. If you're vying for a government or big-industry contract or a grant, you usually have no choice other than to follow the given specifications. But in many other situations, you can save yourself a bundle of time.

One way is to build the proposal into the selling process and make it a simple agreement — confirmation of a plan already discussed. You can create a logical sequence to cover what's necessary, or even use a letter format. This approach requires a different selling process because it builds on a personal discussion of the job at hand rather than analysis of a written request.

The first step is to achieve that conversation. As any sales professional can tell you, aim for a face-to-face meeting with your prospect. Then write the proposal based on what you discover. Proposals based on phone conversations, or worse yet, written exchanges, are harder sells. Ideally, you want to gain a second appointment to present your solution — that is, your proposal.

TIP

At the first meeting, rather than aggressively selling your qualifications, hold a conversation. Encourage the prospect to talk. A beginning that often works well is, "I'd love to know how you came to this position." Listen very carefully and use friendly prompts to keep the person talking and gently steer the direction. Ask open-ended questions:

>> What problem would you most like to solve?

>> How is this problem affecting your business?

>> What difference would solving it make for you?

Watch for clues as to how you really can help the organization and how much problem fixes will be valued. It's unlikely that you'll be told the problem you were brought in to discuss is not important, but it's perfectly possible that exploring the fit between you and the prospect will reveal that it's not a good match. It's better to find this out before you're highly invested.

If the conversation indicates a mutually beneficial arrangement is possible, you can prepare your informal written proposal. This can cover

>> The problem you propose to address

>> Why that problem is important

>> What you recommend

>> How you will carry the program out step by step

>> What will result

>> Mutual obligations, time frame, and so on

>> Your fee

At the end, you can add, "Agreed to by . . ." with room for signatures and date.

Here's an example of a common-sense proposal to pitch for an opportunity in my business of teaching business writing:

A Workshop Proposal for Whiteflag, Inc.

From CC Writing Workshops

I am pleased to propose a series of writing workshops to help Whiteflag customer service representatives handle customer complaints more effectively and actively build customer relations through email and letters.

The Problem: Alienated customers

Your recent review of 24 representatives' interactions with customers showed:

- A growing number of complaints from customers unhappy with how their problems were handled

- An abrupt, sometimes rude tone in many outgoing messages

(This list can be longer, but keep it no more four or five)

Impact of the problem on Whiteflag:

The situation is adversely affecting your company. In your own analysis, it is a major factor in a recent 4 percent decline in your customer base.

CC Writing Workshops proposes:

(A step-by-step outline of the proposed workshop series — specific but very concise — goes here.)

Program goals:

The workshop series will achieve . . .

(List the outcomes you aim for that correspond to the problems and note if possible how results will be measured.)

How we will work together:

(Describe the collaborative planning, time frames, and obligations of each party.)

The presenters:

(Indicate who will deliver the program and their credentials.)

Fee structure:

(State your project fee or hourly rate, which should protect you from "scope creep"; for example, cite extra charges for work that exceeds the parameters you set.)

Agreed to by: _____

The entire document can be just a few pages. If you want it to be really informal, format it as a letter that begins with a salutation — "Dear Jane" or "Dear Ms. Brown." Some more standard sections, like the "presenters" section that describes staffing and credentials, can be done as a separate add-on.

TIP

Your tone and language for an informal proposal are just as important as for a formal one. After all, you've spoken personally with the individual who might hire you. You've also seen how he presents, what his office looks like, how he communicates, what sparks his interest and concern, and how important the problem is to him. Be alert to all these clues and picture him in your mind as you write. (Chapter 2 gives you ways to consciously analyze your audience and align with it in your writing.)

Ultimately, most contracts and assignments are won in person — see Chapter 8 for ways to prepare for this — but writing is the essential first step toward most opportunities. You rarely get in the door without a first-rate proposal. Good writing and the good thinking it reflects can be a great leveler. I know personally many cases where a small David beat a smug Goliath to win stellar opportunities, and companies that have built their entire success on very good writing.

A good letter introducing yourself — another kind of proposal — can work wonders in many circumstances. This may seem like a simple task, but often, the less room you have to frame an "ask," the better you need to think it out.

Applying for grants

In most ways, applying for grants is similar to answering business RFPs. Grants bestowed by government agencies, foundations, and large corporations typically involve completing very explicit questionnaires that must be followed to the letter. Smaller grant-givers, such as volunteer-run organizations that award modest amounts to local nonprofits, typically supply their own application forms. These vary widely in both the nature of the information required and how to present it. However, following some common-sense guidelines will maximize your chance of winning a grant.

REMEMBER

Partly to make the process as efficient for themselves as possible, and help ensure that the most deserving projects are selected, most givers sponsor applicant training sessions. Even if attendance isn't mandatory, be there. The whole application process is a chance to build relationships with the grant giver. In addition to showing up when asked, you can pose good, thoughtful questions by telephone, or in writing as the second choice, to humanize the interaction. Financing a non-profit initiative involves a lot of trust: Investing in an organization to support a good cause is more personal than hiring a service or investing in a product where ROI (return on investment) is the main consideration.

Therefore, ask questions, judiciously, that enable givers to provide you with the most useful information. Never ask a question that a close reading of the instructions answers. And use your best writing and editing skills to communicate credibility, expertise, and integrity. Here are some specific ideas about applying for grants to supplement my advice on drafting formal business proposals. (I'm assuming you want to fund a project or program. If you've worked in the nonprofit arena for any length of time, you know that funders generally prefer investing in a new project or extend a successful program rather than contribute to operating expenses like staff salaries and facilities.)

>> **Align with the funder's mission.** Thoroughly understand "what's in it for them." Why is this company or foundation or government agency investing in this set of projects? Each giver has its own mission to accomplish. A foundation focuses on one or many causes, carefully articulated in its print and digital materials, so always scour these. Many companies support causes that align with their own commercial interests. An eyeglass manufacturer, for example, may choose to help sight-impaired children live fuller lives; or it might adopt a community cause, or one that resonates with its employees. A governmental entity typically identifies unmet needs of its citizens.

TIP

Once you identify the funder's mission, align with it as closely as you can. How will your activity help the giver fulfill its own mission? Build your application on the answer to that question. If you can't do this, you may not be applying to an appropriate funder.

» **Aim not to bore your reader.** I've written grant applications and also screened them. Both processes are hard work. Whether the readers are paid professionals or volunteers, plenty of red-eye activity is usually called for. The requestor pile is big. When a reviewer becomes bored, the application gets a skimming at best. Therefore, consider these guidelines:

- *Frame your information as a story.* Know your core message — what you want to achieve, who you are, what you will do, and what this will accomplish. Even when using a formal prescribed format, figure out how to tell the story in that framework, even if it must be told in increments by answering questions in the order given. (See Chapter 9 for story-building approaches.)

- *Let your conviction shine through.* As in every sales situation, your own belief in your cause, and the project you want funded, is your greatest selling point. Don't mask it with complicated abstract writing. Show heart and energy. If you don't feel that for your project, why should anyone else?

- *Avoid information repeat.* Don't start all over again for every question if there's any way around it. Different people may or may not evaluate various parts of your proposal, but it works better to assume one or a series of readers will evaluate the whole document. If you must repeat, find another way to angle the idea or reword it. The dull repetitive proposals usually lose.

- *Establish the problem without dwelling on it.* If hundreds of sight-impaired children live in your community and need help with vision aids, certainly say so, with good documentation. But write about the program that will address this challenge rather than unnecessary details that crowd out your solution. If you can, assure the funder that the program will be sustainable — something you can build on rather creating a flash in the pan.

- *Stress outcomes, not process.* Funders are usually more interested in what will change or improve than in the details of how you will do it. If you want to train the sight-impaired children to use special devices, for example, do explain how you'll accomplish that — for example, with a series of free small group workshops — but don't over-present the logistics: where the workshops will be held, how the instructors will be hired, and so on. Rather, paint a full picture of how 175 children's lives will be improved.

- *Use good graphics to support your words.* Well-presented material is always more closely read and given more credibility. Take the trouble to make your application look good. Charts, graphs, or tables can make data more easily understood. Relevant photographs and video can be effective for many good causes — but they may be prohibited on the application, so be sure to check.

» **Think long range.** As always, building relationships takes time. A grant application tells the funder who you are and what you do. Be sure you represent your own organization effectively in what you write and how you write it. In the suitable place, explain your mission, what you've accomplished, and what you hope to accomplish. Introduce the key players well and their relation to the project. Include a carefully developed budget as requested.

TIP

A good application that doesn't get funded is still a door to future possibility. You may well get a better reception next year, or the year after. Reviewers do notice your persistence and sustained interest. In some cases, it's acceptable to inquire why your project wasn't chosen and how you might do better next time. Some funders supply this information routinely, and if so, scrutinize it carefully.

WARNING

If your proposal is funded, don't number among the great majority of grant recipients who fail to say "thank you." Express appreciation. And follow up! The people who gave you money want to know how well your program succeeded and they deserve to. In practical terms, demonstrating results is much more likely to help you qualify again in the future.

Writing an Executive Summary

Readers are summary-mad these days. Whether scanning the capsule-size rundowns at the beginning of articles, or digesting multipage introductions to complex content in reports and proposals, people love summaries. Don't you?

And no wonder: Summaries save so much time. They tell you quickly if you need or want to read the actual material. Even if major decisions hinge on a report or proposal, many people may never read the entire document. CEOs make untold numbers of decisions based on executive summaries alone.

TIP

When a piece of your future hangs in the balance with a long-form business document, make the effort to write a first-rate executive summary. Always reserve time to think them through as documents on their own. Never treat executive summaries as an afterthought you dash off after writing the larger document. Write them as original, complete, logical, and interesting statements. See them as a way to get people on your side by communicating what's most important and, perhaps, what you recommend.

Every summary has its own set of goals, but first know its role and what it needs to accomplish. Almost always, aim for summaries that

>> Generate interest — excitement, if possible — to lure readers into reading the report, proposal, or other material.

- >> Integrate the document's main points into a cohesive story that readers can easily understand.

- >> Put the larger document in perspective for your target audiences so that they know why it matters to them.

- >> Say everything that matters most with energy and lively language.

- >> Use a reader-friendly format that is *not* based on bullets.

- >> Create a call to action, rather than a pile of passive information from which readers are left to draw their own conclusions.

Giving perspective to complex material

Good reports, proposals, and other business documents are read and often acted upon. Bad, boring ones are trashed faster than yesterday's fish. They may even be used to wrap the fish.

A strong executive summary makes the difference. It starts you off on the right foot with your audience and can keep you there by establishing interest in the rest of your material.

TIP

A helpful writing sequence is to first write your document, then write the executive summary, then review the main document to ensure that it lines up with the summary and thoroughly supports it. Or, you can write your executive summary first, and then back it up with the full document.

Both processes work because developing the summary helps you figure out your real story. This truth applies to a range of reports and proposals as well as white papers, grant applications, business plans, and most other business documents.

REMEMBER

Your aim in the executive summary is to predigest the information and give the reader a meaningful perspective. You accomplish these goals by understanding your own material in depth.

Suppose you're reporting on what you did last month. Two quick tricks presented earlier in this chapter can trigger your thinking for the summary:

- >> Without looking at the already-written report, ask yourself: What settles out as important, interesting, provoking, promising, or enlightening about what you covered? Write that down.

- >> Imagine your partner or a good buddy was away for the last month and upon return asks, "What happened in your work while I was gone?" What would you say? Write that down.

If you're following a report format that your company or department prescribes — with preset categories (trends, new projects, profits and losses, and so on) — try one of these shortcut processes for each category. Also, take time to determine what matters with a bigger-picture brainstorming so that you know what perspective to give the full report.

Determining what matters

Your executive summary should not march through a series of mini-versions of the larger document's sections. After the opening statement — think of it as the summary of the summary — follow the document's sequencing and integrate the material and ideas for a crystallizing statement.

Figure out what's important — what is most worth sharing — especially in terms of your readers' interests. If you're writing a report, review your answers to the questions presented in "Focusing reader attention" earlier in this chapter; if it's a proposal, look back at "Writing informal proposals."

For models of how to handle an executive summary, check out the best. Warren Buffett, the financier, is justly famous for his crystal-clear communication of tough material. His "To the Shareholders of Berkshire Hathaway" letters strike readers as honest, but at the same time, present a point of view very persuasively. Back in 2007 when the U.S. housing market was beginning to implode, his letter began:

> Our gain in net worth during 2007 was $12.3 billion, which increased the per-share book value of both our Class A and Class B stock by 11 percent. Over the last 43 years (that is, since present management took over) book value has grown from $19 to $78,008, a rate of 21 percent compounded annually.
>
> Overall, our 76 operating businesses did well last year. The few that have problems were primarily linked to housing, among them our brick, carpet, and real estate brokerage operations. Their setbacks are minor and temporary. Our competitive position in these businesses remains strong, and we have first-class CEOs who run them right, in good times or bad.
>
> Some major financial institutions have, however, experienced staggering problems because they engaged in the "weakened lending practice" I described in last year's letter. John Stumpf, CEO of Wells Fargo, aptly dissected the recent behavior of many lenders: "It is interesting that the industry has invented new ways to lose money when the old ways seemed to work fine."

Buffett goes on to explain the housing crisis in a paragraph, then moves on with sections titled: "Turning to happier thoughts, an acquisition"; "Finally our insurance business"; and "That party is over," warning investors to anticipate lower insurance earnings, and more.

The whole introduction occupies seven paragraphs. It sets readers up to read the full report, with all the statistics, charts, and financial detail — in the frame of mind Buffett chooses.

REMEMBER

Notice how Buffett's quoted statement aligns with the principles of good writing as shared in this book. His goal is obvious: to reassure his investors that his company is on solid ground despite troubling financial events. To make that view convincing, he takes account of the negatives as well so the picture he presents appears to be balanced. Understanding his audience — Hathaway investors — makes obvious why he chose a fact-rich lead as his first paragraph. While not catchy, the comparative numbers are nevertheless riveting to those whose eyes are glued to his (and their own) bottom line.

Buffett's use of colloquial language helps everyone relate to his subject. His assurance that "we have first-class CEOs who run them right, in good times or bad" is both conversational and confident. The 2007 letter ends with a paragraph about how lucky he and his partner feel: "Every day is exciting to us; no wonder we tap-dance to work." You're never too successful or sophisticated to share your passion and enthusiasm. In fact, it's essential for getting where you want to go.

Try This: Check out a bunch of Buffett's letters online at www.berkshirehathaway. com. Even if you have no interest in the financial details, you can appreciate his clear, concise word choices and organized presentation style. This complex information is delivered at a tenth-grade reading level. Notice how much better this simplicity works than if he used the impenetrable prose we expect from a financial wizard. Notice too how he creates each letter's tone, and spend ten minutes analyzing what makes him such a credible writer and how he conveys trustworthiness, even when reporting bad news.

One more recommendation for executive summaries: Don't call it "Executive Summary," which is sleep-inducing. Give it a real headline that says something concrete about your content, positions it, and promotes reader interest. You can still use the words but amplify them:

Executive Summary: How the Audit Shifts Company Priorities for Next Year

The next section looks specifically at using headlines and subheads.

Putting headlines to work

To make all your business documents more engaging and reader-friendly, adapt some good journalism techniques. One energizing approach is to stop thinking of section headings as labels and to start writing these elements as headlines.

TIP

The difference is that labels are static, dull, and uninformative. Headlines, on the other hand, tell readers what's happening right now and pique curiosity for what they're about to read. Headlines have a feeling of action and movement.

You can use headlines to begin sections of reports, proposals, white papers, and business plans. They are easy to write when you think about delivering information rather than naming a category. Here are some labels transformed into headlines:

Label: *Admissions: Results compared to forecasts*

Headline: *September admissions exceed forecast by 10%*

Label: *Overall financial results*

Headline: *June starts disappoint — collaborative action needed*

Label: *Calumet Program case history*

Headline: *How the Calumet program turned an oil company's image from black to green*

If you're responding to given categories and must use them, simply add a headline after the label. Adding a colon at the end of the standardized label line can help:

Admissions Performance:

This year's enrollment leaps 19 percent over last

TIP

Most reports, proposals, and business plans benefit hugely from working in subheads as well as headlines. Try this method to solve organizational problems. As I suggest in Chapter 6, write a series of subheads before drafting the material itself and then add the appropriate information and ideas under each.

Breaking long sections of big documents into sequences of smaller sections with subheads pulls readers along and helps them make sense of what you're presenting. Plant these guideposts to help focus your audience on what is most important for them to know, and what you want them to know.

If you have a multipage section on financial indicators, for example, write a headline to capsulize the whole picture and then a set of action subheads for each topic. For example:

March Indicators Promise Much, Move Little

Skilled worker recruitment loses traction: down .5 percent from plan

Stock price climbs to 126, up 2 percent

Sales jump to 2012 levels, led by Jumex breakthrough

Company economists feel cautious confidence for April

You may question whether the preceding headlines and subheads are too specific, encouraging readers to not look past them. Actually, the more specific and compelling you can be, more of the "right" readers — the ones you target — find your material, and the more they'll read.

REMEMBER

The more clearly you signal where you've located specific types of information in your document and why that information matters, the better the response. People are extremely selective about investing their energy and time. Helping them choose what to read is an excellent technique. Further yet: The headline/subhead technique makes your material look more interesting and helps you look like a more take-charge, action-oriented leader. This is true even when the news you're delivering is bad!

Strong headlines are especially crucial to blogs, so for more grounding in the art, see Chapter 12.

Writing Tips for All Business Documents

For your own line of work, you may need business materials that differ from the specific types I cover in the preceding sections of this chapter. Most of the ideas still apply: to business plans, white papers, RFPs, survey reports, and all the other document challenges you may encounter. Some general writing guidelines and techniques are helpful to keep in mind whatever you're writing.

REMEMBER

Finding the right tone is critical. Important business communications must come across as authoritative, objective, credible, and confident. You're trying to persuade someone to do something, so don't sound ponderous and dull. To the contrary, the more lively and engaging your document, the more likely people are to respond with what you want. Given the mounds of boring material your readers face, they may actually be grateful for a good read.

If you compete for a high-stakes opportunity like a really big contract and someone tells you to write expensive-sounding, verbose, grandiloquent prose, shut your ears. You want a transparent writing style that showcases your thinking, not fancy or puffy language that calls attention to itself. Employ all the good writing techniques at your disposal. Chapters 3, 4, and 5 cover a bounty of useful strategies, but pin this list to the top of your proposals file:

Minimize use of:

>> Stiff, pompous tone

>> Arrogant or self-aggrandizing atmosphere

>> Passive, indirect statements

>> Long, complicated words

>> Jargon, acronyms, and buzzwords

>> Complicated, meandering sentences that demand two readings

>> Abstractions

>> Empty hype, including flowery adjectives and unproved claims

>> Hedge words and qualifiers: *might, perhaps, hopefully, possibly, would, could,* and the like

>> Extra or extraneous material that doesn't support your point

>> Mistakes in grammar, punctuation, or spelling

Maximize use of:

>> Conversational but respectful style

>> Low-key, quiet confidence

>> Straightforward, clear sentences, average 12 to 18 words, with action verbs

>> Short, basic words

>> Short paragraphs of three to five sentences

>> Rhythmic flow of language (read it aloud)

>> Concrete, graphic words and comparisons

>> Proof/evidence: Facts, statistics, images, and examples

>> Positive language that doesn't qualify or hedge

>> Story line: Have one and stick to it

>> Correct spelling, punctuation, and grammar

Now that you've seen how to create high-impact business materials, the chapters in the next chapters take a look at how to use writing to present yourself effectively, whether preparing for a speech, sharing your business story, or searching for a job.

3

Writing to Present Yourself Effectively

Learn how to give yourself the edge when preparing presentations and speeches.

Understand why effective in-person networking depends on a well-crafted "elevator speech," and see how the goal-plus-audience strategy can help you create a powerful one.

Find your personal or business story to tell people what benefits your product or service delivers and/or distinguishes you from the competition.

See how you can leverage video as a marketing tool to present yourself or your product, show your service in action, demonstrate how to do or make something, create brand identity, or showcase any other creative idea you can think of.

Learn how to apply your writing skills to résumés and cover letters that get your foot in the door and get you hired.

Use messages to network for the job hunt, from requesting informational interviews to saying "thank you."

Chapter **8**

Speaking Well for Yourself

Most people overlook two central truths when preparing speeches, presentations, and scripts:

» They need to be written.

» They need to be spoken.

That may seem ridiculously obvious, but take these rules seriously and you're way ahead of the game, whatever yours is. Many people assume they'll rise to the occasion and wing much of what they say when they're on stage or just introducing themselves. Or, they write a speech as if it were a piece of literature and then are surprised at how hard it is to deliver it well.

Whatever the length or importance of your spoken piece — from an elevator speech that lasts just a few seconds to a formal presentation — the planning and writing process I cover in this chapter gives you the foundation you need. I also show you how to give yourself the edge in situations where you need to think on your feet. The stakes can be high when you defend a viewpoint or confront opposition. You can prepare just like business leaders and politicians do: by creating *talking points*.

I start with a basic tool of your communication arsenal, the Elevator Speech. It needs to be short but powerful!

Building Your Elevator Speech

An *elevator speech*, also known as an *elevator pitch*, is an indispensable business tool you need when interacting with the outside world, whether you're an employee or work for yourself. Sometimes you need it for the "inside" world, too, especially if you're employed by a large organization with multiple departments that don't understand each other well. The name comes from this challenge: If you found yourself in an elevator with someone you wanted to connect with, how would you introduce yourself in the time it takes to travel from a low floor to a high floor? Or vice versa. What would you say to the other person to find common ground?

Think of it as a speech in miniature to introduce yourself. Effective in-person networking depends on it, so don't leave what you say to chance. Plan it, write it, edit it, practice it, adapt it. Most successful businesspeople and professionals obsess about this self-introduction, and work constantly to evolve it. Once you nail it, take your personal pitch everywhere. If you don't think you need it, you're not getting out enough!

The challenge of the elevator speech is to create a super-concise spoken statement that tells the person you're talking to who you are, what you do, and how that relates to him or her. It's the same basic question we encounter in writing a good email: Why should that person care?

TIP

Not that long ago, the usual recommendation was to create a pitch about 30 seconds long. Then 20 seconds became the preferred norm. But things keep speeding up. Including elevators. My best current advice is to aim for 15 to 20 seconds. You can keep an additional 10 seconds or so in reserve and use it if you sense a good audience reaction. But the 15-second version must stand on its own. Some trainers teach people to have their say while holding a lit match. If they haven't finished by the time the match burns down, well . . . .

REMEMBER

Fifteen seconds leaves a lot unsaid, so you must drill down to your core message. But brevity is good. Effective elevator speeches are conversation starters. If you can provoke a little curiosity and generate a question, you hit the mark.

To create a new elevator speech or improve an existing one, use the same framework that works for emails, proposals, and blogs. Ask and answer: What is my goal? Who is my audience? How can I best connect the two? Essentially you need to crystallize your competitive advantage and communicate what you uniquely offer. Chapter 10 focuses on how to do this in the context of job hunting, and Chapter 14 talks about identifying value propositions for companies. I recommend reading one or both chapters and using the process to find the heart of your message. The following sections tweak the ideas to suit the style and demands of spoken communication.

Defining your goal

Every person and every situation may differ, but generally, aim to connect through your elevator speech with someone you don't yet know — or even more important, *someone that person knows* — who may share an interest or link you to an opportunity you want. A good self-introduction is part of your overall marketing. It helps you build referrals over the long run.

Notice what happens at meetings when people are asked to introduce themselves to the group one after another. When someone positions themselves effectively, the delivery is often low-key, but almost always, you'll observe that at least one person will seek the speaker out to follow up and ask for a business card. And a memorable pitch — one that's right on the mark for the audience — is remembered and may be acted upon by more people later. Using the process I lead you through, you can generate this kind of interest yourself.

WARNING

In using your mini-speech, remember that it's only a first step in building relationships. Trust that there is nothing you can say that will land you a job or consulting offer on the spot. Rather, aim to relax and find meeting ground. Contact points may be purely professional, or more personal (like a shared interest in opera or antique cars). If the outlook is promising, you can then identify an opportunity to pursue the acquaintanceship.

Defining your audience

You can't do a good job on an elevator speech unless you think through your audience's perspective: what interests them, what they want to know, their pain points, and why they'd want to know you. A good introduction is more about "them" than about "me."

For this reason, expert networkers always encourage someone they've just met to speak first. They listen intently, with full focus, and look for ways they can adapt their own introduction and concrete ways to benefit the person.

Of course, when creating an elevator pitch, you seldom have a single person in mind. So start by thinking in terms of group characteristics: what members are likely to have in common. The concerns of bar association members are very different from those who belong to a medical or architects' association, for example. If a group consists of your peers or customers, you know a lot about them and can easily create a useful profile of the group.

Try This: A good way to spark your group profile is by visualizing your ideal client or connection. Think about what he or she is most interested in and how you align with that. What keeps her up at night? What are her problems and how can you help her solve them? This will give you good ideas for putting yourself in focus with people in the same line of work.

TIP

Analyzing your goal and potential audience gives you a big bonus: It shows you where to show up — the places, events, and occasions that enable you to network with the people you want to tell your story to. This strategic thinking leads you to avoid a mistake many businesspeople make: investing all their time with people similar to themselves. If you're a real estate agent, certainly you can learn a lot from your fellow agents and enjoy their company, and perhaps form strategic partnerships. But if you want to market, it's smart to go where your buyers are. Take time to figure out where your prospects congregate. (A good information source is www.meetup.com, which exhaustively lists interest groups in your geographic area, by subject. Online research will also turn up relevant business and professional associations.)

Strategizing your content

If you work on your personal value statement, as I spell out in Chapter 10, you are well on your way toward a good elevator speech. Scan through your core message to find a statement that comes close to expressing the single most important point you want to get across. Then reimagine it in words that work for the ear. For example, here is Jed's value statement, which I use as a demonstration in Chapter 10:

> *Artist, art historian, and administrator with experience and advanced training in archiving, preservation, and photography. Special expertise in designing computer systems to accomplish administrative work more efficiently and economically. Excellent interpersonal skills, adept at training people to use new technology cheerfully.*

If Jed went to a meeting of museum administrators, he might adapt this to say:

> *Hi, I'm Jed White. I'm an arts technology specialist. I build computer programs that save museums a ton of money. Recently, for example, I showed Archive House how to convert a lot of work done by hand to digital methods. And I train people on new technology so they're happy with it. Right now, I'm looking for a staff opportunity.*

Jed's task here was to recycle the content into a conversational, easy-to-say, specific statement that centers on his most important asset for this audience. I clocked this speech at about 20 seconds — delivery speed varies a lot depending on the region where you grew up, which influences your speech. Note how much you can get across in that time.

REMEMBER

The first imperative of a good speech, whatever its length, is to *write* it — on paper or your computer. This lets you look at, rethink, edit, and refine it. The second imperative is to *say* it. There's no substitute for speaking it aloud, because it's ultimately an oral communication and must be polished based on sound.

Of course, you want your speech to seem spontaneous, especially if it's an elevator pitch, so there's a third imperative: *practice*. When you think you're ready, try it out on friends and see how they react. Then refine it further.

But you don't necessarily need to recite what you crafted word for word. More important, you need to completely internalize your message so without stress, you can listen to your conversational partner with all antenna out and adapt it on the spot.

TIP

Whether you've worked on a core value statement or are starting on your elevator speech from scratch, think intensively about whom you help. Whatever your product or service, ultimately someone benefits. Figure out how, and what those benefits are. Think also about what in your work you're passionate about, and what makes you feel proudest.

Tailor elevator speeches to the audience and occasion. A search engine optimization expert may tell this to an audience of marketing directors:

> I'm Marian Smith, and my consulting group is SEO-Plus. My mission is to get businesses right on top of Google search results. I'm the marketing department's secret weapon.

While to a roomful of entrepreneurs, she may say:

> I'm Marian Smith of SEO-Plus. My company is a one-stop shop for online marketing, websites, and social media support. We level the playing field for small businesses — and know how to do it affordably. And we're whizzes at SEO.

Here are a few more representative elevator pitches to stir your thinking:

> I'm a personal trainer, and I work with older women who feel out of shape. I design custom programs they're comfortable with and teach them to do it on their own. A few sessions with me often makes an amazing difference in their lives.

I'm a financial planner. I believe financial planning is so important for everybody, it shouldn't be a service reserved for the super-rich. So I work by telephone to make good advice affordable. I give people what they want to know — how to pay for college, finance retirement, or buy a house — whatever their goal.

TIP

Note how a brief elevator speech can generate questions. Keep the answers in your mental pocket. A sample exchange:

Dentist: *I'm Melanie Black. I'm a dentist and I specialize in preschoolers. I figured out how to give them a good experience so they won't be scared of going to the dentist. That way they'll be happy to take care of their teeth all their lives.*

Listener: *Hmm . . . how do you do that?*

Dentist: *I take plenty of time to show them all the equipment, which is painted in bright colors. I give them a playset of tools to take home. I minimize any pain, of course, but tell them the truth if something might hurt for a few seconds. Almost always they accept that. May I give you my business card if you think of anyone with small children who would appreciate this approach?*

TIP

Actively observe what works well in your own industry environment and what you respond to. Experiment with your own mini-pitches and evolve what works best. Here are some surefire strategies:

>> Be specific and concrete about what you do and who it benefits; generalizations make you sound like everybody else.

>> Use short words and sentences, and craft them to sound like natural speech, not a memorized statement.

>> Make your pitch memorable and easy to repeat.

>> Rev up your spirits and voice to sound positive, enthusiastic, and lively.

>> Infuse your words with your passion for what you do.

>> Support your message with good body language and facial expressions.

>> Practice it to the point where you sound spontaneous and can adapt it on the spot. It's the idea you want to communicate — you can express it differently every time to suit the conversation and occasion.

Welcome the questions your listener may ask and be prepared to answer: "How do you do that?" "What kind of opportunity are you interested in?" "How does it work?"

Elevator speeches lend themselves to closing with a direct question of your own. To any of the examples I cite, you can with suitable variation say, "Do you know anyone who needs that?" Or at least, "May I give you my card?"

In many situations, it's perfectly fine to ask for what you want. If you're looking for a job or a career transition, add that to the end of your introduction or bring it up further along in the conversation. Help your listener by being specific about your need. "I'm looking for a marketing job" is far less likely to gain a nibble than:

> *I'm a five-year veteran of the financial services industry. Right now, I'm working on an extra degree in marketing because that's what I really want to do. I'm looking to move into marketing now at a place where my experience would be of value. Can you think of anyone I might talk to?*

No guarantees, but if you're in the right place, the person you're speaking with is likely to glance around the room to find you a match or give you a lead.

If you're brand new to the job market or almost so, it's also perfectly fine to say that. But be aware of your own assets and speak from strength. And talk about yourself as a professional!

> *I'm a marketing specialist about to graduate from the program at Tennyson. I've worked as an intern at several companies. Last summer I worked at PepsiCo. I'm especially interested in pursuing what I learned there — how to integrate social media with traditional marketing. Can you suggest anyone I might talk to about this?*

Most young people underestimate the value of in-person networking and the enthusiasm with which professional associations and groups customarily welcome them. Many associations are developing programs to connect with students, who are vital to the industry's future, and the association's. They often have a reasonable student membership rate, and in many cases, you can go to meetings without paying for membership at all.

In recent years, some associations have begun accommodating out-of-work professionals in their fields in similar ways. Whatever your age and professional status, if you're aiming for a transition or need job leads, show up!

Representing your organization and yourself

When you introduce yourself as a representative of your company or other organization, you speak for it. Often focusing on yourself isn't appropriate when you're talking to potential customers or industry groups. But do identify your role. For example:

> *I'm Nancy Williams and I'm the head of business development for Brash and Brumble. We're a local company that helps attorneys develop their branding through new social media strategies My role is . . . .*

Your description of the organization should ideally be a 15 to 20 second expression of core value created in much the same way as a personal elevator pitch. It should meet the same criteria — memorability, sharp focus, enthusiastic tone. Your company may have a ready-made pitch, a way of explaining the organization that you can adapt.

If you're the owner of a one-person enterprise, you can speak in your own name or the company's and use the editorial "we" if you wish:

> *I'm Mark Smith, and my company is Four Legs on the Run. We transport horses all over the country for races and competitions . . . .*

REMEMBER

Don't forget, in an elevator speech situation, the people you talk to are just as eager as you are to make a new connection and to be heard. Listen with both ears. If you sense an opportunity to follow up by helping someone else in even a small way, take it. Great networkers pursue a relationship by sending a relevant clipping or link, or information about a travel destination or something else that came up. Or if the exchange is mutually promising and common ground is clear, they suggest coffee or a more formal meeting.

If developing a good elevator speech sounds like a lot of trouble, consider the side benefits. Distilling who you are gives you a great focus for all your communication, including your website, online profiles, and the about-you credit when you write a blog or article. Some people use a version on their letterhead or email signature. And you've practiced the same methodology that will serve you well for all the presentations you may give that are more than 20 seconds, which I discuss next.

TIP

The magic of learning good communication techniques is that they work for everything you're called on or choose to write, and everything you write well helps you tell other people who you are and what you can do. Know who you are, and the rest follows.

Preparing and Giving Presentations

As presentation coaches often point out, many people view public speaking as literally worse than death. I've never seen the research on this, but it does seem that the prospect of presenting terrifies most people. But effective presenting is more and more essential to today's business culture, so if you're among the fearful, you need to get over it!

Opportunities to speak directly to your audiences abound as never before. Anybody can mount a webinar, a teleseminar, or an online workshop via video, Skype, Zoom, or other emerging video conferencing software. You may need to give speeches or conference presentations. Or you may be invited to appear on seminar panels or share your expertise or viewpoint less formally.

Generally speaking, the more truly interactive a presentation, the more on-the-spot thinking is needed as opposed to when you deliver a monologue. But you need to be just as prepared in order to carry it off. Therefore, I address the most demanding presentation mode that readers are likely to encounter: delivering information and ideas, or sharing your know-how, with a large or important audience. You're not necessarily standing on a platform: You may deliver your message in a conference room or corner office. You may deliver it by video. But whatever the channel and formality, when the occasion matters, you want to be your best.

The tried and true classic way to present well and comfortably boils down simply: preparation followed by practice. Adapt the ideas to the situation. They center (of course) on how to strategize content and use writing, but I give you some delivery tips as well.

Planning what to say

Just as for an elevator speech, make decisions for a presentation based on your goal and your audience. What do you want to do: Motivate? Inspire? Sell something? Share information? Impress with your expertise? Change people's opinions or behavior? Each goal calls for different content, whatever the subject.

REMEMBER

The more closely you define your goal, the better the guidance you give yourself. For example, when you want to share information, think through *why* you want to share it. Helping your audience work harder and smarter is different from aiming to sign audience members up for one-on-one coaching. The first goal demands that you motivate the audience and deliver practical how-to information. To accomplish the second, you'd calibrate how much information to give away so that audience members are enticed to want more.

The *audience* to whom you're giving the information is the other half of the planning equation. If you're a scientist, you naturally present different material to other professionals as opposed to a lay audience interested in something useful or fun. Give real thought to what your listeners wants to know, what they worry about, and what they care about. How will what you say solve problems? Or make life better, even if just a tiny bit?

WARNING

Unless you are a technical professional talking to people just like yourself, presentations are not usually the medium for deep, detailed, complex material. Despite how most teaching is still done, oral learning by itself is not very effective. And on-screen visuals and video in the way that most people use them don't help much.

Always the best rule of thumb: Keep it simple. When you plan a presentation, start at the end. What do you most want your audience to walk away with and remember? The best teachers aim to increase their students' knowledge and understanding incrementally rather than in giant leaps. It's best not to be overly ambitious and try to pour everything you know into 15 minutes of fast talk.

TIP

Try to crystallize a *theme* for your presentation — a basic message. Framing your material with a point of view, and putting things into perspective, is far more effective than giving people "just the facts." Most of us feel we're already drowning in information. We want to be told what the data means; what the product or service does for us; what will be different if we adopt the idea or invest in the belief.

Try This: To crystallize your basic message, try it the Hollywood way: Figure out a way to express it in a single sentence. In fact, billion-dollar movies may be funded based on pitches such as, "Boy robot and girl robot fall in love and want a baby." A business equivalent? Perhaps for an audience of talent managers, "Invest in our cross-cultural communication workshops — managers who take them perform 19 percent better." For a new product, your theme can be as simple as "Invest in this gizmo because it shaves 11 percent off your production costs."

Beginning well

Build your talk with the classic, simple structure — beginning, middle, end. As with most written materials, the lead — how you open — is the most important piece. It sets the tone and audience expectations. Aim to to engage people and capture their attention. An opening anecdote is one way to do that. But it must be relevant, and you must be sure your audience will receive it well.

Ideally, find a useful anecdote in your own experience. Or try what many professional speechwriters do: Ask all your friends if they have a good anecdote about the subject, the venue, or your audience's profession. But never tell a joke that can be interpreted as laughing at the audience. It's okay to laugh at yourself.

REMEMBER

Often, however, you don't need to be super-clever. You can rivet your audience and generate an attentive mood by simply telling them directly why they should be interested. You might paint a picture of the problem you'll address and refer to your solution; connect with the audience through a personal experience related to the message; pose a rhetorical question that leads to your solution; or give them a vision of how much life will improve once they know what you're about to share.

You can't really miss if you know the heart of your message and the biggest benefit the specific audience will reap by paying attention. Recently I presented a workshop to an audience of business writing teachers, a mandatory subject for the college program. I'd been asked to explain new techniques for building writing skills. But in decoding advance conversations, I decided that student apathy was the biggest problem, and that both students and teachers needed first to feel that learning to write better was both important and interesting. So I opened with, "I find that a lot of students are bored by learning business writing, because they don't understand how critical it is to their careers. Here are a few ways I've thought of that they'll really relate to."

It proved to be a good start that generated great conversation without the teachers feeling criticized.

Remember the WIIFM principle — what's-in-it-for-me — and act on this understanding.

Middling well

Just as for an email or other document, brainstorm the solid middle content that will accomplish your goal with your audience. Keep to your theme and organize the material in a logical, easy-to-follow sequence. Remember that you don't need to deliver the universe. There can definitely be too much of a good thing, so set limits for yourself.

One organizational method that works well for presentations is to create a list of the areas that relate to your subject, much like creating a list of subheads for a written piece, which I explain how to do in Chapter 6. If you were a doctor introducing a new medical device to an audience of investors, for example, you might list:

1. The problem Device X solves: Why needed?

2. What we're asking for and why

3. Who device will help: The numbers

4. What it will replace and its advantages

5. How idea originated and was developed

6. Where things now stand

7. Next steps: Financing we need, how it will be used

8. Future vision: Anticipated market

If you were presenting to fellow doctors, you'd omit the financial information, but might add more technical data, pros and cons, and detailed trial results. "Future vision" would center on offering a bigger toolset to help their patients. If you were addressing senior citizens who might benefit from the new device, you'd talk in depth how it will help them, who would qualify, and how they can follow up. "Future vision" would be the better life they could enjoy and when and how that can happen.

As with every presentation and written piece, the more interesting you can make your information the better, no matter the audience. For the medical device, there might be anecdotes, examples, "fun facts, " or surprising discoveries to incorporate along the way.

TIP

For many subjects, a numbered approach works well and keeps you organized: "Here are the six most important changes that will affect your future in the advertising industry." Or "Four ways this new software will help you handle project management." Most audiences love this strategy because they can tick off the items as you move along. Numbering gives them a sense of accomplishment and is easier on the brain. Staying attentive for more than a few minutes is hard work for adults!

Ending well

As appropriate, state your grand conclusion, sum up what you said, and reinforce the takeaway you want. You might bring home to your audience why your subject matters to them and, if relevant, how to take the next step or put it to work in their practical lives. If appropriate, close with an energizing vision of the future as it relates to your talk. But don't rehash the entire speech and bore your listeners. Keep your ending brief.

REMEMBER

As the saying goes, it ain't over till it's over. A good ending often requires that you prep for questions. Preparing for the Q&A session afterward helps you deliver more confidently, too. If you inspire tough questions, see that as a plus. But have answers ready. Brainstorm, with colleagues if possible, to figure out the likely questions. Especially try to anticipate the one question you hope no one will pose, and know what you'll say. Use the "talking points" process I give you later in this chapter to do this.

Crafting your presentations with writing

REMEMBER

Other than rocket science and brain surgery, perhaps, no thought is so complex that you cannot express it in clear, simple language. If you find it a challenge to be simple and clear, take it as a signal that you may need to understand your subject better. Or rethink it entirely.

Writing helps you think through your presentation content and approach, so start with a piece of paper or your computer screen. Depending on how you work best, you can:

>> Draft a full script, based on your subheads if this method works for you, or create an outline that covers all your main points. Many people recommend building on no more than three main ideas.

>> Identify a set of idea chunks and sequence them in a natural way so you can deliver your content in logical order, but plan to create the actual language on the spot.

Spelling it all out with Option 1 may seem more secure, but consider that you'd either have to read it verbatim — the worst presentation technique — or completely memorize it. This is very hard, and struggling to remember what you memorized always turns of the audience. So you'll need to boil your script back down to cues to the material you want to deliver.

TIP

Option 2, then, is often the best way to go. You must be totally comfortable with your material: Know your stuff, and know your audience. Think through each area you want to cover and speak to it one piece at a time. You can remind yourself of your topics with an index card or two or what you put on the screen.

Delivering this way makes your content seem fresh — and it is, because you're framing the words as you speak and responding to your audience's expressions, gestures, body language. If as you talk it sounds like you're figuring it out, that's fine, unless you're really slow: a thoughtful delivery brings the audience along with you and typically matches their learning speed.

Try This: A useful compromise between memorizing-the-whole-thing and creating-it-as-you-go is to script and carefully rehearse your opening so you start off with maximum confidence. Be sure to experiment with friends before the event.

Neither the draft nor outline should accompany you to the venue. If the event is so formal you need to read the whole speech, find out if there's a teleprompter — but understand that using it well takes real practice. Another approach is to type the speech in a large font with pauses built in so you can look up often. For example:

Four score and seven years ago

our fathers brought forth

on this continent . . . .

However you achieve it, always remember that maintaining audience contact is much more important than remembering every word, or even every thought.

Techniques to keep in mind:

>> Use basic, natural language as you do in conversation: short words, short sentences. You want to be instantly understood and trusted.

>> Build in natural pauses — the oral equivalent of white space — between ideas, sections, and important sentences to help people absorb what you say.

>> Say your words aloud as you write and listen for an easy cadence; when you find awkward hard-to-say patches, or you run out of breath, rewrite and check the sound again.

>> Avoid using too many statistics or numbers, because they dull the senses and numb the brain.

>> Use metaphors and other comparisons to make your point: "The applicants could have filled half a football field" is better than citing a figure.

>> Use graphic language whenever you can to engage the emotions and paint pictures. Check a thesaurus for alternative words to spark things up.

>> Time your presentation to fit the probable space, allowing for introductions and Q&A, as applicable. Identify areas to skip should you run on too long so that you don't shortchange your close.

>> Have a few content options in mind: When you see your audience losing interest, switch tracks and move on to something else.

Integrating visuals

Notice that I've not yet mentioned Microsoft PowerPoint, Prezi, Google Slides, or their younger cousins. And for good reason: Despite all too common practice, visuals should always be treated as support for your message, not the main show.

WARNING

Don't use PowerPoint or any other presentation system to plan and write what you'll say. Your message becomes distorted when you try to jam it into a limiting, structured format. Resist making decisions about what to include or omit based on preallocated pieces of space or flashy templates.

Plan and write your presentation and then think about supporting visuals. Or work out possible slides simultaneous with the copy as you go. When you prepare the slides, don't cut and paste onto them the editorial content you wrote: Treat each slide as an individual communication and figure out what (few) words should be included and what visuals help make the same point. Avoid throwing your whole speech onto the screen.

REMEMBER

You are — or should be — the central focus when you speak. People are there to see and hear you, not stare at a screen. Never read from your slides. And don't distribute your handout before you speak, because it distracts your listeners, who leap ahead to the end and then wait impatiently for you to catch up.

Here are a few basic guidelines for integrating visuals:

>> Keep every slide simple and easy to absorb at a glance: no long lists of bullets and sub-bullets, no complex charts and graphs, no sets of statistics.

>> Use visuals to translate those statistics or ideas into graphic form — for instance, if you're trying to explain the size of a nanometer, show comparisons such as a human hair and other objects.

>> Keep fonts simple and BIG so that people at the back can read the material. How big depends on the size of your room and audience, but generally, don't go below 24 points.

>> Keep graphics simple and consistent in format, style, colors, and type of illustrations. Mixing photographs with cartoons, for example, is usually jarring. Check for legibility *before* you present to an audience to be sure the text projects well and is easy to read.

>> Use the "action" feature of presentation systems for dynamic visuals to show — for example, how one element of a graph line moves over time. But use animation features sparingly so they are not distracting.

>> Incorporate video clips as available to liven things up, but be sure they're worth the watching time and support your message. Short is usually better.

>> Test everything out before show time to make sure the technology is working, especially if you emailed the slide deck or are using unfamiliar equipment. Video clips in particular may come undone. The savviest presenters stand ready to deliver without PowerPoint and Internet access altogether because you just never can absolutely depend on them.

Don't drive yourself crazy by getting absorbed in the mechanics of presentation. Focus on the substance. In fact, a good way to stay grounded as you speak is to use your slides as an organizational tool. Set up headlines and subheads that key you to remember important points. This keeps your audience with you, too. For example, use a succession of slides that just say things like: The Problem, What We Did, How it Worked, Our Conclusions, What's Next — each with maybe just a few lines of copy. Wouldn't you rather they listen to you for the answers rather than trying to read them?

Standing and delivering

When you do your homework and shape your message to audience expectations and your own goals — first in writing and then by practicing the message to internalize it — you have the right content, and have earned confidence to boot.

Practice is how dancers, musicians, actors, athletes, and CEOs remember what to do when they're on stage or in the sporting arena. Rehearse as many times as necessary to master your own material and feel very comfortable with it. If you can't speak without notes, use cue cards as reminders, but don't stare at them for minutes or rustle through them to find your place.

Try This: There are a great many elements involved in creating and giving effective presentations, which you realize if you know an actor, have worked with a voice coach, or have given a formal speech. Practice won't make perfect, and doesn't need to. But some useful techniques can go a long way. Following are my ten favorite ideas for feeling professional and confident:

>> Warm up. Many professional speakers have an easy exercise routine they do before presenting to help them feel relaxed and limber and get the energy flowing; and many warm up their voices as well.

>> Stand, don't sit — even for an elevator speech when practical.

>> Keep your posture straight and balanced, but not stiff; no rocking or fidgeting or pacing (but natural hand gestures and natural body movement are excellent).

>> Breathe deeply, from very low in your diaphragm. This takes practice.

>> Radiate positive energy and pleasure at being there.

>> Vary the pitch and tone of your voice, and be conscious of pacing: Avoid speed. The best pace may be a little slower than in a natural conversation.

>> Maintain voice energy. Don't trail off at the end of sentences or end with an upward inflection that sounds like you're asking a question. Pause before and after a major point.

Try This: Experiment with any or all of the following techniques to help you relax and project enthusiasm when you are about to present.

- **The I like you trick.** Remind yourself before going on that you like the people you're about to address and that they are eager to hear what you'll deliver.

- **A hypnotherapist's trick:** Right before you are to speak, imagine you've already delivered your talk and it was hugely successful. Imagine how that feels — how you'll stand, smile, walk, hold your head, and look around at the expectant faces. See the experience and feel it. Practice it so you can call it up when you want. Before speech time, take a few minutes to re-create the warm feeling, then carry it with you into the moment.

- **An actor's trick:** Just before beginning, or at key points, say to yourself, "I'm about to share something exciting with you." Your enthusiasm grows, and it shows.

>> Focus on one person at a time as you speak, perhaps for five-second intervals — don't let your eyes dart around or look to the sky for help.

>> Notice how people react. If eyes glaze over, or half your audience is looking at their smartphones, slide into a new direction.

>> Don't sweat what you forget. Even if you skip a major point, you're the only one who knows. Just focus on saying the rest with conviction.

TIP

If public speaking is important to you professionally, perhaps as an excellent way to grow your business, give yourself some solid grounding. Many good speakers value their experience with Toastmasters International (www.toastmasters.org). And courses in voice and presentation techniques are often available through local colleges, other educational centers, and private sources.

Composing Talking Points for Live Interaction

So far, this chapter has covered techniques for preparing presentations, whether an elevator pitch or speech, as one-way communication. Basically, you talk, they listen. But writing is also an invaluable way to prepare for interactive situations. You don't want to give a great speech and then flub the Q&A. If you ever wonder how CEOs and politicians equip themselves to win debates, be good interviewees, and prepare for press conferences, the answer is *talking points.* Many organizations also use talking points to ensure that all executives, or the whole staff, are on the same wavelength with a consistent message when talking for or about the company.

Talking points give you a beautiful personal tool for any kind of confrontation, including a media interview, Q&A session, cross-examination, or any situation where you need to think on your feet.

TIP

The method is simple: Preferably with a colleague, friend, or small group, sit down and brainstorm the main points you want to communicate for a given scenario. Write them down in telegraphic form. For example, if you're preparing for a job interview, think through your best matching points and examples. Then write them out, preferably just a line or two for each, limiting yourself to a single page. Someone applying for a sales manager job might list:

Seven years' experience in a similar industry; know many people

Achieved 14 percent increase in my territory's sales over previous person

Appointed assistant sales manager a year ago

Named local "Salesperson of the Year" three times

Train new sales recruits

Leaving job because of limited upward opportunity

Hold business degree from Martial U.

Captain competitive sailing team

Active in community: Board member of local Heart Association, former school board member, play Santa Claus in school pageant every year

TIP

Of course, you have more to say on each point, but the idea is to *know in advance the essentials to get across* during the course of the interview and write just enough for each item to trigger your own recollection of the full idea. Then you can draw on this ready-to-use material to make points in your favor and answer questions well.

There's no need to cover points that turn out not to fit the actual situation, but with a checklist of your "advantage" points in your head, you can draw on them to answer questions that give you appropriate opening, compose a good "who are you" explanation on the spot, and gracefully add a major point that didn't come up at the interview's end ("You might also like to know that . . .").

You can also use a politician's trick to "bridge" past a question you'd rather not answer, or can't, to something you do want to say (for example, "I don't have direct experience with that strategy, but it's more important to know that . . ."). However, take care not to appear evasive if you bridge this way. Most people have become very aware of this politician's technique and it arouses suspicion. It's important to convey that you are straightforward and honest. A "soft" version might work: "I haven't yet used Latex49 software, but I did work with the 48 version for three years and learned . . . ."

TIP

The talking points approach helps you plan for confrontation, especially if you expect to be asked difficult or hostile questions. Say you're advocating for something and expect to be questioned, or even attacked, by people who disagree. Look at the situation from your opponents' perspective and brainstorm: What questions can they possibly ask? What are the nightmare questions? Be sure to include those you most dread. Once you have a full list and can't think of anything else, march through, question by question, and figure out the best concise answer you or the team can produce.

This systematic preparation gives you invaluable confidence for handling whatever follows. You're able to listen more intuitively to the other side and create good responses as needed. Moreover, it enables you to communicate in the calm, assured manner that so often helps win the day instead of sounding defensive.

REMEMBER

Another significant use of talking points is to drive agreement. Government agencies, for example, forge talking points around an issue, often involving a combination of stakeholders in the process. Once a consensus is formulated, the page is distributed to everyone concerned with the expectation that they will act in accordance.

Similarly, a corporation under pressure creates talking points and supplies them to all representatives so they stay in line with the expressed position. In a high-risk situation, the result maybe distributed to a number of employees so that everyone speaks in the same voice. Sales departments often prepare talking points for the people in the field so all are well informed and on the same page.

Keep in mind that talking points often evolve through several versions if reviewers are given the chance to contribute input or raise questions.

Try This: Talking points are immensely versatile. When you intend to ask for a raise, hold a difficult conversation, sell something, air a problem, disagree with a position, or recommend an unpopular course of action, underwrite your success by developing talking points. But don't take them with you! Review them before the event to remind yourself of what you want to communicate.

REMEMBER

My last word on public speaking: *Smile when you say it.* You can write the best elevator speech or presentation or sales pitch in the land, and answer tough questions glibly, but if you deliver without conviction and enthusiasm, you won't succeed. Write what you believe — and believe in what you say.

The next chapter continues the adventure of presenting yourself memorably by showing you how to find and use your personal or business story. This helps you center and energize all your communication, including through that growing essential, video.

Chapter **9**

Telling Your Business Stories

I f you're an employee of a business, nonprofit, government agency, or any other type of organization, presenting a positive interface with the world is part of your job. If you're in business for yourself, success demands that you present your best case in every situation. You may think of yourself as a freelancer open to almost any opportunity in your field, but if you want more than an occasional gig to fall your way, best think of yourself as *in business.*

And just a like a big international organization, a one- or two-person business must understand its central message and deliver it consistently. This message may remain unsaid in everything you communicate about your business, but it's your essential infrastructure. It should underwrite every page of your website, your blog, your tweets, your profiles, and everything you post on social media that is not purely for friends or relatives. And I wouldn't be too sure that what you write to friends shouldn't meet this standard. Today the lines between work and play blur increasingly, and a friend might be your next employer or referral source.

This chapter shows you how to find your message, tell stories that embody it, and use it in a medium that can carry it well: video. As every part of this book stresses, good writing demands that you know *what* to say as well as *how* to say it. Whether you're writing an email, resume, proposal, or marketing video, the first imperative is to strategize your content. Substance rules. Style follows.

Finding Your Core Business Message

The key to everything from marketing campaigns to sales pitches, proposals, and résumés comes down to crafting your core message.

REMEMBER

The *value proposition* or *unique selling proposition*, as marketing and sales people call it, is the central statement that tells people what benefits your product or service delivers and what distinguishes your business from its competition. I prefer the term *core message* or *keystone message* because it makes the concept clearer and more practical.

For companies, core messages may be internal documents, but smart enterprises invest in their creation and stick with them to frame all communication and remember when making pivotal decisions. A good core message is a living all-purpose touchstone for an organization, whether staffed by one person or thousands around the world. It also serves to unite all employees so everyone is on the same page, and hopefully, enthusiastic about it.

Is a core message the same as a mission statement? Ideally, yes. But often a mission statement is a superficial identity for the public that bears little relation to reality. Whether they're produced by the CEO, a small committee, or with wide employee input, mission statements are often so general they mean little to either the employees or the outside world.

My favorite example of what a sense of shared mission can accomplish is a story told about John F. Kennedy. In touring NASA in its early years, he encountered a janitor in the hall, introduced himself as the president, and asked, "And what do you do?" The man answered proudly, "We're sending a man to the moon." This was probably not NASA's formal mission statement, which probably sounded a lot loftier, but it embodied the sense of employee buy-in that the best business leaders dream about.

WARNING

I experienced some good examples of what happens when this unity goes missing when I produced videos for a large educational agency. It operated more than 100 services for local school districts, such as co-operative purchasing, technology support, and teacher training. The services had to be marketed to prospective users and that's where the videos came in.

Many productions were successful, but I found that creating good videos for some programs was much harder, sometimes almost impossible. Eventually I realized these programs had something in common: lack of mission and message clarity. The managers tended to say things like, "We'll provide whatever our customers want." A tough and ineffective message! This problem also came up in trying to create both print and online marketing materials for the programs, but perhaps because video comes closest to portraying reality, it can be more difficult to cover up a subject's deficits. The resulting videos felt uncentered, just like the programs.

I will not kid you — creating a meaningful core message is real work. But it's critical for everyone who sells a service or product or aims to establish a business. And even if you're an employee who's not directly responsible for selling — surprise! — you need a core message, too. See Chapter 8 for details on how to craft a personal core message.

To shape your message, aim to tell your audience what you offer in that audience's own framework. It instantly shows that you're on the same wavelength. You can't communicate your message successfully by throwing around clichés like "state-of-the-art" or "most innovative" or "best buy in town." Dig down and scan wide. Figure out your truest value to those you want to connect with. This enables you to identify your best-selling points and build on them. When you create whatever marketing materials you need, in any platform, you already have in hand the essence of what you want your readers to know, how to relate to their concerns, and how to build a consistent brand.

Here's the difference between just juggling words and writing a message that directly relates to customers. Suppose I own a consulting firm that helps businesses create their core messages. I can say:

> *Keystone Messaging helps you tell your story to the world so it resonates with customers. We find the right words to liven up your sales pitches, website, networking messages, and more. We save you time and bring a full set of creative skills to this challenge. The results energize your sales team, attract more people to your website, and brighten all your presentations. Our staff of experts . . . .*

Not that terrible? But suppose I start this way:

> *Keystone Messaging works with you to find your company message — the message that crystallizes what you alone offer and aligns you directly with your customers' bottom line.*

This concreteness suggests a different follow-up from the first one's vague claims. It sets you up to cite evidence. For example:

> *International research shows that organizations that communicate well are 1.7 times as likely to outperform their peers. Our clients in industries similar to yours document that using their core messages generates a 10 to 20 percent increase in website traffic . . . .*

The first message may read okay but it's just words: "resonates," "livens up," "creative," "energizes," and "brighten up." These are *process* words rather than results words, and customers don't care about them. Customers don't want to know what you do — but what you can do *for them*. The second message addresses your customers' basic agenda: Improve the bottom line.

A good rule of thumb for marketing: Identify your value and then prove it. Your business may be less abstract than Keystone Messaging, or your product may lend itself to quantifying results more easily than a service. Whatever your business, your customers may be able to give you real numbers for ways that you helped them. If not, or your venture is new, do some research and cite industry statistics. Or cite one outstanding example of how you helped a customer. Or do all of these things.

Searching for true value

You can get in touch with your organization's true value in a variety of ways. Choose one or more of the following processes based on what suits you and your business:

>> **Ask your customers or clients what you have accomplished for them and what they most value.** If appropriate to your industry, ask for specifics, especially in bottom-line terms. They may be more prepared to deliver this information than you think; if you're a repeat or long-term supplier, they may be quite aware of their ROI (return on investment). For ideas on how to frame good questions, see the sidebar, "Questions to ask your customers."

>> **Brainstorm with an internal group.** Working with your immediate colleagues or representatives from different departments gives you the advantage of advance buy-in from different stakeholders. Or work with a business-savvy person or two whom you trust. The sidebar, "Questions to ask your team and yourself," gives you material for this process.

This "inside route" to identifying your strengths can expand and solidify your ideas about what's important and what to concentrate on. It also gives you a broad foundation for a communications program. Additionally, the answers can give you a head start on storytelling for your business, which I talk about later in this chapter.

If you choose to use the inside team approach, consider supplementing it with at least a few outside opinions. Doing so gives you a reality check on whether you're moving in the right direction and staying aligned with your clients.

>> **Do it yourself.** Ask yourself probing questions — or create a small circle of colleagues from other organizations who can also benefit from exploration within a group setting. CEOs from top companies meet this way to share problems and solutions, and you can, too. Focus on building a core value statement for each of you, one at a time.

QUESTIONS TO ASK YOUR CUSTOMERS

Try This: Seek out insights from customers to help craft your core message. Use written questionnaires, have telephone conversations, or conduct in-person meetings. Whatever your method, interpret these questions, add some, and subtract others to align with your particular operation.

In addition to a base for your core message, plan to emerge with great testimonials for your website and other materials. (Gain customers' permission to use their words, of course.)

And while you're at it, pay scrupulous attention to any performance shortcomings that emerge and be prepared to follow through and improve.

- What do you most value about our product or service? Why?
- Have we helped you increase profitability? How? Can you quantify that?
- Have we helped you increase market share? By how much?
- Have we saved you money? How much?
- Did you use the money saved another way? What resulted?
- Did we help you cut costs? How?
- What problems have we solved for you?
- Have we helped you reach new markets or audiences? Which?
- Did we increase efficiency? Systems?
- Did we help you reduce mistakes and errors?
- Did we improve relationships between staff members? Does this prevent conflict? How does that matter?
- What do you like about working with us? What don't you like?
- Did anything surprise you while working with us?
- When would you call us in the future?
- What would you say about us to a colleague?
- Did we meet your expectations? How can we improve? What can we do better?
- Did you know we also offer service X?
- Should we add to our services in any way?

>> **Work with a business counselor.** If you're a one-person operation, a trained business counselor can help you reach productive conclusions. Seek out business development service agencies in your area; local libraries may be able to connect you with free or low-cost services. Local colleges often house business guidance centers or resources for entrepreneurs. Or a growing number of business advisors and coaches can help with paid services.

REMEMBER

If you approach clients in the spirit of checking on their satisfaction level and seeking input on how to improve, they're almost certain to respond positively. Don't see the research as an imposition, but as a relationship–building opportunity. And don't be surprised if what you discover differs from what you expected.

QUESTIONS TO ASK YOUR TEAM AND YOURSELF

Try This: Uncover insights that can contribute to your core message by brainstorming with partners or collaborators and if your organization is large, with representatives from different parts. Or work with a business counselor or a team you create — colleagues, partners, friends — who can amplify your perspective. Without outside input, you risk overlooking your best opportunities or may reinforce a misdirection.

Only some of the following questions may be relevant to you and your organization. That's fine. You're trying to tease out what makes *your* organization unique and how to position it powerfully. If questions don't apply, skip them, but spend some time adding ones that do.

- What makes us special?

- What do we do that's different from our competitors?

- What sparked the idea for this enterprise?

- What's unusual, interesting, or surprising about our history?

- Do we feel a sense of mission in what we do? What is it?

- Do we have a philosophy or company culture that distinguishes us? What is it?

- Is this a satisfying place for our employees to work? Do we actively developed their capabilities and help them grow?

- What are we most proud of (achievements, problem solving, creative thinking, collaborative skills, industry leadership, reliability, and so on)?

- Does a particular person epitomize our history and values? How?

- What does our total body of work say about us?

- What's the best example of our extraordinary service?

- What is special about how we work with clients or customers, volunteers, or donors?

- Do we have a high satisfaction rate? How many of our clients come back?

- What was our toughest, most complex project so far?

- How do we help clients solve the problems that keep them up at night?

- How can we prove how successful we are in carrying out our mission?

- How might the world (or industry) change if everyone hired us or used our product?

- Has our growth pattern been steady? What has affected it?

- Why are we better than our competitors and should be chosen?

- Where would we like to be in a year? Five years? Ten years?

- What would you most like our customers to say about us?

- Does what we do make the world a better place in any way?

Notice that a thoughtful process will inevitably identify shortcomings as well as competitive advantages. When you clarify what you are trying to accomplish on a basic level, you also clarify the criteria that tell you how well you're doing. Many successful organizations use truth-telling exploration to help chart next steps and identify deficits to plug.

Making your case in business terms

Your true value statement must connect with your customers and prospects, and this may take some translation. Reaching businesspeople in their own terms is not really rocket science. It's often about dollars and cents. Use this truth to make your core message more powerful.

Try This: Start developing your core message with a thorough look into work your company has done that solves problems. Look for ways to show that you can:

>> **Increase revenue and profitability.** For example: Grow market share, retain customers, find new markets, reach a wider audience, make marketing initiatives more productive.

>> **Cut costs and streamline.** For example: Reduce expenses, increase efficiency, cut redundancies, reduce mistakes, redeploy staff, reduce turnover, minimize product returns, cut red tape.

>> **Improve positioning.** For example: Build the client's or product's cachet, improve public or customer perception, raise company profile, minimize complaints, increase customer satisfaction.

>> **Change behavior.** For example: Train staff to work in teams or communicate better, promote adoption of organization's core mission and values, shift unproductive systems and behavior to productive ones.

REMEMBER

Important as it is, money isn't everything. Identify your clients' pain points and think about how you address those, especially in different ways from your competitors. Perhaps you have evening office hours to accommodate those who work; wash dogs in their homes; train those who buy your equipment; or provide free ten-year warranties. If you're in business, you probably already offer specific amenities. The idea is to think about value more systematically so you can communicate about it and sharpen your focus.

Every industry is different but all share the same imperatives, though they may take different forms. Increasing revenue for a nonprofit may mean upping donations, sponsorships, or grants, or recruiting more volunteers. A government agency typically wants a larger share of the government pie, which may be achieved by better articulating the need for its service, demonstrating new efficiencies, or increasing client.

TIP

Don't overlook the "good citizen" part of your organization's message. Most people today, especially the younger generations, value enterprises that support and contribute to good causes in the community and beyond. Are you helping people? Making the world better in even a small way? Nurturing your own employees? These may be important elements of how you do business and deserve to play a role in your communication.

Finding, Shaping, and Using Stories

Today's modern technological world, perhaps ironically, has come full circle to value storytelling, the oldest communication art, as the best way to deliver messages. Experts in marketing, branding, advertising, public relations, sales, and education now advocate stories to communicate ideas, values aspirations, and competitive advantage.

The idea makes perfect sense: Human beings have told each other stories for millennia, and as neurological researchers now demonstrate, we're hard-wired to respond to them. Specific areas of the brain process stories, and when vividly told, these tales excite the same circuitry as actual experiences, making us feel we are living other people's actions and emotions ourselves.

REMEMBER

For children, stories make sense of a complicated world and at best, are inspiring. They serve the same purposes for adults. Given the chaotic and random environment we find ourselves in, it's no wonder we crave good stories that put things in perspective and have a beginning, middle, and end.

Stories bring presentations alive, stay with the audience, and create a bond between teller and listener. They can make abstract ideas real and vivid. They offer endless opportunity to individualize and humanize an institution or leader. And stories reach us on the emotional level where, many economists and psychologists agree, we make most decisions, big and small.

Naturally you want to harness the power of stories for yourself and your enterprises. The problem comes in applying the idea. Where can you find a good story that embodies your mission? Can you buy one at the mall? Should you take a fiction writing course? Or hire a novelist to create one for you? The short answer: No.

TIP

Here's a simple and practical way to think about stories for business messaging: A story tells what happened. Sometimes it tells what *can* happen. Your story is implicit in the way you built your business, the reason you chose your career, the way you've helped other people, and much more.

The New York Times publishes a series — now morphed into an online video feature — called "One in 8 Million," which is based on the idea that "New York is a city of characters." But of course, outside New York, too, there's always a story. True, some are more naturally interesting than others, but you can usually find something fascinating if you dig below the surface.

In terms of your business message, you can build a story that communicates the heart of that message — and the other way around. You might already own a story line that can help you understand the meaning of your work.

Finding your story

The value of story-telling is in its multitude of uses: You can use them as anecdotes to spark a speech (see Chapter 8) or website, blog, or profile (Chapter 12), but I focus here on the *lodestar story* — one that epitomizes your business and guides how you think and communicate about it. These stories often evolve over time and must embody the core value idea I explain earlier in "Finding Your Core Business Message."

REMEMBER

Stories can take many shapes, but it's helpful to think about four basic types that work well for organizations:

>> **Discovery:** How I started my business, discovered my talent or passion, found my mission, developed a way to match my values to my work

>> **Bumpy road:** Obstacles I faced, mistakes I made, weaknesses I encountered, how I overcame challenges and grew the business

>> **Success story:** How I used my skills, product, or service to help someone else achieve what she (or an organization) wanted or solve a major problem

>> **Big vision:** How much better the world will be when everyone reaps the benefits of my service or product — or when a disease is cured, a needy group is helped, and so on

All four story types basically revolve around people. Good stories generally do. And of course, your story must relate to the specific people you want as your audience. If you're explaining why you're passionate about your work, it must be work that relates to your readers. A bumpy-road story must have a message your audience cares about — perhaps how you equipped yourself to solve your audience's problems. A success story should center on somebody just like your audience so those people can relate. A big vision should connect with your audience's needs — perhaps by promising a solution to an important perceived problem.

WARNING

Framing your experience and practicing selective memory is legit when you build a story, but *never* tell a story that is not fundamentally true. First of all, you're unlikely to tell it well, and moreover, you kill your own authenticity at the outset. Trust that the materials are there.

TIP

A good way to build a story is to start with the core message you want to deliver and scan your experience for a piece of history that illustrates it and lends itself to one of the story formats. If you've not yet created a core message, this is another good reason to do so.

Building your story

For fiction writers and playwrights, just as for journalists, the hard part is the lead: where to start. Don't be surprised if your story presents the same challenge.

A good beginning is not usually a chronological one. When you start at the first event and proceed forward in time, a story lacks suspense and doesn't provoke the curiosity that keeps people reading or listening.

TIP

Look for an interesting in. A surprise or a built-in contradiction is a good way to start. The fact that Steve Jobs dropped out of college and built Apple fascinates. Similarly, the story of how Facebook was born in a college dorm, XYZ startup began with $20, and a 17-year-old sold his software for $37 million all grab people's attention.

You don't have to blow away your audience. Discovery and turning points in your own life or career make good lead material, too.

> It's Saturday night and I'm hunched over my only table in my one-room basement apartment. Alone. My cat ran away yesterday. There's nowhere to look, no windows, always dark. I stare at my last jar of peanut butter. I set it down with a thud on top of 127 publishers' rejection letters. They're all I have to show for three years' work.
>
> Then I remember this ad I clipped out . . . .

In effect, the story starts at a pivotal point in the middle of the teller's personal saga (no, not mine, but a hovering possibility for most writers, artists, and so on). You might then speak to what got you to that low point and then how you moved on and overcame all those obstacles. The same approach works when you're telling someone else's success story to demonstrate how you helped.

Recounting a eureka moment where you or a customer learned something vital can work. A colleague who teaches presentation skills workshops opens by sharing her first day of teaching. She felt awkward and uncomfortable, and knew she was not connecting with her students. At the first break, one young woman approached and quietly gave her the magic clue she needed — "just be yourself." She then briefly recounts how she gradually learned to become a strong speaker and is now equipped to help other people become their best selves as speakers.

Story-writing tips

The following ideas come from the fiction writer's portion of the writing spectrum, but they can help the business storyteller, too. Use these approaches with both written and oral communication:

>> **Show, don't tell.** Rather than sticking to straight narrative or piling on the descriptive adjectives, put readers right into your scene so they can draw their own conclusions. Paint a detailed picture of the situation, event, place, or person.

Try telling the story in present tense rather than past, bringing it more immediate and alive for you as well as the reader or listener. Immerse yourself in the detail and speak from inside the re-created experience.

>> **Engage the senses.** Use vivid, graphic language to activate people's sense of smell, hearing, sound, touch, and sight and make them feel as if they are there themselves. Research shows that specific areas of the brain light up if you say hands are "leathery," for example, rather than "rough."

>> **Use dialogue and first-hand quotes.** Rather than, "My sixth-grade teacher told me I would be a failure," try, "One day, I'm sitting at school, looking out the window, and I look up and there's Mrs. Dim, my sixth-grade teacher, staring down at me. She says, 'Jeremy, when I look at you, I know I failed to teach you — and that you will fail in life.'"

>> **Be concrete and specific.** Take time to pin down details and the right words. Abstractions don't resonate with people. "I teach people to improve their writing" accomplishes less than "I show entrepreneurs how to create messages that win more hearts, minds, and contracts."

>> **Use simple, say-able language.** Rely on short words, short sentences, and plain structures. This especially applies to written stories because you're tapping into an oral tradition that generates its own expectations. Who doesn't listen up when you hear or read, "Once upon a time . . ."? Think about that natural story cadence and try echoing it. Or try using the words to spark your brainstorming, and perhaps even keep them in your delivered message: "Once upon a time I put on my first suit and went out on my first sales call . . . ."

>> **Stay positive.** Highlighting your mistakes and setbacks along the way is effective; people relate to this sharing and may even mentally cheer you on toward success. But be sure your story has a happy ending — one that leaves the audience with a good impression of you. Park any ironic jokes, told at your own expense, at home.

>> **Know your point.** Be sure you know why you're telling your story and that this moral aligns with the core message you want to get across. In fact, many people write the ending first and then build the rest of the story toward it. You might bring the point home, as in "I know now that following those side roads is what prepared me to set you on the right track." Or you may decide to let the story make the point on its own. A big-vision story might end, "I see a world where no one has to struggle for clean air and all children are healthy" or "My idea will solve the industry's data storage problem and save millions of dollars, millions of trees."

Try This: A good way to explore storytelling is to exploit its oral basis. Identify something that has stuck in your mind, whether an experience or small incident, and then tell that story to someone orally. You may find that after a minute or so, you can immerse yourself in a specific place and time and relive what happened to a surprising degree. See where the story takes you. Because the incident comes to mind, it may shed more meaning than you expect on your career or a particular decision, action, idea. Then create a written version.

Stories are everywhere around us. Develop your awareness of good storytelling techniques in presentations you attend, what you read and what you listen to. NPR and the BBC both have storytelling programs, and it's especially illuminating to hear well-crafted stories read aloud well. On a more down-to-earth level, take a look at Quora, "the best answer to any question," at www.quora.com. On this site, anyone can pose a question and have it answered by interested people ranging from "ordinary" to celebrities in their fields. You may be surprised at how effectively popular answers are in setting the stage with a line or two, drawing you in to click on the rest.

Putting stories to work

REMEMBER

You may be your own most important audience. A strong story tells you where you've been, where you are now, and where you're going. It solidifies the relationship between who you are, what you do, and where you want to go. That's why therapists use story-building to help people understand and reframe their life experiences. It's energizing to recognize that your life and career are still in progress: You can adjust course to change the ending! Stories work similarly for organizations. They communicate a shared history or vision serve as the glue that unifies people and keeps them on the same track.

On the practical level, your own story gives you a versatile tool that can be adapted to:

>> The "About Us" section of a website

>> Website pages that focus on good-cause accomplishments or needs

>> An elevator pitch

>> A job application cover letter

>> Online profiles

>> Pitches for investment or other support

>> Brochures and marketing materials

>> A speech or presentation opening

>> A media feature about your business

>> Special event promotions, like a company anniversary

>> Posting in your office as a framed piece

>> Exhibit handouts for trade shows and other public events

>> A blog

I recently saw several good stories told on restaurant placemats. Each basically relates who the founders were, where they came from, how the restaurant was born and evolved, which descendants are running it now, and what makes it so great. These sorts of stories are hard not to read while you're waiting for your food! Look for suitable opportunities (not necessarily on dinner placemats) to share and tell your own stories.

REMEMBER

For nonprofit organizations, stories can provide the entire key to fundraising, volunteer recruitment, and more. They can make the mission real and important, even exciting. Some nonprofits do this through the "founder" story, effective when that person is famous or charismatic. Often, charitable causes tell moving stories about the people who need their help and/or success stories about those they have helped. The most effective ones revolve around specific individuals.

Many nonprofits are good at embodying their sense of purpose and accomplishment in stories. Companies can learn a great deal from them about humanizing abstract ideas to touch people and make their organizations memorable.

TIP

Stories can be prime tools for carrying a corporate message about its good works, such as the charitable causes it supports or its efforts with sustainability, green building, and conservation. Demonstrating corporate responsibility is a must for all businesses today, and telling stories is a great way to do that.

Telling Your Story with Video

Video is (for now) the ultimate storytelling vehicle. Like film, it compels our attention by integrating moving images, voice, and music. Ways to use the medium are expanding way beyond the traditional because the production process has transformed so much. Today, just like we are all photographers and all journalists, we are all video producers.

Are we good video makers? That depends on how you look at it. A communications professional told me that after realizing that his agency's expensive, beautifully produced videos drew only a fraction of the YouTube fans of his mailroom clerk's videos, he put the clerk in charge of production.

Are production values — good picture, sound, and scripting — dead? We like the power of creating a 10-second video to share with friends, but we also like our movies and television shows to be beautifully shot and technically excellent. In some venues, like YouTube, do people prefer rough amateur video made on smartphones? Often, I think, we do. They strike us as "authentic" and real. Of course, our smartphones and other devices are become amazingly sophisticated in handling the moving image, at least in short bursts. And ways to share our experiences and imagination grow along with the technology.

Social media like Snapchat and Instagram surface a lot of creativity in using images, including video, to communicate visually. And the easier and more affordable it becomes to produce video, the bigger the role it plays in longer form vehicles for both classroom and online learning, entertainment, and marketing.

I focus here on both practical ways to create and use do-it-yourself video and high-end, more traditional video, because knowing those techniques will help you succeed better when you wear all the hats specialists hold: director, scriptwriter, cameraperson, sound specialist, voiceover talent, editor, animator.

WARNING

This "democratization" of video means that to reach people and accomplish business goals, as opposed to sharing something charming or cute or shocking online, your video has to be good. Use the ideas and techniques appropriate to your goals and audiences. Adapt them even for your solo smartphone shooting and editing. If you want higher production quality and have money to invest or a team at your disposal, these ideas will help you know how to invest your resources.

Deciding how to use video

Social media services do endless surveys to prove how important images, and especially moving images, are to reach target audiences. The last statistic I saw was that people are 40 times more likely to open a posting with video than without. The statistics boggle the mind. At the time of this writing, Facebook reported it generates 8 billion video views per day. YouTube claims more than a billion users who spend 60 percent more hours watching videos year over year.

There is an unquenchable appetite for video. But most of that is created for entertainment purposes. As with social media, businesses are getting better at producing video that has audience appeal while it promotes their goals at the same time. You can do this, too. Like social media, video is another route to leveling the playing field for small businesses, startups, professionals, and independent workers. The price of entry is more one of time and creativity than big bucks. Here are a few ideas of how you can use video:

>> Present client testimonials and stories.

>> Demonstrate a product.

>> Show your service in action (for example, teaching a workshop, fixing a bike).

>> Introduce yourself, your team, your company.

>> Deliver a company VIP message to share information or inspire.

>> Demonstrate how to do something.

>> Demonstrate how you make something.

>> Train or recruit staff.

>> Create brand identity.

>> Record "live" FAQs featuring you, or different staff specialists.

>> Support a pitch for funding or crowdsourcing.

>> Share expert opinions (for example, review new products in your field).

Any of these basic ideas can be done short (a 15-second customer testimonial) or long (a 2- to 15-minute demonstration). And how you use any of these formats is limited only by your imagination. Digital magic allows you to endlessly recycle your video material, which often more than justifies the time and financial investment. Most of the listed video products can be used on your website and posted on YouTube or another public venue. A product demonstration can be used in these ways and also taken along to support in person sales calls. You can use them to liven up blogs and just about every social media site.

You can go further afield with whatever idea suits your business. For example, invite user-generated video contributions by customers who can speak for the value of your service; live-stream industry events or occasions at your own work-site; produce video surveys by taking your camera to the street or an event to record answers to your planned questions. A man-in-the-street survey of what brands people prefer in your niche market, for example, can give you interesting material that highlights what people value about the product.

If yours is a service business, you might create glimpses of what you do and how, for example. If you run training workshops, clips of the action are far more effective for marketing than endless descriptions. A nonprofit can showcase its accomplishments, focusing on people its work has helped. Heartwarming interviews with grateful beneficiaries can touch viewers in ways that miles of brochures will never do. Needs can be made graphic by showing, for example, victims of a natural disaster, a child in need of financial help, or a ruined landscape calling for remediation.

Video is also a powerful tool for fostering team unity. International organizations use it to deliver messages from headquarters and make the CEO "real" across international waters. One smart communications department produces short features that each focus on a single employee talking about his personal interests and passions. This humanizes the work environment and makes it more collegial. Staff members feel important and appreciate that they are working alongside interesting individuals. Other companies invest in video to showcase their contributions to good causes, and their employees. This promotes good feelings both inside and outside the company.

Using video for marketing

Corporations and nonprofits alike create an endless number of full video "shows" to use in a range of venues, from sales presentations to speeches and special events. Marketing professionals love video because it can bypass customers' rational side and go straight to the emotions. Even a good 30-second television commercial can do that. However, both commercials and video marketing shows are accomplished through expensive planning, shooting, and postproduction work with large teams of specialists. But today's technology enables you to do quite a lot to promote yourself and your business, even without the expensive equipment and large team of specialists.

REMEMBER

Like every communication format, video is best used strategically. Consider these basic guidelines to orient you for producing useful video for your own purposes, on whatever production level you work with.

>> **Know what video can do well, and less well.** By integrating picture, sound, voice, and at times music, film and video have enormous power to grab us emotionally. But they can be less effective as learning tools. Visually based instructional material can show us how to do something, but it isn't suited for the kind of detail, or abstract information, that print media can deliver.

>> **Regard video as one more tool to integrate into your overall marketing strategy.** Unless you just want to have fun or produce random bits that might find an audience online, think through how what you want to produce fits into everything else you do, how it can be used to carry your core message, and how it can amplify the power of that message.

>> **Pre-think all possible ways you might repurpose the video.** If you are shooting a customer testimonial for your website, brainstorm other potential uses for the material, such as a marketing piece for your website, blog, or Facebook page. It's much easier to shoot a little more and cover the extra territory at the same time, especially if you won't have another opportunity. Don't underestimate the time that a quality goal-oriented video may demand.

TIP

>> **Script your video before you start shooting.** It's like everything else in life: How can you get what you want if you don't know what that is? Regardless of production values, video improves dramatically when you use writing as the base.

REMEMBER

Even if your final video is purely visual and contains no words at all, you still need them in the thinking and planning stage (called preproduction). Video or film that's more than a few seconds long requires planning, and I don't know a way to plan that doesn't require language. Any medium that delivers a message beyond a general mood, or to provoke an emotion, must first be expressed or imagined in words. Then we translate those ideas to visual form. Completing the circle, the viewer translates it back to language because that's how we ascribe meaning.

Further, if you're collaborating with anyone else, you need to write the script so the different specialists are on the same page and everyone involved can contribute refinements based on his or her own viewpoints and expertise.

Scriptwriting is a special kind of writing challenge because it's multidimensional. The picture must be planned right along with the narration or live sound. This becomes obvious the first time you work on a video project that is more than 15 seconds long. During my first experience, I came to the editing room with 15 pages of carefully written and recorded voiceover and a few days of on-site shooting. The editor laid down the first two minutes of sound and said, "Okay, what's the picture?" We had only 30 seconds' worth of relevant footage. Out went the script.

REMEMBER

Know what you want to accomplish at the earliest stage and plan based on *simplicity.* It's wise not to get overly ambitious. Pick subjects that support your goals and that you can handle with the equipment and know-how on hand. Know your content options.

According to the nature of your project (and budget), content can include:

>> Talking heads (people speaking directly to the camera)

>> Live action (such as demonstrations of a process or something happening)

>> Cutaways (close-ups of models, charts, or details of the scene)

>> Secondary footage called B roll, for background and transitions

>> Still images, which can be manipulated to give an impression of motion

>> On-screen titles, animation, and more

>> Archival material from your own files, a customer, or commercial source

Introducing yourself with video

Video of the company leader is a powerful way to liven up a website or social media page, even if you're a one-person operation. Someone — perhaps you — talking on camera about your business, product, service, or career dream is a much more personal introduction than plain old written copy. You and your business become real to the viewer and he feels he knows you personally.

WARNING

However, not everyone comes across well in living, speaking media. Video is especially high-risk if you plan a talking-head speech with the camera focused fully on you the whole time. You can work out a simple version of a teleprompter, such as cue cards or pages with notes outside the camera's view, rather than reading. Be prepared to find this a lot more difficult to do well than you might expect if you haven't tried it. Coming across as warm and natural without some talent or training is difficult.

Try This: Record yourself for a few minutes speaking directly to a camera and then take a hard look at how you come across on video. Ask colleagues for honest input. If the piece doesn't show you off to advantage, either:

>> Scrap the "Here I am" video for the time being.

>> Do a really short version.

TIP

Twenty or 30 seconds of video is usually plenty for an introduction. Think of it as an elevator speech with a camera. Your actual elevator speech, which I discuss in Chapter 8, may give you the core of your video message. Also consider drawing on your personal value statement (also Chapter 8), or your personal story, which I talk about earlier in this chapter.

What often works best is to find something about your work that ignites your own genuine enthusiasm or passion. I once reviewed a script for a travel agent that began, "Hello, I'm Viola Smith, and I run a full-service travel agency that takes care of you all over the world." I suggested instead, "I'm Viola Smith, and what I love about my work is rescuing people from the travel adventures they didn't expect."

After your lead is in place, the rest falls naturally. Viola went on to give a few examples of extreme rescue, like finding a flight from Afghanistan for a family at four in the morning, and replacing a traveler's stolen money and documents in time for him to get home for his daughter's birthday. In less than a minute, the video demonstrated Viola's problem-solving skills and above-and-beyond service, which connected well with prospects. Who hasn't had a disastrous travel experience and doesn't anticipate another? Viola's message was a reassuring, "Don't worry, I've got your back and I'll do whatever it takes. And I love doing that."

A simple line or two introducing yourself is fine for a video opener — you don't need a flashy introduction or magical words. But use your best writing-thinking skills to find the substance that you can communicate with great conviction. There's a good quote from Theodore Roosevelt that applies: "Nobody cares how much you know until they know how much you care."

Sharing expertise with video

Most people today go straight to the Internet to learn things: how to fix a computer problem, how to treat a pulled muscle, how to make a quilt. If you're good at something or have specialized knowledge, you probably already possess excellent subject matter for how-to videos.

Disseminating such videos may be well worth your while to establish expertise or authority in your field. The Internet offers an astonishing number of videos, just like blogs, that share knowledge purely for the satisfaction of doing so. I think that's great, but bear in mind how much competition is out there. Think through carefully how to communicate your knowledge or advice as clearly as possible. Create a step-by-step set of visual-plus-narrative instructions.

How-we-do-it videos are also especially good enhancements for your organization's website or blog. Whether you make boots or art glass, teach yoga, or fix carburetors, how-to tips can interest your target audiences. They can also communicate what makes your product unique and perhaps expensive: special materials, a demanding process, long experience.

If like most of us you've searched online for a way to solve a problem, you've probably found that most how-to videos are badly produced: out of focus picture, poor sound, hard to follow. Use common sense and pay attention to production values as best you can. If given a choice, we'll all watch the better-quality video.

TIP

If you don't have a team of specialists to work with, build one with colleagues who have good ideas and a willingness to experiment. Ingenuity and imagination can, to some extent, make up for specialized technologies.

If you're basically your own crew, rely on the following production essentials:

>> **Lighting is the big difference between interesting, clear video imagery and indifferent visuals.** Invest in a light you can position and adjust. Take the time and effort to light your subject carefully.

>> **Sound quality counts hugely.** The biggest technical complaint about home-grown video is poor sound. People can apparently forgive not-so-good picture but hate having to strain their ears to catch or interpret the words. Seriously consider investing in a good, versatile microphone.

For more tips on achieving quality and using a step-by-step production process, see Chapter 17.

Articulating your special value, adopting the techniques of storytelling, and applying some video know-how can amplify your communication toolkit nicely. The techniques will come to your aid in many situations where you are selling yourself in some way, from building a unique online presence to job hunting, my next subject.

Chapter **10**

Writing for the Job Hunt

I f the U.S. Bureau of Labor Statistics is correct, today's average worker stays at each job for approximately 4.4 years. But most Millennials expect to stay at a job for less than three years. If you were born after 1980, that means you'll probably hold 15 to 20 jobs in your lifetime. But taking account of how fast industries appear and disappear these days, some futurists predict that today's young people will hold 40 different jobs — in ten completely different career paths — over the course of their lives.

REMEMBER

Whichever statistic you buy into, I recommend you face this fact: Your career will demand countless résumés, cover letters, interviews, and networking messages. It's hard to imagine new technology will change this situation much. Good written communication is becoming more central than ever for accessing opportunities. Unless you regularly dine with a CEO, you're unlikely to leap into a job without a résumé, a cover letter, and in many cases, effective messages, and a written test or two.

This chapter shows you how to apply your writing skills to showcase yourself advantageously. Especially because job hunting will be a constant part of your life in an ever-evolving workscape, I believe your first imperative is to have a solid sense of who you are and what you offer. Even when you're on the job, you may have to keep demonstrating your value and keep competing for the opportunities you want, so this self-assessment always matters. (Chapter 7 looks at adopting this entrepreneurial mindset.) Let's start by talking about how to identify and articulate your value.

Knowing and Expressing Your Value

Marketers call a message that expresses your or a company's value a "core value statement." It's also called the "value proposition" and "unique selling proposition." For an organization, such a message is the crystallization of what the enterprise contributes to its customers, and the world in general, that no other entity provides. A company might, for example, offer extraordinary service in its domain, an innovative or superior product in its niche, or a unique way of solving a problem.

REMEMBER

The most effective branding is based on the concept. An organization communicates its central value in a systematic and consistent way, using whatever channels it chooses — websites, ads, print materials, and all the rest. You can use the same thinking. A personal core value message clarifies your sense of identity and keeps you on target toward your goals. Just as a core message guides a business, nonprofit, or other enterprise, a personal one helps you always know who you are, what you're doing, and why.

TIP

Holding fast to your central identity is especially important in a flux-dominated world that demands chameleon-like responses. You may need to bring different parts of yourself to the fore when applying for particular jobs. Knowing your own uniqueness has a solid impact on how you communicate in résumés, cover letters, and online media.

This sense of self supports you in-person as well. Imagine going into a job interview with a secure conviction of what makes you valuable. You own an effective message about *you*. Knowing and believing in this message gives you the confidence to deliver it well. You're prepared to answer interview questions without floundering. You can field whatever is thrown at you and respond appropriately, while staying grounded by your sense of intrinsic value.

Consider, too, that when you hold a job you want to keep or advance in, you are bound to encounter new department heads or a manager who's looking for people to cut — or promote. How can you justify the company's investment in you? Show you're capable of more? If you start with an internalized core value statement, you're certain to fare much better than your colleagues. Let's see how you can develop one for this moment in your life.

Pinpointing your personal strengths

Smart leaders put a lot of energy into figuring out their company's value proposition. One way they do this is to ask their executives, employees, clients, customers, themselves, and perhaps the general public and others, questions that reveal what the various stakeholders value about the organization. Then they analyze and distill all this input to determine the company's central value and find the language to communicate it. (Chapter 9 discusses how organizations do this.)

I offer you here a process that adapts this corporate approach to your personal needs. Don't view this as an assignment worth a casual ten minutes. Good answers may take shape over time, and often arise when you're doing other things. I recommend experimenting seriously with this process because it can radically improve the content of your job-hunting communication. Good substance is always the first imperative of good writing!

TIP

A good way to engage in this process is to work with one or two other people you trust and with whom you feel comfortable. Determine in advance that each of you will emerge with your own core value statement and give each person equal attention. I guarantee you'll be happily surprised at what you learn about yourselves. This is an uncovering process!

Try all or some of the following approaches:

>> **Explore your past history as a story.** Imagine someone asks you, "So, how did you get here?" What would you say? Think about your life overall as well as your career path so far. Try answering orally. Notice what comes to the fore. Jot it down. (Chapter 9 offers more specific guidance on finding your story.)

>> **Analyze your experience in writing.** This pushes you to think more deeply. Start at the beginning of your career — or close to it — with facts such as where you were born, your family situation, your education, your first job, and subsequent jobs. Can you identify turning points? Milestones? Obstacles you overcame? Connections between your personal life and work choices? Write down achievements, recognition, and honors of any kind in all of your life arenas.

>> **Focus on your assets.** What natural skills did you bring to the table? What skills have you developed? What assets do you value in yourself, and what do you believe others value in you? How would you describe your ideals? Write these things down, too.

>> **Ask other people for input.** If you're working solo, frame some questions to ask people who know you from various standpoints: friends, ex-colleagues, partners, maybe a former supervisor. For example:

- *What do you think I'm good at?*

- *What do you like about being my friend (or colleague or boss or partner)?*

- *Do you believe I have any qualities that make me different from anyone else?*

- *What would you say about me to a prospective employer (or friend or colleague)?*

- *Does knowing me benefit you in any way? Make your life different in any way?*

Then ask yourself:

- *What am I passionately interested in? What do I care about?*
- *What am I most proud of?*
- *What is my highest ambition?*
- *How do I want other people to see me?*
- *What have I contributed so far to my employers? Friends? Family?*
- *How do I want my work and life to fit together?*
- *What do I want to contribute to the world?*

Try This: Here's a fun activity that may bring some useful ideas to light. With a group of perhaps eight to ten people, choose a scribe. Then focus on one person at a time by name. Each person in turn quickly says a single word or short phrase that he or she feels best captures that person. The scribe scribbles each contribution down on a single sheet of paper and at the end, everyone is given his own page with the full group input. You may see a surprising consistency, and equally probable, a set of personal qualities or assets you would not have attributed to yourself.

Pulling your ideas together

Review the results of the exploratory work you did. What patterns do you see? Are there more correlations between your personal life, background, and career than you expected — or fewer? How closely does your self-image accord with how others see you? Has your career path been straighter than you thought and moving in the direction intended? Can you see yourself as more persistent and effective in overcoming obstacles than you imagined?

WARNING

As human beings, we share a tendency to dwell on negative experiences and discount the positive. Psychologists tell us this is built into our brains, perhaps as a survival advantage. For thousands of years, expecting the worst from unfamiliar people may have helped negative thinkers survive better than their more optimistic cohort. If you find yourself taking a negative slant on your history and value, think again! Give yourself permission to see the positive and you will. Look past the "mistakes," missed opportunities, and setbacks that may bog you down. Psychotherapy depends on the idea that we can shift perspective on how we interpret the past and see the present.

When you've reviewed your findings, write a one-paragraph statement. Every one of us truly is unique; there isn't a specific formula for doing this. The statement is just for yourself, and it's provisional, so don't get stuck in the wording. Here are a few general considerations to take stock of:

>> **The light that other people's perspectives shed on your personal qualities, assets, and skills that you haven't recognized, take for granted, or tend to discount:** What did they uncover about you that you didn't see in yourself?

>> **The proofs of success you identified in different parts of your life:** In terms of work, did you find a way to save your employer time or money? Manage or contribute to a successful project? Are you the go-to person for something?

>> **Degree of alignment with your work:** Do you have the scope to exercise your ideals, talents, and abilities? Use your best skills? Do you see progress toward your goals, or a need to correct course?

>> **Personality factors:** Often, they are more readily recognized by other people: a sense of humor, adaptability, kindness, resilience. What are the qualities that make you special to the people in your life?

>> **Your passionate interests:** Do they find expression in your work? Do you want them to?

TIP

Here's a practical lens for reviewing individual experience: Identify a combination of skills and interests that make you unique. I know a psychologist who combined her love of horses with her career as a psychologist, and now helps patients by having them work with horses. A musician who studied business management, a lawyer with a medical degree, a dancer who loves photography . . . disparate-seeming skills can make an individual especially marketable and lead to a highly satisfying career. Think also about how a hobby or strong interest might multiply your unique value. And think about what you might learn that gives your expertise a whole different dimension.

Try This: A straightforward way to follow up your exploratory thinking is to write a simple list. Create headings such as:

My deepest interests:

My combination of skills:

My accomplishments and successes:

My proudest moments:

My personality assets and strengths:

The talents and skills I want to develop:

My vision for the work and life I ultimately want:

LEVERAGING YOUR PERSONAL VALUE STATEMENT

In the workaday world, your value statement gives you a healthy advantage as a job seeker. It's a compass for making good decisions about what jobs to look for, how to match your strengths against job specifications, and how to present your qualifications.

A young man I know, Jed, is an aspiring painter with a set of degrees in the fine arts. He took practical courses along with fine arts and with a natural affinity for computers, gained work experience helping a historian archive photographs. Ready to launch an independent life, Jed needed a full-time job that would support the life he wanted. No one was hiring studio painters.

Jed used a version of the process described in the preceding section to review his abilities and experience. He consulted other people to collect their observations of his skills and assets and composed a simple list of his interests and strengths. His goal immediately clarified: find a job within the art world that would expand his thinking about his avocation and give him a base for a career he could enjoy. Jed soon spotted a posting for an administrative job in a museum. He reviewed the job specifications and adapted his core value ideas to align with the opportunity this way:

My background and interests make me completely comfortable with the museum world and its people. I bring training and experience in archiving, preservation, and photography.

My special skill is with applied technology. Everywhere, I become the go-to person when computer problems crop up. I can assess technology systems quickly and create better ones to do the work. Recently, for example, I did a project for a photograph archiving company, and in the process designed a computer-based system that does in minutes what used to take hours of work by hand.

I also like training people to use new technology in friendly ways that make them feel good about using it.

Jed built his application cover letter around this idea, backed up his claims in the résumé, and was able to speak well for himself in a series of interviews. He competed for the job successfully, and this additional credential helped him obtain the next opportunity and prove himself further. He's now a well-rewarded technology specialist for an international art gallery.

Cut or add categories that relate to you and fill them out in as much depth as you choose. This brings you well on the path to understanding your value and potential. What could be more interesting? Inspire yourself!

Let's look now at the job-hunt components one by one.

Writing Résumés That Win the Race

If you like to imagine that résumés are no longer necessary in an employment market where online search and hire is the norm, I must tell you that's a fantasy. Employers need a standardized way of evaluating candidates more than ever because so many applicants respond to online help-wanted postings.

For both sides — employer and job seeker — making a good match is a real challenge. An outstanding résumé is your best offensive. Let's see how analyzing the usual suspects — *goal* and *audience* — can help.

REMEMBER

Your résumé's *goal* is not exactly to get a job — rather, it's to move you past the first filter to the next step of the hiring process. What can you put "on paper" to make you stand out and achieve an in-person or online interview, or at least, gain you further scrutiny?

You must show in writing that you

>> Understand the organization and the job's demands

>> Offer a good match for that job and will bring value to the company

>> Can prove your credibility with proof of accomplishment

Beyond these basics, you must communicate that you are an energetic and proactive person who can be relied on to solve problems, take the initiative, work well with others, rise to challenges, and perhaps lead. On a technical level, you must meet tangible demands such as using keywords to survive prescreening.

TIP

To accomplish all this, your résumé needs your best thinking and writing skills. In fact, demonstrating that you communicate well is in itself necessary because those skills are high on employers' wanted list, whether the ad says so or not.

In considering *audience*, note these three points:

>> **Making the match is your responsibility as an applicant.** This means that the employers' needs matter more to them than yours. Face it: They don't

care that you require "an interesting position in the field I love that will use all my skills and help me grow." They want to know what you can do for them.

>> **You must customize every résumé to the specific job and employer.** One size doesn't fit all. You can create a general résumé that's adaptable to different purposes. You can produce two or more résumés that are slanted differently if you're open, say, to either a marketing job or a public relations spot. But always, if a job is worth an application, you need to customize it.

>> **It's smart to do your homework.** Inform yourself as well as you can about the organization: its history, products, industry standing, challenges, and problems. Infinite information is available through the company's own website, its social media presence, online conversations by employees, career sites such as Glassdoor (www.glassdoor.com), or a simple Google search. And don't forget to scour the job ad for all the clues it offers as to company needs and candidate qualifications.

WARNING

Consider also what else your target is reading about you! Do you have a LinkedIn profile that paints a different picture of your experience and interests? Do you have inappropriate photos of yourself partying on Facebook? Does your Twitter feed include nasty remarks to or about people you don't like? (Chapter 12 offers advice on cleaning up your virtual act.) Assume the people hiring will search all this out, as might your current employer.

Let's look concretely at how to produce the winning résumé you need. There's a lot good advice on writing good résumés out there (including another Wiley title, *Résumés For Dummies* by Laura DeCarlo), so here I concentrate primarily on format, content choices, and writing style.

Choosing a format

Traditional résumés, with variation, generally cover your life this way:

Contact information (name, email address, home address, telephone)

Job objective/self-identification (for example, Senior Project Manager, Nonprofit Sector)

Summary statement of your qualifications

Reverse chronology of your work experience with title, overview of each position, achievement highlights, and dates

Education

Skills, knowledge, certifications (may also be called "key competencies")

Other categories as relevant: honors, awards, recognition; special interests; publications; volunteer experience; affiliations

TIP

A substantially different format option is the "functional résumé." This opens with a much more detailed version of the summary statement — perhaps half a page — that highlights skills and capabilities rather than specific job experience. It works well for consultants, freelancers, and other non-staff workers because someone hiring for a project wants to know what a candidate can do, rather than her work history.

Even if your goal is full-time, on-premise work, adapting aspects of the functional résumé can solve a host of planning problems if the traditional format doesn't showcase you effectively. A functional résumé is organized this way:

Contact information

Title and/or company name if there is one (for example, Mark Brown, Freelance Copy Editor; Amy Green, Inc., Social Media Marketing Consultant)

Full summary overview that specifies relevant skills

Sampling of clients and projects

Background experience (for example, former relevant positions)

References

Adapt elements of this format if it helps put the emphasis where you want it. It's a good way to minimize any perceived deficits. The traditional presentation can also be juggled to put you in the best light. For example:

>> **Right out of school?** If you lack relevant work experience, use the traditional format, but put the education section first and amplify it with your coursework and any honors. Focus on what relates to the job.

>> **Long-term unemployment, or gaps in your work history?** Use the expanded functional résumé version of the summary statement and write a good narrative about your capabilities and achievements. But you do need to explain the gaps and indicate your activity during that period (more on that later in this chapter).

>> **Feel you're "too young" or "too old" for the job?** Minimize the dates visually by adding them in parentheses after the job description rather than placing them in the margins. If you're on the older end and want to avoid making the point, no law says you have to include everything. But don't undersell yourself: Communicate your experience and knowledge with pride. And because

eventually you'll have to show up in person, it's shortsighted to mislead the reader too much in any case.

>> **Trying to transition to a new field or role?** Adapt the functional résumé approach and focus on producing a strong summary statement that translates your practiced skills to the prospective job's demands.

>> **So many jobs you look scattershot?** Find a category for whole groups and cover them with a singe time frame. For example, the job title might be, "Retail Job Experience, 2012 to 2015." Below that give each job a line of its own, such as "Managed Icy Treats Shoppe for two summers, coordinating staff of three, operating cash register, tracking inventory." Internships can be grouped this way, too, and present a strong collective impression.

REMEMBER

Bottom line: Customize every résumé you send out to match you up with the job specifications, and play to your strengths and assets.

Writing the summary statement

To guide readers to review your qualifications in the light you want, begin your résumé with a strong three- to five-line narrative capsulizing why readers should be interested in you. Rather than telling your readers what kind of job *you* want, tell them why you match what *they* want.

Effectively done, the summary embodies your job target and makes you eminently qualified for it. This can take a lot of thought so don't be surprised if that is the case. But if you worked out your core message, as I recommend in "Knowing and Expressing Your Value" earlier in this chapter, you can easily adapt it to the purpose. For example, my young friend who applied for the arts administration job might write:

> *Arts Administrator, Art Historian, Practicing Artist*
>
> *Experience and advanced training in archiving, preservation, and photography. Special expertise in designing computer systems to perform administrative work more efficiently and economically. Adept at training people to use new technologies cheerfully. On every job, recognized as the go-to person when computer glitches happen.*

TIP

A helpful way to develop your self-summary is to start with the job you're aiming for, the more specific the better. If you're not applying for one right now, scan online to find help-wanted postings in your field and look carefully at the requirements. This tells you what matters to the employer. Then review your own experience and see how well you can align it with those skills and qualifications.

Try This: An interesting exercise is to invent an ad for your ideal job. Put yourself in the head of the hiring manager and describe the opportunity in detail — the role, responsibilities, and challenge; essential "hard" and "soft" skills; desired experience; and other qualifications. Then answer the ad you wrote. Besides giving you some useful insights into your résumé content, this helps you define what you want more closely. And in turn, this helps you recognize the right opportunities and identify ways to get there, such as learning something new.

TIP

The best résumés make it look as if the candidate has been preparing for the job all of his or her life. You achieve this not by misrepresenting your skills and qualifications, but by looking at them within the perspective called for. Strategize what deserves the most emphasis for each job, and which factors count in your favor. Often you must creatively translate the value of a skill learned elsewhere for this job. Don't expect the reader to do this for you.

Discriminate among the parts of your own experience. In Jed's case, for example, he knew that his main interest — painting — was not what would engage his target job market, but rather, his practical skills. Yet the fact that he is himself an aspiring artist is relevant, so he mentions it but doesn't elaborate.

REMEMBER

The summary statement is almost always the first — and perhaps last — part of your résumé that will be read. Use it to communicate your value to the people hiring so they will be drawn to read more, and orient the rest of the résumé as backup.

Building your work history section

Whether you call it Professional Experience, Employment, or Work History, this section must prove the claims of your summary statement. A reverse chronology is standard. Start with your current or most recent job and present it more or less in the following order (I point out variations you can choose):

>> **Job title, company name and location, employment dates:** You can take a little liberty with titles — for example, if you were officially Third Assistant Manager for Technology, but your main job responsibility was troubleshooting, you are (in my opinion, but use your judgment) justified in calling yourself Technology Troubleshooting Specialist. If you feel guilty about this, user lower case letters to make it generic. Regarding dates: If for any reason you do not wish these overly noticed, put them quietly at the end of this line, or the end of the description, rather than thrusting them into the margin in bold face.

TIP

Include a phrase explaining the organization as necessary and helpful. If it's a company few will recognize, identify it. For example, "Whitehead Hats, largest Midwest wholesaler of top hats with $200 million revenue." If it's GE, sure, people know the name, but don't really know its scope, or the specific piece that employs you.

>> **Narrative overview:** Don't start a job description with bullets! You first need to provide a succinct perspective on your main responsibilities. Use bullets to present notable achievements. If you have trouble writing the overview, look for the most general and encompassing bullet you wrote and you can likely expand on that. For example, a magazine editor might write:

Directed the editorial, design, and production of the martial arts supply industry's leading publication. Produced 12 120-page monthly issues with a staff of nine. Increased ad revenue 19 percent over five-year tenure.

>> **Bulleted achievements:** Each bullet should provide a detail of the job and whenever possible, be achievement oriented. It's not about just being there — the responsibilities you carried out that nobody complained about — it's about how you made difference. The editor might say:

Responsible for coordinating work of sales and editorial departments.

But he shouldn't. This is better:

Created integrated team of sales professionals and editorial staff to collaborate on issue themes and facilitate ad sales.

That sounds a whole lot less passive and boring. But better yet:

Introduced collaborative sales/editorial team system to create issue themes, securing 17 new advertisers in the first six months.

REMEMBER

The last version is better because it quantifies an achievement. Do this every time you can because it speaks every manager's language — call it *bottom line-ese*. Did you save time or money? Increase efficiency? Solve a problem? Introduce something successful or innovative that accomplished a specific goal? Flaunt it! If you've done a decent narrative overview of your current job, as described in the preceding section, you can use bullet follow-ups to highlight your best contributions.

TIP

Mentally brainstorm the whole experience at the job to identify those crystallizing specifics that prove your value. One useful way is to review projects you've led or been part of, because those typically start with a problem and end with a successful resolution. Also look at everything that produced a tangible result: "Built a landing page that doubled the conversion rate in three months."

Try also asking yourself, "What would have been different in my unit or organization had I not worked there?" Some of your accomplishments might be of the "soft skills" variety that are harder to translate into time or money. Get as close as you can — sometimes an anecdote or testimonial will work. For example: "Office restructuring idea identified by the CEO as among the 10 best ideas of the month"; "Class op-ed writing assignment published in regional newspaper"; "Managed intern program rated 92 percent effective by participants."

Treat earlier jobs similarly, with a short opening narrative amplified with bullet points. Logically, each previous job merits less territory than the more recent one.

Showing off strengths

In addition to adapting format to showcase your main selling points, choose to highlight the best content for the job. Here are a few more ways to adapt the presentation to your strengths and the job's demands:

>> **Create a Professional Highlights section.** This is especially useful if you want to minimize the impact of your chronology. You can make a Highlights section a star attraction by putting it right up front before a job listing to focus on your capabilities. You can follow this section with a simple rundown of the positions — in effect, where the experience was developed. This is a good tactic for a highly experienced job-seeker, a career switcher, or someone reentering the job market.

>> **Work in testimonials.** If your professor said you were the best accounting student he ever had, or a former boss agrees to acclaim your contributions, use the accolades to strengthen your hand. Sometimes even a coworker or friend who looks to you for related help can add spice. Give some thought to graphic presentation for testimonials. You might add a statement at the very bottom, or box it in a good place.

>> **Add an areas of expertise section to clearly communicate your skills and abilities.** Or, add a Professional Development section if you're in a fast-moving field like technology. Even if you're in a slower-changing field, indicate that you care enough to keep taking courses, workshops, and training opportunities. This dedication speaks to your value.

>> **Include a Community Service section.** This is a good way to go if you've been out of work for a long time, or if thus far, it's what you mainly have to show rather than work experience. Unpaid work is indeed work and can be relevant! If you taught free classes in tax preparation while out of work as an accountant, that's a lot more impressive than looking like you sat around the house. Unrelated activities also help you come across as a caring, involved person, and who doesn't respond to that? But don't call it volunteer work. Call it *community service*.

>> **Explain employment gaps.** Why leave those unaccounted-for years open to interpretation? Naturally the reviewer will want to know how you spent them. Basically, tell the truth. Most employers are much more open to relatively erratic career paths today because so much is out of the individual's control. If you were caring for a relative, say so. If you tried your hand as an independent

consultant, that's fine, no matter that you didn't wildly succeed. But be prepared to speak of the experience and outcome, as well as your preference for a staff job.

>> **Make the most of your progress.** If you were promoted after three months, say so. If you were the youngest regional manager ever appointed, say so. Especially if you've held one or more long-term jobs, it's important and inspiring to make your progression obvious. You can incorporate these successes in the job narratives, or in a highlight statement.

WARNING

Do not include any information that trivializes your experience. If your administrative assistant duties included organizing meetings, overseeing supplies, and filing, leave out filing, unless you're going for a job as a file clerk or manager. You do not need to include everything you've ever done or every detail of a job. Doing so tells the résumé reader at the least that you can't discriminate the wheat from the chaff. Worse, people tend to see you as the lowest denominator you offer. So, once again, we see that less is more.

For more résumé-writing tips, see Chapter 16. Next, let's look at the cover letter that introduces your résumé.

Succeeding with Cover Letters

TIP

Take time to write a good, original, targeted cover letter for every job application you submit. A well-crafted cover letter is essential even if you're responding to an ad that say cover letters aren't necessary. (Exception: If the posting says "absolutely no cover letters," don't disobey.)

Writing effective cover letters is tough, but worth the trouble. It's your chance to talk in the first person — "I" — about yourself as an individual. Use the letter to supplement the basically dry information of an application form and résumé. Cover letters also set up your reader to give your submission the perspective you choose. You can provide a context for your accomplishments, point at what's most relevant, add depth to a noteworthy qualification, or create your desired tone.

The following sections show you how to organize and execute a cover letter that strengthens your application.

Planning a cover letter

The basic decision-making system I introduce in Chapter 2 and apply to email in Chapter 6 works for cover letters, too. Start by focusing your goal. While your ultimate purpose is to get a job or secure a contract, as I say in the case of résumés, you rarely achieve this result from paperwork alone. The letter is best viewed as an introduction to your résumé. Or, in some cases, it may serve as the whole application.

WARNING

Never treat the cover letter as an afterthought. Most of your competitors invest all their energy into résumés and tack on careless, perfunctory notes rather than letters. In more than a few cases, a bad cover note eliminates someone from the running altogether because tired reviewers welcome the chance to "just say no" to an applicant. The planning process gives you insights on how to stand out.

Use the strategy outlined in Chapter 6 for email: Brainstorm a list of the points you may want to make. Consider the following questions to find content ideas:

>> What personal facets are you unable to include in the application that would animate your bid?

>> Do you have any connection with your reader or the organization worth referring to — a common acquaintance or alma mater, for example?

>> What key qualifications and qualities is the organization looking for — and what are your most salient match points?

>> How can your cover letter embody the qualities the organization seeks (for example, creativity or attention to detail)?

>> Why do you want this opportunity? Can you say something genuine and positive about your motivation? Exhibit enthusiasm?

>> What can you say that is genuine and positive about the person or organization you're applying to? And why do you think this is a good match?

Opening with pizzazz

It's always worth taking trouble with your letter's opening sentence and paragraph. Like email, letters should get to the point as quickly as possible and focus on what most matters to readers so they are enticed to keep reading. But often, letters need context. If you're responding to a job ad, you're probably impelled to begin along the lines, "I'm writing in response to your ad for an SEO specialist in the *Daily Techie*'s July 1 issue, page 13."

TIP

If you're delivering the letter as an email, use the subject line to identify your reason for writing: "Application for Software Engineering Job #1465." But if it's a physical letter, avoid a boring lead. Here's a way around it: At the top of the letter, preferably on the right, type "In application for the SEO specialist job, *Daily Techie*

July 1." Then you can begin the letter more this way: "I began inventing computer software at the age of 9 using a flashlight in the dark because I was supposed to be in bed." Or a simple, straightforward statement is often called for (use your judgment): "As a Topsy Software developer with seven years' experience, I see your job opportunity as an ideal match."

To create a strong opener, look for clues in the brainstorming list you assembled in the preceding section, then see which other points help tell your story in a few tight paragraphs. What do you most want the reader to notice in your résumé? What will make you more "real" to the reader, more individual? What's your best matching point with the job?

Avoid repeating word for word statements in your résumé. That wastes people's time and bores them.

Another caution: Be scrupulously courteous. Always address a specific human being if you possibly can, using his or her last name and title. Close formally: "Sincerely" is best.

And yet another caution: Edit and proof the letter ten times. Ask a friend to review it. Read it backward. Let it sit overnight and read it again. A spelling or grammar error in a cover letter comes across as even more disrespectful than in a résumé, and may consign your whole application to the wastebasket.

Networking with Messages

You may often send spontaneous messages for online networking, but when you're job hunting, see such messages as letters that deserve TLC. If you're requesting an informational interview, reference, or introduction, you're usually asking an influential person to give you valuable time or stake his own reputation on you. If you're writing a thank-you-for-your-time note, you will be evaluated upon its merit, perhaps just as much as how you interviewed. You must do such messages thoughtfully with all your empathy feelers out.

Requesting informational interviews

When you ask for any kind of favor in writing, your message represents *you* to the reader, whether she's met you or not. You're evaluated based on what you say and how you say it. If you send careless, sloppy requests for informational interviews, don't expect people to do you many favors. If you ask in the right way, most people are extraordinarily willing to help. People may choose to spend a half-hour telling you about their experience, for example, either in person or by telephone, if you

>> Target the appropriate person

>> Define and limit your expectations

>> Show respect and appreciation for the prospective conversation

>> Demonstrate that you will be a credit to the person, and his industry, when you interact with others in his circle

>> Come across as someone worth knowing in the future

TIP

Ask the classic "what's-in-it-for-me" question to frame content for any request. If you're asking for an informational interview from a relatively young person, he may be pleased to know you consider him knowledgeable and influential. More established people are often motivated to "give back" — to their alma maters, their professions, or simply in recognition of their good fortune. They may recall someone who reached out on their behalf at an earlier time in their careers. And, many successful people with children of their own take satisfaction in helping young people.

In addition to altruistic motives, smart businesspeople like making connections and bringing worthwhile people together. They value being known for their networking skills. When you craft your messages, you rarely address such "what's-in-it-for-me" factors directly. But being aware of probable motivation guides you to the right tone and content.

If you share a connection, use that entree early in your message — in the lead, if possible. For example, "Our mutual friend Pat Jones suggested I contact you because I'm aiming for a career in your field, biomedical engineering, and would deeply appreciate your advice."

If you don't have a ready-made connection, research the people to whom you're writing and see if you can find one. For example, do you have a college, career path, or professional association in common? Did you hear the person speak at a conference or read his article? Do you have a reason for admiring him?

TIP

Do your homework and make sure it shows in your request. You need to have a good reason to write to a particular person and organization. An individualized message has an entirely different impact from a hit-and-miss email that could be addressed to anyone.

To see what I mean, think about your reactions to the following two messages.

Message 1

Dear Rob Walker:

I'm a new grad with a degree in Business Admin and think I might like to work for an international nonprofit. I see that you do that now. I'm in your area next Thursday available from 2 to 4. OK for me to come in then? Thanx much. —Mark

Message 2

Dear Mr. Walker:

I write at the suggestion of Allison James, who interned with your office this past summer and spoke highly of the experience. I hope very much you might find the time to talk with me about my career path — ten minutes would mean a lot to me.

I've just graduated from Marshall State with a degree in nonprofit management. During the past five years, I've held internships with four international development agencies and feel confident that this is the work I want to spend my life doing. I've spent several months in Nigeria, Sri Lanka, and Peru.

In hopes of preparing for work like yours, directing overseas field volunteers, I see several possible career routes and would appreciate your perspective.

Would you consider scheduling time for a brief telephone interview? I can be available at your convenience almost anytime next week.

Thank you for considering this request.

Sincerely, Melanie Black

If you think the politeness of Message 2 is exaggerated, perhaps so. But if you were Rob Walker, would you talk to Mark or Melanie? Which one sounds like a good investment of your time — not only because of how much the candidate may value the opportunity, but because of that person's relative long-term prospects? Melanie comes across as someone worth helping.

To succeed with network messaging, think through your content options, draft a message tailored to the particular reader, then carefully edit and proof. You may be amazed at what opportunities and people move within reach. If you're performing a virtual introduction between two people, spell out what's in it for both parties — why you're suggesting the connection.

WARNING

Don't use the power of virtual networking to replace or avoid in-person networking or human contact in general. You can sit at your computer all day and exchange written messages, but that's no substitute for a conversation or live interaction. No one hires a piece of paper or an email.

TIP

If you want the best assignments, job leads, and relationships, *show up.* The benefits of networking face-to-face within an industry and through professional associations are huge. Use your writing skills to achieve in-person opportunities.

Saying thank you

Suppose you achieve the informational interview you want and speak to the person. Should you write a thank-you note? Don't even ask: The answer is not "yes," but "always." That applies even if you didn't find the person all that helpful, and it applies every time someone gives you information, advice, an interview, a contact, or an introduction. If you don't write, the discourtesy may be held against you.

A good thank-you note is notoriously challenging. I often ask graduate students in public relations to thank, in writing, a special guest who participated in a seminar. Most are surprised at how much thought a brief note takes.

TIP

To the writing rescue once more — the idea of defining goal and audience! To thank someone for an informational interview, a job lead, a reference, or other favor, your *goal* is to express appreciation and also to keep the door open for future interaction or help. In considering the *audience,* decide:

>> What did the person do that you appreciate?

>> What feedback would this person value?

Consider Roger, whose client, Jen, has referred him to one of her own clients in need of services in his province. Roger sends this note:

> *Jen, followed up the referral to your client Bob Black, went well! Thanks. Roger*

You're probably not impressed because major elements are missing. The information is vague and gives no concrete idea of the interaction or outcome between Roger and Bob. Second, the tone is careless. Added to minimal feedback from Roger, Jen (who staked her reputation on Roger) is likely to feel uneasy about making the connection and reluctant to reach out on his behalf again. Here's a version that works better:

> *Dear Jen,*
>
> *Thanks so much for connecting me with Bob Black. I met with him at his office this morning, and we had a good conversation about his technology update program and how my group is equipped to help.*

Bob asked me to prepare an informal proposal for review by his team. Of course, I'm delighted to have the opportunity.

Jen, I really appreciate your opening this door for me and will keep you updated on developments.

Sincerely, Roger

Besides being carefully constructed and written — itself a necessary tribute to Jen's generous spirit — the note reassures her that Roger made a good impression on her client rather than flubbing it. In this instance, what's-in-it-for-Jen is creating a connection that benefits both parties and makes her look and feel good.

Depending on the situation, consider too whether a more definitive thank you is called for: offering your favor-giver a cup of coffee or lunch, for example. Surprisingly few people actively reciprocate a good turn. Returning the favor at some point is the most effective response, of course. Each thank-you situation deserves individual thought.

TIP

If your thank-you note is written in the wake of a job interview or pitch for a project, it probably becomes part of your application package. Treat the thank-you note as a test of your communication skills and a chance to customize what the decision-makers know about you. If you spoke to someone on site or experienced the environment, you have new insights on what qualifications the organization most values. Or perhaps you realize you didn't mention something important in writing or in person. Such additions are first-rate material for thank-you notes. The note is also a good way to reinforce your belief in how good a match you see between the company and what you can do for it.

Odd as it may sound, take the time to thank someone for the opportunity even when you don't win the job, contract, or grant. The same people are likely to make the decision next time, and your positive attitude may pay off. Thanking someone for the opportunity underscores your professionalism and makes you a bit more memorable. Many people positioned to bestow jobs, projects, and other awards find the world discourteous. Act as the exception and see what happens.

In the next chapter, I focus on skills that are especially useful for people who work independently and as part of a virtual team; or earn their ways as consultants, freelancers, and professional specialists. But if you're an employee, skills in collaborative writing, virtual teaming, decentralized work systems, and marketing tools benefit you as well. All these activities depend on . . . good written communication!

4

Evolving Your Writing for Online Media

Learn how to create the online presence you want no matter your business goals by strategizing your content and adapting your writing for each medium.

Decide which digital platforms are right for you: websites, blogs, Facebook business pages, LinkedIn and/or Twitter accounts, email.

Learn techniques for writing long-form digital content and see why making your content look like easy reading is the key to snagging readers' attention.

See how to build website content from the ground up.

Determine your best blog subject and how to capture the right tone and style.

Discover tips for networking with Twitter, writing online profiles for LinkedIn, and engaging with other social media sites.

Chapter **11**

Writing for the Digital World

The Internet is like a magic door that democratizes communication. It empowers you to reach almost anyone, anywhere, and offers you virtual space to represent your own interests. The price of entry for online action keeps coming down. If you have more money than time, you can hire teams of specialists to plan, write, design, and produce a website, like in the early days. But the tools become more and more sophisticated, and today, almost anyone can produce an effective site and do all or most of the work himself. You can put up your own blog in an hour or two. Or post comments and ideas on other people's blogs with a click.

The windows opened by social media evolve even more dramatically. A decade ago, few people expected that 92 percent of employers would use social platforms to hire, and that three out of four would screen candidates online. Nor did we know that more than half of all purchases would be made electronically, and that social media would influence an estimated 70 percent of consumer buying decisions.

Many of us depend on online media to know what's happening in the world, share opinions, and find communities. More and more learning is done online, too, whether we want to polish a skill or learn how to cut an avocado. We look online to hear what our business and political leaders are saying. And digital media has transformed the world of advocacy. Social movements, massive protests, and common causes originate and are managed online.

From a career perspective, whether you see your future as an employee in a series of jobs or as an entrepreneur, contractor, or freelancer, the profile you build with your online content may be critical. If you view the digital universe more personally — as a way to explore an interest or passion, connect with new and old friends, or expand your thinking — you, too, need to understand the tools.

Realistically, the digital age challenges all of us. If you're a "native" user who grew up with the Internet, you probably take it for granted as the basic infrastructure of your personal life and perhaps a big part of your work life. If you're an older user, you may feel pressured to transfer your skill set to the newer media, and are scrambling to catch up with its lightning evolution.

Everyone has a learning curve. Baby Boomers and to varying extent Generation X'ers are pulled to transfer their communication know-how and people skills to new channels. Most Millennials, if they are to achieve what they want, need to deepen their thinking about communication and marketing. This chapter and the one that follows are dedicated to helping you create the online presence you want, whatever your business goals and whatever your facility with new media. Writing is the common ground. To be effective with digital media you must know how to strategize your content and adapt your writing for each medium.

Positioning Yourself Online

When I wrote the first edition of this book in 2013, I observed that the Internet had leveled the playing field for those willing to learn its ways. People could scout for jobs and be discovered by recruiters, reach a VIP with a click, or compete with big well-funded businesses armed only with a good idea and a website. Everyone gained the power to be not just an author, but also a commentator, editor, and publisher. No more gatekeepers!

WARNING

All of this and more remains true. But there's a snag: Today almost everyone has landed on that playing field. You're competing not only against people in your industry, but also with hordes of talented, well-paid communication specialists. Most companies dedicate in-house or outside resources to manage their websites, blogs, and tweets, and to produce videos, create infographics, and post cleverly on social media. The advantage no longer belongs with the early adaptor.

TIP

But you can certainly succeed if your online life is strategic and well-executed. Creative thinking, reflected in good writing, is your ticket to today's digital universe.

But, I hear you asking, what about visually based media: Facebook, Snapchat, Pinterest, Instagram, and new platforms that are brewing as I write this?

REMEMBER

As I point out when talking about video in Chapter 9, ideas start with words. Imagination translates those words into images. Often, the corporate posts you may love are not bits of spontaneity, but carefully crafted messages created by teams working within an established marketing frame. They often use those most traditional tools: writing and storyboards. What you ultimately see may contain few words or none at all, because the message is carried by imagery.

Sometimes a platform's visual orientation is in part illusory. Pinterest, for example, which collects and displays images based on themes, nonetheless delivers plenty of information as infographics. These typically involve extensive planning, research, writing, and graphic design.

However, if your aim is to entertain your friends, or share moments of your life, strategic thinking is a lot less necessary. For many people the value of digital media is the spontaneity the technology underwrites. If you want to communicate "look what I'm doing," or "here's where I am," or "isn't this funny, or beautiful, or inspiring," that's absolutely fine.

TIP

If you want your messages to support larger aspirations, they must be strategic. Random tweets will produce random responses. Carefully written blogs won't help your cause if they don't tie to your goals. Spontaneous social posts won't build a following that matters if you don't have a plan.

Everything you put on the Internet adds up to a unique social profile that can bring you opportunities, or if you're careless, lose them for you. Therefore, you must know what you want to achieve and whom you want to reach.

Strategizing Your Platform Choices

A character named Pogo in an old cartoon famously said, "We are surrounded by insurmountable opportunities." Used strategically, online channels consume time. They can drain you of energy and creativity, and even shift your focus away from the "real world" to become counter-productive. So be selective about your activity.

I talk about using specific social media platforms in Chapter 12, but it's smart to consider your options and decide how to budget your energy and resources. Possibilities include:

>> **Build a website.** If you're in business of any kind, hunting for a job now or down the line, or spearheading a community or charitable cause, chances are good that a website is indispensable. It can be a complicated multipage

ecommerce site or a blog — the two have become fairly indistinguishable. You can build a site with all the resources it can take and spend money, or you can put in time and build it yourself with online tools such as Wordpress.com, Wix. com, or Web.com. Take into account that an effective website needs to grow and change, not treated as a static brochure.

>> **Create a Facebook business page.** This is useful for a wide range of enterprises, since people of all ages have learned to enjoy sharing this way. However, even Facebook's business pages are geared to be visually entertaining and news-oriented, so a business page is not the place for detailed promotional material. But Facebook is a great way to build a fan base, launch contests, share interesting and timely happenings, and show a company's personality.

>> **Start a blog.** Regular blogging helps you establish trust, credibility, and authority. You can post blogs on media such as Medium.com, or LinkedIn if you prefer not to mount your own blog or want to supplement it. Experts often advise that to establish a following, you need to post new material predictably, preferably twice a week. But today there are so many blogs (some estimates say 152 million) that they must deliver substantial content. Research finds that surprisingly, 2,000+ word blogs are better read and valued than the short blogs that used to be recommended. The current outlook is less quantity, higher quality.

>> **Become active on LinkedIn.** LinkedIn is the professional's networker, and other than more personal job hunting venues like social media, LinkedIn is the best hiring center for recruiters and employment managers, and therefore, job hunters. For the consultant, contractor, and professional, LinkedIn is essential because potential employers find and check out candidates here. There are numerous industry-specific sites worth considering as well, and international versions, too.

>> **Post on Twitter.** This 140-character messaging system is far from the flash in the pan predicted a few years ago. Who knew that presidential campaigns, and many lesser causes, would turn on this mini-messaging system? Many reporters and editors use it as their story source. And it isn't just words anymore; images and video are starting to dominate. A strategic Twitter program consumes 5 to 20 tweets per day, and some widely followed users post hourly.

>> **Use social media.** Here the plot thickens, as people sometimes say about films that become complicated. These apps are the most moving of targets. They not only proliferate, but constantly change features to maintain and grow their fickle audiences. Each platform has its own personality and tools. Facebook, Instagram, Snapchat, and their cousins, current and future, are best seen not as *media outlets* in the traditional sense, but as platforms where users can express themselves and engage in conversations. Organizations

that want to build their brand with Generation Z and younger Millennials need to be here and figure out how to be part of the fun.

>> **Send email.** I devote a whole chapter to email (Chapter 6), but I mention it here because it should not be overlooked as a marketing tool. Email is ubiquitous and interweaves so well with online media. Many businesses of every size depend on email's reach. Some of the most influential bloggers deliver posts via email or embed a link inside a curiosity-provoking message. Notice too how sales-funnel strategies on blogs and websites are designed to collect email lists. To receive the giveaway or subscribe to a newsletter — also sent by email — you must provide your email address. Then they know where you are! Like it or not, don't rule this workhorse system out of your mix.

TIP

How to begin designing your program? Some experts advise focusing on a single platform, or a small coordinated set of platforms, and doing them well. Be realistic about how much to expect of yourself. Create a written plan to develop your ideas and make the most of your personal investment. Consider three factors: your goal, your audience, and your capabilities, which includes your time as well as skills.

Breaking down your goals

If your overarching goal is to market a product or service, brainstorm how the Internet can help you do that. Objectives might include:

>> Establish your credibility, trustworthiness, and likability.

>> Prove your expertise and authority in a field.

>> Interact in real time with customers and contacts.

>> Maintain connection with current and past clients.

>> Connect with new prospects.

>> Humanize your business.

>> Participate in conversations to understand your market and customers better.

Amend this list and add to it as appropriate. Then think more concretely about how you might accomplish your set of goals. For example:

>> Become an active member of an existing online community.

>> Cultivate your own community of loyal followers.

>> Attract customers and prospects to your website, blog, and social sites.

>> Educate your customers, prospects, and other people about your work.

>> Offer "inside" glimpses of your firm's people and what they do, or how products are created.

>> Organize and promote events — live ones, webinars, online meet-ups.

>> Find ways to generate positive word of mouth.

>> Partner with influencers — people who already reach your audiences and are listened to.

TIP

The more narrowly you identify your goals, the better you can identify your best media options — and the more ideas you'll generate for using them. If you want to listen in on your customers, for example, research where they're hanging out and actively plug into that channel. To present a friendly, accessible persona for yourself or your firm, consider Facebook, Snapchat, and Instagram. If you have the expertise to teach people how do something, YouTube is a prime candidate and perhaps brief videos on social apps.

Keep the long range in mind. No matter how secure your present situation feels, you will benefit from the support of a personal following or a community, and from networking with people in your field. You might at some point want to find collaborators, test the waters for a business idea, showcase your abilities, or develop ways to turn a passion into a living.

Knowing where your audiences are

I cover audience analysis in several chapters because it's central to writing suc-cessfully in every medium (see Chapter 2 in particular). But for online platforms, this staple take some additional twists. Knowing where your audiences are, you are able to:

>> **Aim directly at your target.** As never before in history, you can reach your audiences without intermediaries. Do you want more customers like the ones you have, or prospects from other arenas? Do you want to reach people who share a passionate interest or a specific age group, like Millennials? Analyze where to find your targets and invest in channels that reach them. Each platform offers detailed information on its demographics and ways to find groups. A simple Google search tells you which sites are currently popular with your audiences. *The Internet is all about using easy-to-find information to locate your communities.*

>> **Tightly define your audience.** The more closely you know who you want to reach, the better you can draw them to you. Consider the fishing analogy. The ocean teems with fish and each kind has its own food preferences and

habitat. Once you're clear on which fish you're after, find out where they spend their time and which food they like. Then you can go where they are and create the right bait. Be specific: If you want to reach "young women," for example, you'll find an over-abundance of possibilities. A 15-year-old cares about very different things than an 18- or 21-year-old, has different interests, and spends time on different platforms. Whom do you want to talk to? *The Internet is all about narrowcasting.*

>> **Lead people to your online content.** On the Internet, you need to help interested people track you down quickly through SEO (search engine optimization), which is a process of identifying your content in the ways people are most likely to look for you. You can also drop breadcrumbs in your various sites to lead people to your website, blog, special offer, or Snapchat or Twitter account. *The Internet is all about cross-promotion.*

>> **Expand your audience through shareability.** Delivering content valued by your connections gives you extraordinary potential to reach others who are like them, and thus, build your following. In every venue people look for material they can share with their own connections by re-tweeting, reposting, or incorporating links to your messages or sites. Make it easy for readers to do this. The lucky few succeed in a post that "goes viral," but it's impossible to aim for that. More important: *for marketing, the Internet is all about generating word of mouth for a product, or service, or you.*

LEARNING TO LEVERAGE THE POWER OF SEO

Search engine optimization (SEO) is critically important to online writing because you want to be found when people look for what they need. Search engines such as Google rank content by its degree of value to users. Because searchers rarely look past the first page of the list that comes up, everyone wants to be one of the first ten results.

Engines continually refine their criteria and algorithms to reflect their perception of highest value. For website and blogs, the perennial values are appealing content that changes often, number of inbound links (links to your site from other sites), and the effectiveness of your keywords and search terms. Lots of expensive professionals are available to help you optimize your site by adjusting your content and search terms, as well as plenty of books. Here I give you a brief overview.

To dig into SEO, seriously brainstorm your enterprise to come up with the language your target audiences are most likely to use when searching for your service or product

(continued)

(continued)

or posts. Try for a pool of at least 30 terms that include your product or service names, location if relevant, and any industry specifications people might think of (for example, Gary Smith Photography, Pittsburgh plumbers, ABC certified dieticians). You want to use the most popular search terms — but on the other hand, if everyone in your category is using them, your business may be buried. Many people look for a balance between the obvious and obscure, and cover both ends of the spectrum.

Help is available via Google itself. Try entering a search term, then click on "Related searches" to see what competitors are using. Also look into Google Insights (www.google.com/trends) and Google AdWords (https://adwords.google.com/keyword-planner). Another good learning resource is Moz (https://moz.com).

Once you settle on your search terms, use them liberally! "Frontload" your headlines by putting the keywords at or near the beginning. Sprinkle them through your website and blog content, and use the most important ones in the first paragraph. Some specialists recommend using three to five per page, but recent algorithms mostly credit those used in the first few paragraphs. Each website page should have its own set of terms to distinguish its content. Keywords are also important to social media bios and posts — savvy people pack even the one-line Twitter bio with keywords as well as hashtags. Fortunately, your groundwork for websites or blogs gives you what you need, adaptable to each platform's guidelines.

The trick to all this is to make what you write feel natural and read well, despite the search terms. Even working in three keywords on a page can undermine your message's impact. If you jam in so many search terms that they interfere with reading and enjoyment, you've defeated your purpose.

Always think of the reader first, then the search engine and its crawlers.

A few trends to note:

There's a shift toward "long tail" search terms, the more natural way people might look for what they want — closer to the question they would ask. Instead of (or in addition to) "formal bowtie," for example, "tie you wear with a tuxedo." This is in line with the growing use of voice search — as in asking Siri or Alexa to find something for you.

A second big tilt is in favor of mobile communication. If people type in a keyword, it must be short and to the point. On the other hand, if they voice their question, they are apt to use long-tail search terms. Mobility also creates more demanding criteria for your content. The smaller the screen, the tighter, more relevant, and fat-free must your writing be. Use this book's strategies to distill your meaning without losing the energy.

Keep in mind that optimization is about content first, then SEO to promote distribution of that content. Keep your material fresh and alive.

Assessing your skills and potentials

REMEMBER

Most Internet channels raise issues that have more to do with time than with money. Rather than trying to do more than you can reasonably handle, review your commitments and priorities. Realistically appraise how much time you can invest in this part of your life and its relative return-on-investment. Consider your people resources, too, if you're part of a company or a team.

Assess your skillsets. The various channels require different mindsets and talents. It makes sense to choose those with which you are most comfortable and will be most productive for achieving your goals. If you don't like to write more than necessary, why commit to blogging twice a week?

TIP

If you're a visual thinker, your day has come! Those who can plan visual content are in high demand because photos and videos are the best open-sesame keys in all digital media. Today's tools make it so easy to produce, edit, and use visual material that you can build your skills by practicing them. But if you do have graphic training or talent, flaunt it!

Social apps offer an ideal way to explore your potential strengths and talents. You may discover a gift for humor or for creating surprises. If you simply love to spend time on the Internet and find good things others are doing, curation may be up your alley: Scout for material of interest to your audience and share it (always with suitable credit).

Social media give you plenty of room for some trial and error, but aim to choose platforms you can sustain over the longer run and that will most benefit you.

Writing for Digital Media

In this section, I offer general guidelines for online writing that apply to relatively traditional content: blogs, profiles, newsletters, websites. These are considered "long form" media, and long form is in! These techniques adapt to the various social platforms, which I address in the following chapter, along with specifics on creating websites and blogs.

REMEMBER

Does good writing matter online? Absolutely. Those fish I talked about in "Knowing where your audiences are" earlier in this chapter won't snap up your offerings otherwise. No matter how much you know. Moreover, it's indispensable for establishing credibility and trust. People may not consciously evaluate writing excellence, but it's how they automatically decide whether a stranger merits their time and trust. Do you buy products that are described in boring, or overly hyped, error-prone language? Or find badly written arguments persuasive? If you do, you're unusual.

The guidelines for print writing presented in Part 1 apply to online writing but more intensively. You need to be more direct, concise, clear, and dynamic. Imagine a formal, stiff, academic-style essay — you may have written your share in college — with long, complex sentences, weighty words, and a dense look that warns of slow reading ahead. You know the piece may take a few readings to ante up its thought nuggets.

TIP

Try to write for online media in exactly the opposite way. First, snag attention. Then make it look like easy reading. Writing that looks and is complex works poorly online because reading anything on-screen is physically harder. Our eyes get tired, we blink more, resist scrolling, and bypass anything that looks hard to access. As readers, we expect speed and immediacy online — not meandering messages that take work. Strive for simplicity and brevity.

Loosening up

TIP

Online writing can ignore many formalities of grammatical correctness. Contractions are fine: for example, *won't* rather than *will not*, *I'll be* rather than *I will be*.

DIGITAL WRITING CHECKLIST

Good online writing gets right to the point, reads fast, and reads well out loud. Strive to include as many of the hallmarks of good writing for digital media as possible:

- Informal, friendly, conversational style
- Warm, personal, upbeat tone
- Ultra-conciseness: no excess words or thoughts
- Minimal (or no) adjectives and adverbs (very, extremely, totally, innovative)
- Minimal clutter words (in order to, as a matter of fact, at this point in time)
- Lively action-oriented verbs in present tense
- Short, simple, everyday words (mostly one syllable)
- Free of jargon, mystery abbreviations, and clichéd business-speak
- Short sentences: 1 to 12 words on average with few clauses (as signaled by commas)
- Short paragraphs: one to three sentences
- Good rhythm that pulls readers along

Sentences can begin with words like *and, but,* and *or.* Or they can consist of a single word: *Never. Ask. Maybe. Why?* Sentences like these can effectively punctuate copy and make it feel lively.

What your computer's grammar checker identifies as sentence fragments often work well, too:

> *Why web surf? Because it's fun*
>
> *Too many choices, too few good ones.*
>
> *Better than excellent.*
>
> *Hardly ever.*
>
> *Well, you asked.*
>
> *Does it work? You bet.*

But be sure your incomplete sentences are clear in context and don't read as mistakes.

Keeping it simple and visual

If you're targeting general audiences, stay short and simple by stashing complexities elsewhere. Or keep them in a separate section. Of course, exceptions abound. For example, you may pinpoint an audience that specifically likes technical material or sophisticated thinking. As I talk about in Chapter 12, long-form blogs are generally more widely read and valued than short ones. And if you're trying to establish thought leadership, white papers and opinion pieces must treat their subjects in depth.

TIP

Acknowledge your skimmers and speed readers by finding ways to present information telegraphically, at-a-glance rather than as narrative. Descriptions and technical specs lend themselves well to this approach. Use introductory phrases to summarize long lists of information and help readers move more quickly through complex material:

> *Product suited to:*
>
> *Kit includes:*
>
> *Caring for your item:*
>
> *How to reserve your place:*

Bulleted lists work well. But don't make those lists too long or present them without context. Start each item with the same grammatical part so that they read consistently.

What about humor? If you can write content with a sense of fun or surprise, good for you. Often such material is hard work that talented teams labor over for weeks, months, and even years. If you're a writer, of course you want to showcase your skills. But for most websites and other content, good substance presented in a down-to-earth, easy-to-absorb way works just fine.

TIP

If you have a gift for spontaneity and charm, by all means use it. But try your experiments out on your friends before launching them into digital orbit. I'm reminded of advice I once heard given to a new camp counselor: "With children you must always be sincere, even if you have to pretend."

Communicating credibility

If you use the Internet to promote yourself or a business, everything you post must convey that you're authoritative, knowledgeable, trustworthy, reliable, responsive, open to input, and a nice person, too. Viewers scout for clues to your credibility. In addition to writing your best and proofing meticulously, convey your trustworthiness with these techniques:

>> Include only verified information and keep links updated.

>> Use technical language sparingly and only as audience-appropriate.

>> Provide clear, easily found contact information.

>> Identify your credentials and highlight any sign that your authority is recognized.

>> Use attributed testimonials to show you've met other people's needs.

>> Invite input in specific ways, and respond to it.

WARNING

And never, never, ever:

>> Criticize anyone on a personal level.

>> Conduct personal arguments online.

>> Reveal anything about yourself you don't want the world to know.

>> Post photos or videos that may embarrass you if your grandmother or a future employer sees them.

>> Use offensive language or an angry tone.

WARNING

Do not use Internet platforms for blatant self-promotion more than appropriate to the medium. A website, for example, naturally includes product information and a purchasing pathway. A Facebook business page is intrinsically commercial in a soft-sell way. But for social media, the message is best supported by creatively interpreting the subject to connect with audience priorities: What might your readers want to learn? What entertains them or makes them laugh? How can they be part of the action? Scout the channel to see how companies and individuals do this successfully.

REMEMBER

Ultimately, you can only reap rewards from Internet platforms if you deliver value in their own terms. For the more purely social platforms this may mean sharing a smile, a bit of inspiration, a behind-the-scenes glimpse, a special moment. On long-form platforms it's giving your readers useful information, teaching them something they want to know, or expanding their world.

Whatever the medium, *always share your best.* The Internet is an overwhelming source of information and entertainment. Followers must be earned with authentic contributions. Most successful ecommerce specialists give a great deal away through blogs, videos, webinars, and ebooks. This makes sense. As a buyer, why would you send money to a total stranger you'll never meet, who may be thousands of miles away, and will be hard to hold accountable if you're disappointed? You must prove value and reliability to sell. People who are impressed with your expertise want to know more and may become loyal customers.

Cutting hype, maxing evidence

A century of traditional advertising and public relations may have dulled our sensibilities to highly promotional writing. Although most people claim to hate ads and marketing pieces, they may still skim through blurb-ridden printed material to find kernels of interest. But not on the Internet! Online readers strongly resist the clichéd, overblown, and hard to credit. Combined with our limited attention span for on-screen reading, the overwhelming supply of good material leaves us with no patience for wordy, overwrought, self-promoting content.

WARNING

Cutting out the dross is even more imperative now that so much reading is done on tiny screens like smartphones, watches, and tablets. Skip the flowery language and use your imagination to puzzle out what will deliver your core message and prove your value to the readers you want in the most concise but non-boring way.

REMEMBER

Begin with this simple principle: Make no claims you don't back up. Nobody believes those empty statements like "the most innovative breakthrough in the entire twenty-first-century technology powerhouse" anyway. Tell readers as specifically as you can why and how your whatever-it-is improves their lives in some way.

Try to eliminate nearly all adjectives and descriptive words. Use statistics, facts, testimonials, case histories, and visual proof as appropriate. Cite benefits rather than features. Of course, you can include the features or technical specs that readers may want; just place them so they don't distract from the central message and its flow.

Devising nonlinear strategies

I once had an argument with a video producer about a storyline I scripted. The sequence was getting out of order in the editing process. "It's A, B, C, D," I insisted. "No!" he shouted. "Don't you understand that there's no more *linear*? No more beginning–middle–end? That's *over!*"

I've since decided he was right, and he was wrong. In the context of the Internet, everyone has become an information surfer. You may land on any page of a website or in any part of an online conversation, and you don't care about logical development of the entire site or interaction. You don't intend to read it through like a novel. Because the material probably won't be read as a sequence, it must be modular — presented as pieces that make sense on their own.

TIP

You must accommodate online reader behavior with matching writing techniques:

>> "Chunk" information into easily absorbed units so that readers in motion can swoop in and grab what they want.

>> Make sections self-contained so readers aren't required to read other material in order to understand the piece currently in front of them.

>> Repeat some information as necessary so that readers can get what they need.

>> Provide different access points to the material so readers can find and enter the site from different angles.

>> Offer choices: links to other parts of the site with more depth or breadth, or different angles on the subject, and links to offsite information sources.

>> Build in a call to action on every website page and every post: Find out more information here; fill out this form for the giveaway; call me today to talk about your problem.

WARNING

But don't take modular, nonlinear structure to mean that you can present disjointed bits and pieces that add up to less than the sum of their parts. Every page of a website, for example, must make sense on its own. It must also flow logically through a cohesive plan. A blog post needs a beginning, middle, and end.

Incorporating interactive strategies

The biggest difference between digital and print media is the power they give you to interact with readers. People are now so accustomed to responding to what they read with their own ideas, experience, and opinions that they expect you to invite input, and respond to it in turn. Today's audiences want to be actively involved, not passive bystanders. Interactive tactics are especially critical to communicating with Millennials and younger generations.

TIP

The digital world is all about creating relationships. Accomplish this by involving readers in every way you can invent.

>> **Blogs:** Invite responses and be specific. What do you think? Has this happened to you? What would you do? Do you vote yes or no? Did you have a similar experience to share? Do you have a solution to this problem? What else would you like to explore?

>> **Websites:** Offer tangible things people can request: free information, an e-newsletter, a discount. Invite them to buy something, join something, contribute something, or spread the word. Or ask people to rate a product or experience, send a recipe, or submit a photo of a given subject.

>> **Social media:** Encourage creative interaction. Companies that use social platforms well monitor customer conversations and participate in them. They offer the latest news and inside views of their brands. They listen and respond to complaints, ask questions, and run campaigns and competitions.

REMEMBER

Organizations are enthusiastic about *user-generated content* for good reason. Today, younger people particularly welcome invitations to send images, selfies, and snippets of personal experience. A travel-related company might ask you for the funniest thing you saw on a trip, the most interesting person you met, or the best (or worst) food you ate — a universally popular subject. User-created content is the ultimate interactive approach, and since it's virtually free, an alluring way to feed the Internet's endless hunger. Brainstorm ways for users to contribute their stories or images; participate in special promotions or games; write about favorite movies, books, or sport experience; and so on, as long as the activity connects to your purpose.

Of course, be sure you're equipped to follow through — and do so. Send the freebie, share the results, pay attention to input, respond to comments (definitely including the critical ones), feed the forum, and prod it along. Yes, all of this takes time.

Translating text into visuals

The statistics and predictions are hard to ignore:

>> People form a first impression in 50 milliseconds.

>> Posts with images produce 650 percent higher engagement than text-only posts.

>> People are 85 percent more likely to buy a product after viewing a video of it.

>> Tweets with images earned up to 18 percent more clicks, 89 percent more favorites, and 150 percent more re-tweets.

>> An estimated 84 percent of communications will be visual by 2018.

>> An estimated 79 percent of Internet traffic will be video content by 2018.

How to handle this transformation in your own communications?

If you're among my younger readers, you're probably moving in this direction without hassle via Snapchat, Instagram, and other current platforms. Many older-than–Millennial businesspeople and communicators, however, must rethink how all their messages can be reinforced or reinterpreted visually. To jog your thinking, consider that the nature of online reality creates the demand. Some factors:

>> **Images attract attention.** In a digital world that's more and more competitive, you want readers to choose your particular tweet or blog or Snap from a million choices and not only read it, but find it worth sharing with their networks. If you're selling something you want your audience to take a step closer to trusting you or ultimately, put up real money or time for something you offer. Visuals engage people instantly.

>> **Images reach us emotionally.** A description of a high-fashion shoe triggers a visceral reaction from its target audience — impossible with even the best description. This does not mean that the written material doesn't count. The shoe photo on its own probably won't close the sale, unless the reader is already a fan of the designer and trusts the distributor. She wants information about quality, fit, ease of returns, and so on. The image gets her attention, but the copy must talk her into action.

>> **Images can save you a lot of words.** They're invaluable for any kind of how-to material. They can substitute for a mountain of dull descriptive detail in many situations — to describe the fashion shoe, for example. As I say throughout this book, promoting speedy comprehension is always a goal. Visuals also strike us as more true and believable — after all, "seeing is believing." Watching video of a workshop leader in action is a lot more effective than any words you can bestow upon yourself in writing.

>> **Visuals make things more real to people.** Not long ago we bought all our shoes in stores. We touched them, checked out the colors, tried them on, held them alongside other options. We directly experienced how they made us feel: Comfortable? Beautiful? Young? When you buy your shoes online, however, you have no tangible experience with them. Photographs are as close as you can get. Selling a charitable cause, or an online course, is not so different. We want to see what we're getting: the result of our charitable giving, what people say about the course.

>> **Visuals make *people* more real to people.** Establishing relationships — which is so much of what the Internet is about — is also not so different from our experience buying products we can't touch. We make friends digitally, hire virtual workers, and collaborate with people around the world whom we will never meet. Isn't it more personal to see an individual, whether in a profile photo or social media selfie that expresses personality with stickers and filters?

>> **Visuals can present abstract and complex information with impact.** Businesspeople and scientists have always used charts and graphs and tables to report and persuade, but technology makes it easy now for anyone to create lively, colorful material that entertains us as they inform. Witness the rise of the infographic, to explain everything from how to make a cup of tea to why water quality is declining in different parts of the word. The format makes the data easier to grasp and invites interesting comparisons.

>> **Images enable us to symbolize ideas.** This is in my opinion the trickiest challenge but one worth meeting, particularly for bloggers and marketers. You know your piece will be better read with an image: but how to illustrate something like how to cut red tape in the office? My answer: Adopt a "show don't tell" mindset. You may know the term "objective correlative" from a literature course. It means conveying an emotion, or something abstract, by representing it in a physical dimension. Rather than saying "I'm really mad," for example, a character shows his fury by smashing a precious vase. Rather than saying "I'm cutting myself off from a world I can't handle," a character burns all his shoes.

Try This: Look for an objective correlative when you're presenting something abstract, or practice the technique for fun. In the case of too much problem of too much red tape: An image of people trying to push a boulder made of paper bound by red ribbon up a hill? An office worker at his desk surrounded by darkness, with a single lamp to illuminate a toppling pile of paper? Files overflowing a cabinet and colliding on the floor? Or maybe you want to represent "solution": a scale of justice with a ton of paper weighing down one side, and a tiny hard drive on the other. Or a hard drive shaped like an alligator eating its way through a paper mountain.

TIP

The remarkable thing is that all the visual approaches mentioned are within reach of us average folks. In addition to the good photos we can shoot on our smartphones, we can use better and ever-easier editing and special effects tools right on those smartphones or online. We can access unending resources of free or reasonably priced photos, illustrations, gifs, video clips. (Check out Unsplash [https://unsplash.com] for free high-res photos cleared for social media.) We can create high-impact charts and graphs with the right tools.

We can manipulate images for specific purposes and create infographics with templates in apps like Canva (www.canva.com/create), Infogram (https://infogr.am), and Piktochart (`https://piktochart.com`). We can shoot our own video, edit it, add music, voiceover, titling, special effects. We can create dramatically better presentations with programs that integrate video and movement as well as those great charts and photos. We can Livestream real-time video broadcasts on platforms like Facebook Live, Instagram Stories, Periscope, and Snapchat. And there's endless help with all of this and more in YouTube tutorials.

REMEMBER

The only limit is your imagination. Don't see the challenge of adding visuals as words "versus" images — aim to integrate them and capitalize on what each does well. Use visual media in all its forms to help get your message across and as appropriate to the medium, your brand, and your purpose. Don't restrict yourself to new media: Review your website, product information, and marketing materials to brainstorm where and how visuals can do more work.

WARNING

You are sure to find a lot of text material that can be repurposed and energized by visualizing them, but:

>> Be wary of mixing your styles — be consistent in your branding. If you're using illustrations, don't mix them with photos, for example. (But mixing stills and video is fine.)

>> Don't use irrelevant imagery that doesn't amplify your material just to attract attention or for the sake of it. People don't like it.

>> Don't use bland clip art like a happy diverse team conferring around a conference table. People don't like it.

>> Don't underestimate the time sourcing the right visual material can take.

Try This: To build on this the last point, it can be especially hard to find an existing image that illustrates an idea such as my red tape examples. One way to spark your imagination is to work backward: Spend some time browsing through an online photo resource and you're likely to find a number of images that give you ideas for new subjects to write about, as well as ways to visualize them.

One last "don't": Resist cutting so many words that what you're saying loses meaning and context. A manufacturer once asked me to simplify his assemble-it-yourself product instructions. It proved impossible to streamline the copy enough for him. Eventually I realized he wanted to make the directions purely visual — like some IKEA instructions, which drop explanatory language altogether in the interest of an international market. The trouble was that stripping the copy failed to serve the goal — helping people do the job easily. Always remember your goal and your audience.

In the next chapter I show you how to apply online writing strategies to specific e-media: websites, blogs, Twitter, and other social media.

Chapter **12**

Creating Your Online Presence

Digital communication offers so many tempting options that when writing for business, it's wise to plan an integrated program and set priorities. In doing so, be sure not to leave out traditional communication channels: marketing materials, print advertising, publication articles, and book authorship, to name a few. You can miss a lot of opportunities, as well as a lot of life, if you confine yourself to your digital tools!

Connecting with your audiences in person is always the best way to build relationships and reputation. Consider giving speeches, presenting workshops, networking in your industry, participating in your professional associations and much more. Podcasts, video, and online workshops split the difference a bit between face-to-face and virtual.

Consciously integrating all your communication saves time and money by helping you

» Focus your efforts most productively.

» Repurpose content for different channels.

» Cross-promote your channels to support each other.

>> Evaluate the newest and brightest apps.

>> Fine-tune your program mix to better accomplish your goals.

A coordinated program becomes more than the sum of its parts: Collectively it's all content for building your tribe, as the social gurus say. Center your program by creating your value proposition and personal story, as I explain in Chapter 9. Review your plan continuously because month by month, new trends materialize, particularly in social media.

Once you have a working plan, a number of services are available to help you schedule and automate your posts on multiple platforms, for example, HootSuite (https://hootsuite.com) and Agora Pulse (www.agorapulse.com).

Let's look first at a relatively stable portion of the digital repertoire — the website, which serves as a marketing hub for most businesses. Later in the chapter we look at starting a blog and networking with Twitter and other social media platforms.

Creating a Website from the Ground Up

If you have been in business for a while, you may already have put your website through several generations. If so, think for a moment about how the different iterations were produced. Did the graphic design come first, incorporating some "placeholder" copy, until someone said, "okay, give me some words now to fill the spaces"? That's the trouble with most websites — the graphic appeal trumps the writing.

REMEMBER

A good website needs to be solidly planned and well written. Research bears out that while visuals entice and entertain, most site visitors — regardless of the industry — value the words far more than the graphics. The goal of the technology component of the site is to provide the infrastructure, and ensure that visitors can easily find what they want and navigate the site intuitively. Properly seen, design and technology serve to make the words work. That's where the message is.

The good news here is that given the good, flexible online resources for designing and producing your own site, it's in your power to create an effective one. Sure, it's great to have a team — preferably including a marketing specialist, a writer, a designer, and a digital pro. But if you're a do-it-yourself businessperson with some strategic help, no problem: You're the all-important client. Who knows your business better?

Determining goals, format, and audience

To determine what kind of website you need and to start thinking about content, consider what you want to accomplish. Take a look at Chapter 11 where I discuss breaking down your goals. Consider also practicalities such as whether you want to sell your product or service on the site; whether you're interested in a local, regional, national, or global market; and realistically, how many orders you can satisfy should you generate interest.

Websites have specific sets of goals, too. They need to: be findable by people with a problem you help solve; keep visitors on the site once attracted; educate people about the value of your service; communicate that you are trustworthy, understand their need, and are able to fill it; persuade visitors to close the sale or take other action; and keep them coming back. You also want to reach out to them directly in the future, so collecting contact information is high priority.

Choosing website or blog format

The distinctions between blogs and websites are blurry. Online services have become sophisticated and user-friendly enough for you to create either medium on your own. In fact, if you hire a professional designer for the job, she will probably adapt a template from an online web-development platform company such as Wix (`www.wix.com`), Web.com (`www.web.com`), and WordPress (`https://word press.com`).

Find a template you like and on your own, with some time and patience for the learning curve, you can build a blog that looks like a blog: a page that leads off with a new posting on your subject. Or it can look like and function as a full website: a multipage platform representing your business (or you) that includes a home page and an array of additional pages, perhaps including a blog.

Considering audience characteristics

Chapter 2 offers an extensive list of audience characteristics that may matter with all targeted communication. Supplement this list with demographic and psychographic factors that relate to your business. For example, if you want to sell a new tech gadget directly to consumers, in addition to the basics — age, gender, occupation, economic status — your list may include:

>> The buyer's degree of technological savvy or interest

>> Buyers' purchasing habits (how they shop for such products, where they go for advice)

>> Buyers' information preferences (level of detail, type of information, how it is presented)

>> How buyers see the problem your product solves and its importance

TIP

Marketers recommend creating a detailed persona, or *avatar*, of your ideal customer. To do this, think about your current customers and better yet, talk to them about why they use your product, what led them to buy it, and what they like about it. Just as it's easier to write an email by visualizing the person who'll read it, it's more effective to know in detail who your online customer is and understand her needs, points of resistance, and the problems your offering solves.

You might also consider secondary audiences for the product, such as stores that sell your tech gadget or people who might buy it as a gift. Defining multiple audiences doesn't mean you must create a website that serves all possible audiences and purposes. It's easier to market to narrower niches and deepen your reach over time. Or, of course, create more than one website.

Try This: Mountains of marketing knowledge are available online and in adult education courses, workshops, and books. If you're building a website and/or business on your own, but lack marketing know-how, tap a learning resource. When big companies create or revamp websites, they bring whole marketing departments and long experience to bear on the process. Practice thinking like a marketer and your website, and entire venture, will more surely succeed.

Planning a basic website

TIP

Are you creating or rebuilding a website without a business plan or a concrete marketing plan? You may find it either good news or bad news to know that building a good website compels you to develop (or update and refine) both in the process. A good website forces you to center all your business thinking. It's why so many people pay those big bucks to website developers. Sure, the money supports good design and technical quality, but the heart of the process is strategizing the business.

Let's assume you originate an idea for a service you believe is marketable. Your first thought is that you need a website. You have plenty of enthusiasm, but you don't have a marketing plan or a business plan. Where to start? I show you how a practical process centering on a website can work using an invented service business as an example. The same thinking structure works for selling products or serving a charitable cause. And if you already have a website, I recommend trying out the following process to check if you find room for improvement.

TIP

Do your own plan in writing! Use this basic format. Writing is the only way to push your thinking where it needs to go.

My business idea: Teach elderly and physically limited people how to use the Internet for entertainment, learning, and socializing.

Why. My own grandparents live a thousand miles away and were obviously bored and lonely. I coached them and now they're happy. They feel their world has opened up.

Goal: Make a business of this and sell in-person coaching services.

Audience: Elderly people like my grandparents and their children or grandchildren, who might want to give my service as gifts.

But that restricts me only to local work. Can I think bigger? Why not . . .

- Use online video conferencing or other media to coach people anywhere?

- And how about senior citizen residences — can I offer group sessions?

- And why not rehab centers for people with disabilities?

I'll need to investigate the practicalities for each new idea, and if they prove out, decide whether to pursue them now or make them part of a future plan.

My core message: People with physical limitations don't have to be bored and lonely. With today's super-easy technology, and me to adapt the equipment if necessary, they can make friends, learn, play games, and be entertained. It just takes a little coaching, and I'm especially qualified to do this because . . . . (This is your *value proposition*. Use the process outlined in Chapter 9 to develop this important guiding principle. Think of it as an elevator speech for your business. Whom does it help? Why does that matter? Why *you?*)

Strategizing the message — audience pain points:

- Physically limited people confined to a small world are unhappy and bored

- Loved ones feel guilty for not being there more

- Group facilities are challenged to keep seniors cheerful and entertained

Strategizing the message — audience points of resistance:

The seniors, or their relatives, may think:

- They are incapable of learning

- The equipment will be expensive

- The training will be expensive

- The elders will fall prey to online scams

- Online purchase is risky (why should they trust you?)

A good way to brainstorm pain points and resistance points is by using the talking points method I explain in Chapter 8. Look at both sets of statements as questions and answer them. How will your service address the pain points? How can you demonstrate your ability to do this? What are your best responses to the points of resistance? This gives you good content guidelines for the whole site.

TIP

To further crystallize your thinking, it's wise to consider keywords and search terms at this stage. (See the sidebar on leveraging SEO principles and identifying search terms in Chapter 11.) Assembling a list will help you tell your story more concretely and concisely, and you'll need to incorporate the words on every page. Better to build them in from the start rather than trying to graft them on after the fact.

Once you have your audience, goals, and central message in mind, you can move into building a site structure to embody and reflect these considerations.

Creating the site structure

The next step in creating a website is to think about what pages you will include on the site. Logic suggests:

>> A *Home page* that has a concise magnetic message and supporting visuals to entice visitors to know more

>> An *About Us* page that establishes your trustworthiness, skill, and experience, and introduces or describes other team members

>> A *Services* page that describes specific options

>> A *How It Works* page that explains what you do and how

>> A *Case Studies* page that offers evidence of success

>> A *Contact* page that contains full contact information and perhaps a special offer to grow your email list

>> A *Blog* to establish expertise, make your business more personal, and keep visitors coming back

You might combine some of these pages, like "How It Works" and "Services" or "Case Studies," and add others. Q&As and FAQs are popular with readers and search engines. Your type of business may demand a portfolio, and if events and media are part of your mix, you need an online newsroom. A resources page that links to other sites can support site optimization.

If you think I took the long way 'round to end up with a standard-sounding site plan, you're right! This basic structure has evolved over many years and is commonly used because it works for many enterprises. Of course, you can adapt it to your own needs imaginatively.

But inventing a whole new architecture for a website is rarely a good idea. Audiences come with preset expectations and have no patience for figuring out what you're about or where you put things. Better to focus your originality on what to say within the basic framework, how you translate your message into visuals, and how to use video or additional media with impact. Once your general plan is in place, content for the pages starts falling into place — and you will probably find some gaps in your planning to fill.

The clarity-first rule applies to all your navigation buttons, too. Don't go so far astray of the standard naming customs (for example, About Us, Testimonials) that visitors don't know what you mean, or where to find what they already want.

Assembling and writing a home page

No matter whether you're working on your own or with a team of specialists, the first step for creating a home page is *writing*. If you have a designer on tap, explore your ideas in tandem and elicit his thinking. The back and forth between writer and designer produces the best communication in most media, definitely including websites. If you have a technology specialist, listen to her explanations of what is practical and ask for insights into what else is possible. It's smart to ask both kinds of professionals for choices: different ways to accomplish what you want.

The "classic" way to compose a website calls for:

>> Your business name, preferably in logo form, or something that looks like a logo

>> A tagline amplifying the nature of your business so it is immediately understood

>> A "positioning statement" that tells your target audiences they are in the right place

>> A call to action — where to go next or something more specific — and contact information (some experts advise putting this on every page)

>> An overview of the whole site, in image or words, and a clear way to access all the inside pages

The stumbling blocks for many people are the tagline and positioning statement. Paying attention to your keywords and search terms can help center you.

The tagline needs to identify your business as closely as possible. If your business name is self-explanatory, this is easier. For example, if your name is "Main Street Drop-off Service," you have a lot more explaining to do than if it is "Overnight Apple Repair by Main Street." And remember, you're telling search engines as well as customer prospects who you are. In the case of the vague business name, you'd use the tagline to specify the actual work, such as "overnight repair of Apple products." But if that's already in your name, the tagline can move on to "24-hour turnaround on every laptop, desktop, and iPhone problem."

Taglines are worth a lot of thought. But as an old advertising adage puts it, "Don't be clever, be clear." Suppose our theoretical senior coaching business is named "Golden Years Internet." A tagline might read: *Personal coaching to help seniors and the physically limited connect to the online world."* Or *"Open up the world. Connect. Enjoy."*

TIP

The positioning statement gives you another way to expand on what you do. It's trendy to dispense with this, but ask yourself: Will the visitor I want, who may run across my site randomly (while looking for "nursing home entertainment," for example) or because he was searching for my specific set of services, know immediately he is in the right place?

The positioning statement is a tool for making that match. Unless you're a household name, take advantage of the chance. Actually, even household-name companies take pains to clarify that you're in the right place. They may have numerous and complex websites, so must tell customers they're in the right place to make payments, find information about a product, file a complaint, and so on.

Our Golden Years Internet positioning statement might say:

> *In-person in southern Georgia, or online anywhere: individual or small group coaching that empowers physically limited people to socialize, learn, explore, and be entertained online.*

You might add another line to address the senior's children (for example, "Give your loved one the greatest gift of all: today's best way to counter boredom and loneliness by connecting with the world").

And you could even address your third audience, managers of senior residences: "Entertaining people in their golden years is easy when they know how to use today's inexpensive tools to open up their worlds by Internet."

Another favored home page element is an irresistible offer of some kind — sign up for a free blog, newsletter, ebook, introductory conversation, and so on. This will further your marketing plan. Do you have such materials? Can you create them, and do you want to?

TIP

Once you are clear on your message, think about how to translate it into visual form. You can illustrate it with photographs, but make them authentic — not generic stock photo people but real customers and real staff members. Use video if you can to demonstrate a learning session and to present testimonials from happy customers. Consider introducing yourself to visitors as the warm, caring, expert individual you are.

Writing the About Us page

Did you know that after the Home page, About Us is the most frequently visited website page across industries? Often, it's the make-or-break part of your site that keeps people with you or leads them to click away.

You want to be your best and most trustworthy self on the About Us page. Therefore:

>> Write in first person: Use "I," not "they."

>> Center on the problem-solving core of your business.

>> Deliver your value proposition in reader-friendly terms — what your business provides that no one else does.

>> Tell your story: why you founded the business, why you are passionate about it, what is satisfying to you, what audience success means to you.

>> Translate your skills or product capabilities into benefits for the customer.

>> If appropriate, say why the opportunity is special or why the timing is wonderful — for example, new technology opens up the Internet to almost everyone, affordably.

>> Include a good photo of yourself, looking friendly but confident, and video of you in action if possible.

WARNING

Cite evidence of your authority, expertise, and trustworthiness, but don't lead with it — it's probably boring. No résumé-speak! See credentials as a backup to communicating who you are and how and why you can help. Here is the place to present a vision of how much better life (or something) will be with you in the picture.

A good About Us page prompts the reader to look into the actual product by moving on to your Services, or some other page. It's another good place to offer something free and collect email addresses, too: "Schedule a free 10-minute consultation now!" "Register for our webinar now!" "Ask for my free ebook!" "Read my free newsletter!" "Follow me on these social media!"

What if there is no "us"? Then "Meet Jane" or something similar is fine. But it's not a virtual world for nothing: Most consultants have allies on call and occasional partners according to the gig. Our Golden Years Internet CEO might well notice when writing the About Us page that in fact, he does need to back up his qualifications with other people like an occupational therapist and psychologist. This team should also be introduced on the About Us page.

Writing the inside pages

With your Home Page and About Us drafted, move on to write the rest of the pages your plan calls for. Here are some of the pages most sites need.

>> **Services and How It Works:** Use one, or both, to get across the concrete options and opportunities you offer. Describe your services in a lively, user-oriented way, and counter any predisposition not to invest in you — the "resistances" list you assembled earlier in this chapter. Our Golden Years Internet entrepreneur might need to explain the technology choices and why they are affordable and work for this audience; what handicaps can be accommodated; and different service levels, for starters. Try not to over-burden this section, however. Keep descriptions brief and down to earth. Use images as much as you can to shorthand your words.

>> **Testimonials:** Some sites devote separate pages to first-hand endorsements. Some scatter endorsements everywhere, from the home page on. Some sites do both. In any case, be sure they are real: Never write them yourself, because somehow, they won't be convincing. And you don't know until you ask what clients actually value in working with you (see Chapter 9).

This is a word-of-mouth era for marketing. We believe fellow buyers, not official company statements. Don't overlook this resource and the value that video testimonials in particular can give you.

>> **Contact:** Be real here, too! Use at least a first name for email, not an anony-mous "info@" address; give a phone number if you can; offer phone appoint-ments; cite your special irresistible offers; and collect contact information from your visitors every way you can.

You need to build keywords and search terms into every page of your website. And keep in mind that websites are global. If you have any interest in an interna-tional reach, you have even more reason to create easy-to-read and simple-to-navigate sites.

Graphic tips for websites

If you work with a graphic designer, refuse to be intimidated by her, no matter how good she is! A checklist of do's and don'ts when thinking about the visual nature of your site:

>> **Go for an audience-centric design.** An elderly audience, for example, generally prefers more neutral colors, clear type, big headlines, and, naturally, pictures of people like themselves. There's plenty of research available on viewer preferences — check it out. Neilsen (www.neilsen.com/us/en.html) and the Neilsen Norman Group (https://nngroup.com) do widely respected research on site usability and media habits.

>> **Leave out the flashy introductions and music.** Only include these flourishes if there are obvious opt-out buttons.

>> **Avoid tactics that interfere with easy reading.** For example, tiny type, busy complicated designs, more than two or three main colors, and drop-out type (white type against a black or other dark background).

>> **Don't use long, dense text blocks.** If you have more than a few sentences of text, break it up into short paragraphs (one to three sentences each) and add visuals, subheads, or bullets. Build in lots of white space.

>> **Limit the need to scroll.** People fade off. Break the material into separate pages as needed.

>> **Use photos, illustrations if appropriate, and video as much as you can to help minimize the words.** But never use a visual for its own sake (unless you're an artist or photographer). Viewers resent them.

TIP

"Usability research" is a big and expensive deal for large organizations. They want to know how users navigate their sites, identify stumbling blocks, and understand negative responses. They especially want to know viewers' eye tracking patterns when scanning each page. But you can do this yourself!

Try This: Create your own focus group and test drive your finished or in-progress site. The Nielsen Norman Group recommends a do-it-yourself approach. Assembling one to six people (six is ideal) and friends is fine. Ask them to use your site and watch carefully where they pause, stop, and click. Observe their reactions. Then ask them to talk about their experiences and you should emerge with a blueprint for improving your own site, cost-free.

WARNING

Always remember that today, more and more websites are viewed on smartphone screens and smaller. Every month a bigger percentage of viewing and buying decisions are made on our smallest devices. Yet more reason to get to the point fast — distill the message — and keep your interface simple and easy.

REMEMBER

Finally, always look at a website as an evolving work. It's never "finished." To function as you wish, it must be constantly rethought, and you must invest in new fresh content.

Once our Golden Years Internet coach has his basic site planned, he must further develop his business plan with a program that will bring the site to his target audiences' attention and expand his thinking beyond the website. New questions: What other tools and platforms can I adopt to develop my business: speaking engagements? Free workshops? YouTube video? Networking groups? What online channels should I invest in to cross-promote?

For many people, the first idea to consider is the blog, which we look at next.

Creating a Blog

Whether your goal is to support a business, build a platform to support a book or consultancy, stake a place in the virtual universe, make friends, or influence people, the blog may be your medium of choice. However, blogging is a crowded field these days, and gaining attention for a new one can be tough.

Some alternatives to building your own blogging site are to post on the LinkedIn Publishing Platform (www.linkedin.com); Medium (https://medium.com), which invites you to "tell your story"; or Quora (www.quora.com), which says it is "a place to share knowledge and understand the world." Remember also local or specialized blogs to which you can contribute as a member of an industry, association, or network.

REMEMBER

Whichever distribution system you choose, unless you're into the joy of self-publishing, it is important to invest your time strategically. Know your objectives: for example, to establish authority, keep your website fresh, find fans for your service, and so on. And of course, know the readers you want. Plan on promoting your blog via email and social media, and include it in your email signature and with any articles you write. Track results to see if your time investment pays off, but keep in mind that establishing an audience takes time and posting frequency.

TIP

Opinion varies, but general consensus is that a blogger needs to post new material at least weekly. On the other hand, the trend toward valuing long form content suggests that fewer posts that offer in-depth substance work better. Make the judgment according to the nature of your material, your audience, and personal capabilities.

Generally speaking, less than 500 to 750 words (one and a half to two pages single-spaced) just doesn't interest most people. Research confirms that in-depth blogs around 2,200 words plus (more than five pages singled-spaced) are the most read and most appreciated. That isn't really surprising. Most of us have moved past the "great little nugget" reaction and want real substance that teaches us something.

No wonder some advice-givers now say look to podcasting, a relatively unpopulated medium, or video, which increasingly dominates Internet platforms. But blogging remains attractive and a key part of "content."

TIP

The process for writing articles is much the same as for writing a blog, should you aspire to appear in a print or online publication. Both formats demand solid substance, but an article is a more "careful" undertaking that needs a more traditional structure: beginning, middle, and end. A blog can be more relaxed and spontaneous in tone — more personal. It can focus on one strand of a subject, while articles usually need to take a broad perspective. But these lines are also blurring.

Try This: Write a plan for your blog, using one or more of these methods:

>> **Think through your goals and your target audiences.** What do the readers you want need? What problems must they solve that you can help with? What interests them? What can you share that they will value?

>> **Analyze you own special knowledge, expertise, and interests.** Do you have any special access to interesting sources? Can you tie your expertise into any trends? Are you passionate about something, or curious enough about a subject to seriously learn about it?

>> **Study where your audience already lives.** What are they reading, talking about, participating in? Which blogs are most popular with them, and which subjects? Study competitors' blogs to understand your audience better and look for niche areas that aren't being covered, or at least, not as much.

>> **Look to your hobby or a strong interest.** I know a PR professional who blogs about running and a doctor who blogs about classical music. This works best for business purposes if you want to communicate "personality" or want mainly to contribute and connect with other enthusiasts. Many people who practice this are sure it connects with business interests over time.

TIP

Before committing yourself to a subject, perform a reality check to see how much similar material is already out there competing for reader attention — and how good it is.

Choosing your best subject

During a writing workshop for communication professionals, I asked everyone to create a plan for a personal blog and compile a list of ten topics. Some chose a cause, such as eating nutritiously with prepared foods or high-fashion dressing for overweight women. A number wanted to share their opinions about movies, books, television shows, or life in general.

One young man presented a "here's-what-I-think" idea, and I asked him who he imagined would read such a blog, other than a few friends. Can this blog be so entertaining that people who run across it will care about his opinion? And how to build a following for something so amorphous?

A few questions later, it emerged that the young man had pursued a passionate hobby since his early teens that had paid his way through college. He worked as a disc jockey at parties. Could he think of DJ-related topics to write about? He instantly came up with a long list of ideas for sharing professional tools and techniques.

REMEMBER

An ideal choice for your blog subject may be something you care about because it fascinates you, excites you, prompts your curiosity, or just seems important. Like the amateur DJ, you may have real expertise or ideas to share. Great blogs stem from a focused passion of almost any kind, joined with knowledge and a desire to share.

Will the DJ blog help the PR professional I talked about with his career? I think so because his special expertise makes him unique. Together with his other credentials, it may well link him up with PR for the entertainment industry. The blogger who focuses on her running is less unusual, but if she does a good job scouting new equipment and techniques, rather than just reporting her personal experiences, she has a better chance of establishing a following of people who trust her and a long-term soft sell.

TIP

How-to blogs are endlessly attractive and successful. Ideally, you can provide something new, or at least a new angle on the topic, but people also appreciate round-up pieces that gather good ideas and information for them. Give credit as due by acknowledging the source and linking to it.

When you're blogging to support the organization you work for or your own enterprise, use the same criteria to identify topics. Explore subject possibilities such as:

>> The part of the work or service you care about most

>> Things to which you have special insights or access

- » Inside tips and behind-the-scenes glimpses into organizations (particularly effective if the business or nonprofit boasts a fan base)

- » Highly specialized information for your field's geeks

- » Announcement and analysis of new products

- » Stories and examples of how customers have used or been helped by the product or service

REMEMBER

I shouldn't have to say it but I will: Don't criticize your employer in a blog if you want to keep your job!

Developing tone and style

Write in a simple, straightforward, conversational way. Easier said than done, I know. Use the techniques explored in Part 1 to write clearly, tightly, and transparently. It takes progressive editing to strip the chaff and flowery language that annoy online readers. Don't be surprised if it also takes careful editing to sound spontaneous, unless you have a natural gift for this. To sound informal but authoritative, substitute active, interesting verbs for boring ones and short words for long; and work for a rhythm that alternates long and short sentences and reads well aloud.

TIP

Don't pontificate! You're talking to friends. You may find you have a naturally individual voice. Or you may develop one over time. But don't fret about it. If you're delivering good content in a natural voice, in line with advice throughout this book, you're just fine. Adapt tone to audience, of course. Lawyers and accountants, for example, have not yet noticeably lightened up as a group, so probably require a more formal tone than soccer fans or wannabe DJs.

WARNING

Always be positive and upbeat when blogging — even if you're writing critical reviews of a film, book, product, or idea. Be wary of criticizing anything or anyone personally, or at least be prepared for repercussions. And *never* attack or slur anyone personally. Doing so is bad manners and hurts you every time. Plus, you run an increasing risk of being sued.

Creating magnetic headlines

Headlines are critical to getting your post noticed by both readers and search engines. If you're luring people in via email or social media, they must be explicit and a touch exaggerated. Keep them honest — but a little irresistible.

Start your thinking with how the information benefits the reader: Will they find out how to do something faster, better, cheaper? Improve their lives in some way? Observe what captures you and adapt the approach for your own writing.

Free is always a great promise: *FREE business writing templates make you a star*

Sharing secrets is great: *What your doctor doesn't share that can kill you!*

Saving money appeals: *40% off monthly supplies of your favorite dog food*

A promise to teach readers how to do something tempts: *Learn to play the piano like a soloist in two hours per week!*

A question can compel: *Do you know what your girlfriend watches on TV when you're not there?*

Watch your inbox for grabbers. Here are a few that drew me to click and read today:

> *Increase Digital Trust . . . the "Easy Way"*
>
> *How Experiential Marketing Works: 7 Enlightening Tips*
>
> *How Often Should You Wash Your Clothes?*
>
> *How to Recover from a Long Flight According to Flight Attendants*

The first two are the ever-popular "listicles" — text organized around a list of ideas — that appeal by promising specific, useful information, in a compact and accessible way. The third sounded like fun, and I opened the fourth because I'm soon taking a trip. Timing can be everything — one reason why experienced bloggers recycle material with or without a new angle periodically.

REMEMBER

Don't use a headline to promise something you don't deliver.

If you're trying to reach a narrower niche than the casual scanner, you can be less sensationalist, but adapt the ideas for your purpose. Here's how our friend who runs the Golden Years Internet coaching service might think. He's already reviewed his goals, audiences, selling points, and client resistance points, so he needs a title and a set of topics. A tentative blog title could be, *Internetting in the Golden Years,* and some possible topics:

> The 6 best equipment choices for Internet explorers over 70
>
> Free! 10 online courses perfect for 75+-year-olds
>
> Citizen science: The amazing new way for seniors to help researchers
>
> How to recognize Internet scammers who prey on seniors
>
> Online games for seniors: From checkers to chess, mahjong to Go
>
> Exercise for seniors — the 8 best online programs

Using progressive subheads

Dividing your blog text with subheads serves many purposes: It helps organize your ideas, adds white space, and keeps people reading. If you use the listicle format you know in advance how to write your subheads, one for each of the listed points. Subheads every few paragraphs make the material look easy to read. What's not to like? Even a short blog benefits. Alternatively, bold the first phrase or sentence of each item to produce a subhead-like effect.

Writing good subheads is also covered in Chapters 3 and 6, and see the section on writing strong leads, also in Chapter 6. And yes, search terms apply and should be front-loaded in your headline and lead.

Try This: If you need inspiration for potential topics and headlines, here's a fun way to find it. Experiment with an online headline generator. Here are two I like and the results I received when I entered "business writing" as my topic:

HubSpot's Blog Topic Generator www.hubspot.com/blog-topic-generator

The Worst Advice We've Ever Heard about Email

Portent Content Idea Generator www.portent.com/tools/title-maker

Why Business Writing Is Afraid of the Truth

Networking with Twitter

Twitter has become a serious communication and networking medium despite all the dull "chatter" that still characterizes much of it, and all the pronouncements that it's not changing fast enough and is inevitably doomed. Last I checked, the Twitter community had 317 million monthly active users sending out an average of 500 million tweets daily. Also, about 25 percent of journalists have verified accounts, and so do 83 percent of the world's leaders. There are a good many reasons to actively participate in this platform.

Creating a Twitter presence that's influential and professionally useful takes commitment. For your tweets to make an impact and build a substantial following, the social media gurus advise that you send out at least 5 to 10 of them per day.

And they must be good. If you think writing guidelines don't apply to the 140-character tweet, you're certainly not alone. However, *in a business context*, sloppily written tweets work against you. Hastily written messages make you look like a lightweight. Use all the editing tools in Part 1 to drill down to your message succinctly without sacrificing its life.

Treat every tweet as a public statement that's an indelible part of your online profile. You can use @ before a Twitter handle to send a private message, but it remains findable. Assume that when you apply for a job, the hiring manager will review your Twitter account not just to see if you're posting anything blameworthy, but to see how you think. So be sure you are thinking! I know a number of people hired because the employer found and liked their tweets, and also a few — including high-profile cases — where a thoughtless tweet cost some their whole careers. Treat Twitter with respect.

Make each tweet as clear and understandable as you can to the most people. That means editing them for both writing quality as well as content! No abbreviations or mystery acronyms. Second, create tweets to deliver value, not share your favorite snack food. Third, never write anything that could embarrass you or anyone else now or in 20 years. Look up "disgraced politicians" online if you need a reminder of what can happen.

Planning your Twitter program

Random tweeting produces random results. Consciously build a Twitter program that aligns with and complements your website, blog, video, other social media investments, and traditional media, too (your print materials and presentations, for example). Unlike formal media such as résumés, Twitter gives you the opportunity to show off your personality and individuality. But don't go freewheeling. Try for carefully spontaneous. Make an active decision about who you want to be and make sure that persona is appropriate to your goals and target audiences.

Do you want to establish yourself as an authority in your field? Build a following? Draw people to your website or blog? Find a job? Connect with like-minded people — or influential ones? As with the social platforms I discuss in the preceding sections, strategize whom you want to reach, best content strands, and your degree of investment.

There's never a good side to demonstrating bad temper, a mean spirit, or sarcastic turn of mind — no matter how terrific it feels for ten seconds. If you recognize yourself as someone who's regularly tempted to send out angry or ill-considered tweets, use Twitter's scheduled/delayed posting feature, or an app that delays posting until your better angel has a chance to take back the helm.

Guidelines for tweeting

As with other platforms, keep yourself up to date with trends and features. Twitter has become very "visual" as users find that photos, infographics, and videos exponentially increases the likelihood a message will be read and shared. For most people, being *re-tweeted* is the aim of the game because it's how you grow your audience. Here are more guidelines for tweeting successfully:

>> **Do a good job on the mini-bio and try for a lively description that crystallizes your uniqueness and uses your key words.** Twitter's own Bio Generator helps you describe yourself for this medium effectively. And, do whatever it takes to provide a good photo of yourself as you want to be seen.

>> **Find people and groups that interest you.** Twitter's own search function enables you to find specific people, brands, customers and clients, jobs, hashtagged conversations, and news. You can also search Twitter to find search terms used in conversations you want to follow.

>> **Listen.** Just as you hesitate to plunge into a party conversation before listening to what's already going on, take time to acquaint yourself with what people of interest to you are saying to each other. Notice the conversation's tone and content. Look for niches with which you're comfortable — questions you can answer, for example, or a subject you can usefully comment upon.

>> **Promote re-tweeting.** Keep tweets even briefer than 140 characters, in the 100-character range, to encourage others to re-tweet your messages with their own comments. Use bitly.com (https://bitly.com) to reduce the space needed to communicate links and URLs. Use hashtags (for example, #businesswriting) to identify your subject matter and relevance; this broadens your audience beyond your own followers.

>> **Share substance.** Share anything — news, ideas, tips based on your expertise, insights into events, a snippet from a good lecture you heard, an insight from a conference, links to something of interest, re-tweets of other people's messages — you believe others will appreciate. And share discoveries: blogs, articles, books, other people's comments, an image, an inspirational quote.

>> **Repeat yourself judiciously.** Many social media gurus recommend sending the same or somewhat different tweets out several times per day, because different audiences catch up and scout at different times. Use a management tool to schedule your tweets, which will also signal when you receive a response.

WARNING

>> **Don't constantly sell or self-promote.** Yes, you can call attention to a new blog post, event, workshop, article, book, product, or service improvement. It also can pay dividends to let people know where you are — at a conference or when traveling, for example. But resist the temptation to promote yourself or your organization every time you tweet. You'll quickly be discounted as a self-seeker. Some savvy tweeters follow a rule of thumb: Self-promote one out of four times, max.

You can also use Twitter in ways that big companies find valuable. To accomplish research that would otherwise be very expensive, run surveys, crowdsource. Want to test-run your new website copy? Or a contest idea? Invite your network to visit your website and comment. Need an idea for employee recognition? Or advice on which logo to adopt? Put out the word.

Research on social media and networking sites is intensive, in part because the digital nature makes it so easy to generate statistics. Studies even tell us the best time to use each channel. The most popular time to tweet is between noon and 1 p.m. — but tweets sent in the early morning are more likely to be clicked and re-tweeted. You're more likely to send cheerful upbeat message then, too. Tweets are most often re-tweeted when posted between 3 and 6 p.m. because people are tired then and prefer relying on other people's tweets.

Of course, you can write all your tweets when you're in a good mood, according to your internal clock, and use a social media distribution service to feed them out over the day. Time zones are a complicating factor.

Writing Online Profiles

Online professional networks, such as LinkedIn (www.linkedin.com), XING (www.xing.com), and Ryze (https://ryze.com), are good business connectors for many people and are generally considered the "professional" social media. My tips here apply to profiles for LinkedIn and similar business networking sites.

TIP

To adapt these ideas to other media, read a batch of profiles on the site or service that you're interested in joining and see what approach you feel works best. Use that style and the guidelines of the medium.

In general, an online profile is a chance to communicate more of your personality than in a résumé. Writing in the first person works best because you automatically take a more personal tone and genuine feeling comes across. Write with a sense of where you want to go, not just where you've been and are now. Align your profile with your big goals. You can use the headline area to list what you do and appeal to search engines with search terms. For example:

Business Writing. Magazine Features. Writing Workshops. Publication Projects.

Then create a strong opening statement that instantly tells people what you want them to know about you. Surprise! You can draw this from your core value statement or your story. For example:

When I realized how terrified most people are of sitting in the dentist's chair, I decided to find ways to make the experience more positive — something people would look forward to. Or almost.

If you're trying for a career transition or new job, take advantage of the chance to say so:

I'm a public relations professional with a great background in the entertainment industry. My special love is hip-hop culture. I'm looking to connect my two passions.

Successful online material doesn't follow a formula. Experiment and scout for profiles you like, both in and out of your own field, and draw your own lessons from them. A few tips and possibilities:

>> Share your enthusiasm and passion for what you do.

>> Include the achievements you're most proud of.

>> Skip empty rhetoric and get down to brass tacks; what you actually do and what it means is always more interesting.

>> Know what you want to achieve with this profile — find new customers? Connect with an industry? Showcase creative skills? Establish expertise?

As always, write to specific audiences to accomplish specific goals.

Using Social Media Platforms

Facebook (www.facebook.com), the social media groundbreaker, began as a people connector for Harvard University and spread nationally, then internationally. Eventually the business world figured out that the site was a terrific marketing tool and it's almost obligatory for enterprises big and small to represent themselves with a Facebook business page.

Most of the social media platforms that spring up follow a similar pattern. Young people's enthusiasm for a platform becomes hard to ignore and marketers flock in. No surprise — they're eager to reach a buying audience that now represents 25 percent of the population and resists traditional media advertising by television and newspapers. Professionals learn to use the medium. Then the younger people are drawn to something new and the pattern repeats.

The trendiest social platforms are most likely to be used by teenagers and the big, resource-rich enterprises. More and more of them devote whole departments to social media and teams for each platform they choose. If you're on your own or run a small business, it's challenging to build up the know-how to use the media-of-the-moment effectively, especially if you're not a digital native.

TIP

To use a social app productively, you must keep to the terms set by the audience you want to reach through it. For Generation Z and younger Millennials, the point is to have fun. It's fun to share what's happening in their lives and their friends' lives, or a laugh, or a moment of inspiration; it's fun to find new connections and communities; and it's fun to experiment with a site's features — video, filters, stickers, emoji — and produce original posts that demonstrate their individuality and creativity.

Social media enthusiasts are also happy to learn something, provided it's of practical use and entertainingly presented. And they are definitely buyers if approached in the same spirit of their personal messaging. Overt promotion that isn't interesting is a turnoff.

REMEMBER

Becoming ever-newer and glitzier is the hallmark of social platforms. They change their parameters frequently and, in fact, must do so to maintain their user base and grow it. Also, who knows how many developers are out there in garages and computer labs inventing glitzier new options right now? What holds steady is the need to use the platforms strategically, and develop your own way to stay ahead of the curve and adapt to the next great thing should you choose. Here's my nutshell advice on how to develop a content marketing strategy for social media, as evergreen as I can make it.

Engaging with social media

First, ground yourself with an overall strategy and select platforms based on the factors outlined in Chapter 11. Check out the analysis of generational characteristics in Chapter 2. It's critical that your marketing demographics line up with your platform choices. If you want to reach people under 24, for example, Snapchat is your game. Know your message, as covered in Chapter 9, and then you are ready to:

>> **Invest time in the platform you choose.** Absorb its style, observe the most popular subject matter, identify its conventions, and find and follow industry leaders and brands similar to yours. Find communities that relate most closely to your interests. What content do they favor?

>> **Explore content streams you can create.** Your content should represent your brand in ways that connect with your selected audiences. What can you share that's entertaining, amusing, surprising, thought-provoking, and/or

educational in an interesting way? Rather than one-off posts, look for themes you can develop that will themselves suggest a flow of ideas.

» **Practice the tools of your platform.** Each platform provides some how-to instruction, but scads of helpful directions and hacks are available online, such as Try YouTube. Plan to use social amenities, like hashtags, which function across platforms, and embedded links to bring people to your blog, a special offer, or something of special interest.

» **Create posts that deliver the message visually for Snapchat, Facebook, Instagram, and other platforms.** How can you translate your ideas into visual formats? Infographics give you a good way to deliver written information on sites that are essentially visual, like Pinterest. Photos with captions superimposed lend relevance to images and audience pleasers. A mix of photos and video is popular.

» **Create posts with substance.** Aim to be relevant, entertaining, and interesting, but don't collect likes for their own sake! Deliver something real that your fans will value and want to share with friends. Avoid obvious brand-promotion that users will shy away from. The best advice with all social networks is quality rather than quantity.

REMEMBER

» **Write your best!** The words may ultimately be few, but make them well-chosen and correct. Social style is relaxed and breezy, concise and transparent: Get ideas across in simple, instantly accessible ways. You only have 5 seconds to engage people enough to stick with you even for a short post! If the platform provides space for brief biographies, review how other people write theirs and create one that's appropriate. Include a good photograph when you can. Personalizing your identity is important. Showing some personality and humor helps with this, too.

» **Build in as many ways as you can think of for people to actively participate.** Conduct surveys and report on them; ask questions; invite photos and videos, especially if they offer selfie opportunities; encourage fans to offer opinions or share an experience; or ask them to suggest a subject themselves. Keep in mind that they want to be part of the story and invest their own personality and spin.

» **Respond to comments, questions, input, everything.** Remember, you're joining a community or building one, and either way, you must earn entry and create trust. Look to start conversations and keep them going. Snapchat in particular is geared for fast response because posts disappear after 10 seconds, though options for extending this time frame have been introduced.

>> **Consider paid advertising.** Increasingly common on social media, big organizations are investing more and more in advertising. If you want to do "native advertising," which means promotional content presented in the platform's style, it's best to identify it as advertising or the impact will be negative.

>> **Review results systematically.** Digital media give you unparalleled tracking power. Look at what has worked best for you in terms of responses, number of shares or likes, linking to your other media, and whatever else matters to you.

TIP

>> **Integrate your social media with your entire marketing effort.** You may or may not like thinking of yourself as a "brand" personally, but the concept is helpful. It reminds you that you must always communicate in ways that benefit your reputation and give value to your connections. Social platforms give you good ways to lead people to your blog post, website, LinkedIn profile, and so on. Repurposing content for different media is fine, but adapt it to each one's unique personality.

Exploring content ideas

It's hard to generate ideas in a vacuum. Instead, spend time with the platforms of your choice and see what strategies other people are using that can be adapted to your purposes. And scan content you created for other uses to mine snippets and images.

TIP

It's also a good idea to review any social causes you or your organization are involved with. The generations you want to reach through social media channels like and respect organizations that demonstrate ethics and community citizenship. If you work with a charity event, an environmental cause, or any initiatives that help people, you have prime themes to explore. Angles might include ministories and images of people who were helped, benefits organized by your staff, events, and so on.

Another resource that keeps giving: the people you work with, even if they are few, or collaborate with you on occasion. Social media users enjoy behind-the-scenes glimpses, especially if it's a product they relate to. Show them how ideas are brainstormed, how something is made, what the Halloween party looked like, how individuals spend their spare time, their pets, and so on. Give a face to the organization every time you can.

Crowdsourcing is another ideal source of material. Whatever your business, think of photos or video related in some way and invite your followers to share with you. Opportunities for people to selfie-themselves at the scene engage their interest. Invite video and photos from an event. Ask people to vote for the best whatever.

Some more content ideas to spur your thinking:

- » Invite photos and video from events.

- » Show people using your product, especially in unorthodox ways.

- » Show how to fix a problem related to what you do.

- » Show unusual uses of a product.

- » Connect to seasonal events and holidays.

- » Demonstrate how to do something, from cutting up a mango to fixing a tire to executing a yoga pose.

- » Present recipes with mouth-watering photos or video.

- » Write inspirational quotes on an image.

- » Tell a joke (that won't offend anyone).

- » Present educational tips.

- » Offer advanced tips on a new product or event.

- » Reward followers by showing photos or video of them enjoying your event.

- » Introduce followers to staff members.

- » Curate: Share other posts and snaps generously.

Working with social media successfully takes a special mindset. Immerse yourself in a platform and you may be surprised at what you come up with. Remember your strategic plan, but interpret it creatively and loosely: You want to communicate that you feel the same sense of fun as do the loyal followers you want.

Today's online universe is in many ways a new one of sources and resources, media and platforms, opportunities and pitfalls. It changes so fast that approaches are at best temporary. At the same time, what will help you make the most of so many possibilities are your traditional communication tools — good writing especially — to think, plan, and present.

In the next chapter, I show you some persuasive writing techniques and how to apply them when writing as an independent worker.

5
Extending Your Writing Skills

Learn persuasive writing techniques and how to apply them when writing as an independent worker.

See how to effectively introduce yourself in writing and pitch your services by defining your goal and knowing your audience.

Understand how strategic writing can give you a key advantage as a virtual team member or project leader.

Learn how to communicate well as a manager, including how to write to inspire and motivate, deliver good news and bad, and write requests and give orders.

Look at ways to successfully write strategic messages to higher-ups.

IN THIS CHAPTER

» **Using the tools of persuasion**

» **Introducing yourself and selling your services**

» **Writing tough messages to clients**

» **Communicating in the virtual environment**

» **Achieving media coverage**

Chapter **13**

Writing and the Independent Worker

Today, whether you are an employee, business owner, consultant, or freelancer, building a full range of communication platforms supports your success. More people than ever practice a suite of ways to earn a living, and over time may move fluidly from colocation to virtual office or in-house position to independent status and back. People who hold steady jobs need to keep selling their savvy to stay employed and win what they want. And plenty of people dream that their basement tinkering will skyrocket into a big-time business overnight, or soon thereafter.

The idea of adopting the entrepreneur's mindset is introduced in Chapter 7, which covers creating business documents such as reports, proposals, and the always-useful executive summary. This chapter centers on special writing challenges for the self-employed. But don't overlook these strategies even if you intend never to leave the office or cubicle world. You, too, may need to sell your ideas and achieve difficult goals gracefully.

While all business writing incorporates principles of persuasion, these principles are especially important to the self-employed, who must create connections to win opportunities. Accordingly, this chapter begins with persuasive writing techniques and how to apply them when writing as an independent worker.

Writing Persuasively Cross-Media

Persuasion is a topic that obsesses marketers, communicators, psychologists, neuroscientists, and even economists, who created the field of behavioral economics with breakthrough thinking about how humans make decisions. The nutshell version is that while we may believe we make choices based on information and logic, in truth, our decisions are usually driven by emotion and then justified with rationality. Because analytic thought consumes enormous amounts of energy, we typically call on it only when we more or less force ourselves to take the trouble.

TIP

In business writing, the lesson is: *Whenever possible go for both the heart and the mind.* Look for ways to capture people's imagination, give them a vision, and provide reasons to trust you. Help them back up instinctive decisions with solid facts and evidence. These two elements of persuasion support each other. For example, if you don't establish trust, a long recitation of facts is unlikely to convince your audience to take a chance on you. But likability isn't enough. Aim to satisfy their analytic review.

Some of the following techniques are touched on in other chapters, but I bring many of the ideas together under one umbrella now and expand on them. They include writing techniques to boost persuasive power, and strategic content planning for reaching heart and mind.

Communicating with conviction

REMEMBER

Nothing is more convincing than your own belief. When you write an important message to introduce yourself, for example, or pitch a product, take a minute to reinform yourself of why that product or service is outstanding and why you've made it your life's work. What drew you to do what you do — a passion? A commitment to solve a problem or help people? Why are you certain that knowing about your service will benefit the other person? Or, why are you the ideal person for the opportunity?

Try This: To further reinforce your positive spirit, experiment with proven techniques for calling up your confidence. Actors, presenters, and salesmen commonly use them, and they can help you infuse confidence into your writing. When you're about to work on an important email, letter, proposal, or other document, energize yourself by assuming an assertive but comfortable posture and walk around that way for a few minutes. This technique exploits the mind–body connection, signaling to your mind that you are capable, resourceful, and so on.

Another strategy, drawn from the psychologist's repertoire, is to relive a proud moment from past experience as vividly as you can, employing all your senses to re-create how you felt. Or: put on whatever music lifts your spirits and energy. Carry your conviction and upbeat mood to the writing task.

REMEMBER

Good, well-strategized writing is inherently persuasive. Employ the basic techniques the chapters in Part 1 demonstrate to achieve clarity, brevity, and impact. The best quick self-check is to read your message aloud and identify the stumbling blocks to smooth delivery. Then edit until your copy reads easily and naturally. Humans are attuned to oral communication, and material that reads well aloud conveys credibility and competence. Also:

>> **Write for speed reading.** The faster your message can be read and understood, the more likely people are to stick with it and remember it.

>> **Build sentences with action verbs.** Take time to substitute lively verbs for dull passive ones (an online thesaurus helps you do this in an instant).

>> **Use short, easily understood words that are tangible rather than abstract — things you can see and measure.** They're the words we most often use in everyday speech.

>> **Alternate short and long sentences.** This produces a rhythm that pulls readers along.

>> **Compose short paragraphs.** Write paragraphs that are one to five sentences long, each focused on a single idea. Material that looks inviting and easy to understand gets read.

>> **Minimize the use of meaningless hyperbole.** Exaggerated statements and clichéd words and phrases add nothing (for example, "innovative cutting-edge state-of-the-art breakthrough").

>> **Skip the wishy-washy.** Don't hedge with qualifying words, such as "maybe" or "perhaps," and hesitant phrases, such as "I hope you will find this idea of value."

>> **Edit for totally correct spelling and grammar.** If it looks like carelessness, or a mistake, you've shot your credibility.

TIP

And here's my own secret sauce: Attend closely to all transitions between sentences and between paragraphs. Add extra transitions to help you clarify your own logic: You can always cut some in final editing. When you show clearly how each idea relates to the rest, you create a progressive argument that strikes readers as logical and unassailable (more on transitions in Chapter 5).

Connecting with your reader

WARNING

Whether you're asking for an appointment or writing a blog, the first essential is to get your message read. Assume you have about 4 seconds to entice someone to read your message instead of tossing it. Time yourself if you don't believe me: Scan your email inbox and note how quickly you make decisions about whether to read a message, and note what kind of subject lines and leads draw you in.

Here are some techniques to help you make the most of your brief window of opportunity. Adapt them to your purpose.

» **Characterize your audience before you begin writing.** Imagine the ideal reader you want to reach and think about the message you're delivering through her eyes. Remember WIIFM (what's-in-it-for-me)? Gauge her reading level and what she already knows about your subject, and what she probably thinks of it. The right tone and language will come to you. (More on how to do this is detailed in Chapter 2.)

» **Write action headlines.** This applies to proposals, reports, marketing pieces, and other materials. Online materials, including blogs and websites, also need headlines that attract readers and crystallize your message to establish its relevance. Can you come up with a must-read angle? Use it! In the case of emails, treat your subject line as the headline. (Writing persuasive headlines is covered in Chapter 7.)

» **Write organized, progressive subheads.** Action subheads entice readers along and are worthwhile even in short messages. A good way to produce them, and also stay organized, is to plan them as a series of guideposts that deliver the high points of your message. Even a skimmer will absorb the important points, or may be drawn in more deeply.

» **Keep the reader going with a compelling lead.** Focus in on what is most interesting, useful, or relevant about your subject. Why should your readers care? Answer that question yourself to find your best opening. Professional writers probably spend 20 percent of their work life on constructing good leads. It's worth the time.

» **Use graphics and images to lighten and liven.** In this age of diminishing attention spans, how your message looks is critical. If it appears dense and difficult, few people will dive in. Give every kind of document lots of white space. Keep type and format simple, and use images whenever possible to attract and entertain the eye and promote understanding.

Maintaining reader engagement

Yes, you must capture your reader's wandering eye, but good leads and writing style aren't enough to keep him. For that you need solid substance. Before writing, brainstorm all your selling points and write them down. I address that challenge in many parts of the book, but here's a recap of ways to deliver the message convincingly:

>> **Cite evidence of your expertise or the wonders of your product.** Include reviews, testimonials, statistics, awards, signs of authority such as blogs or articles, and published interviews.

>> **Sprinkle your material generously with anecdotes, examples, and illustrations.** This brings it alive and makes it both real and relevant.

>> **Center on benefits, not on features.** What does the product or service do for people and how does it makes them feel?

>> **Create a vision of how life will be more wonderful.** If your idea is adapted or your product is bought and put to use, how will some aspect of life improve?

>> **Call the reader to action.** What do you want the reader who's made it to the end (or skimmed to get there) to do now? Call? Write? Read your blog? Go to your website? Subscribe? This should be built into your conclusion.

TIP

Here's a favorite technique to help you be your most persuasive: Figure out the main opposing arguments and build in the rebuttals. Take account of opposing ideas rather than ignoring or dismissing them. You become more credible. This affords you good openings for citing evidence, too. For example:

One reservation you may have is that the system requires adapting to a whole new technology. We know there's a learning curve, but we also know that users become 18 percent more efficient. And we have a good training program ready to go.

It's true this strategy was tried 10 years ago, but at that time, we couldn't tap big data to fine-tune each step.

You can produce a new website less expensively. But a Second Opinion site generates twice as many leads for our clients than any of their previous sites.

Giving people time

REMEMBER

When you sell a service, product, or new way of thinking, it's wise not to expect overnight miracles. Decisions are grounded on trust. Think "one goal at a time." A good letter can gain you entrée to meet with someone; a well-crafted email pitch draws people to your website; an interesting tweet leads someone to read your blog; a free webinar brings in people ready to pay for a service; effective blogs lead readers to trust you enough to buy your ebook.

Good teachers aim for incremental learning. They start where their students are and take them, step by step, toward more knowledge and understanding. Experienced marketers also know that persuading someone to buy a different product or adopt a new idea takes sustained effort and a consistent message across platforms. That's what integrated marketing is about: knowing your core message (see Chapter 9) and using a range of communication formats to deliver that message and reinforce it.

Let's turn now to some specific kind of writing you may need in your everyday life as an independent worker.

Introducing Yourself in Writing

When you open a new business in the community, assume a new role in your company, or join or take over a professional practice, introducing yourself by letter is well worth your time. A letter of introduction doesn't replace the value of a good first impression in person, but it's an important step toward building relationships and sounding the right note.

Start by thinking about your *audience.* Suppose you're an accountant and you're taking over as head of a firm specializing in corporate tax counseling. You want to retain the firm's existing clients and build relationships with them.

TIP

Asking "What's in it for them?" helps ground your content decisions. What can you say that will help this audience feel comfortable and well-disposed toward dealing with you, a stranger? Rather than "what I want them to know," consider "what do *they* want to know." Put yourself in their shoes to brainstorm what points to make, remembering that *people want to know how a change affects them.* Here is a list of probable client questions:

>> Will I receive the same level of service?

>> How do I know he'll do a good job?

>> Will I be inconvenienced in any way?

>> Is he a nice person to deal with? Will I like him?

The accountant would then translate this set of needs into a content list:

>> Demonstrate my respect for the former business owner (whom clients presumably liked) and mention why he's gone (but don't give a negative reason).

>> Assure clients that service to them continues with absolutely no inconvenience.

>> Tell clients about myself:

- Where I'm coming from, plus my most impressive affiliation and clients

- My specialized expertise or experience (for example, my early work for the IRS and certification in relevant subject area)

- Honors I've received that prove I am an expert

>> Discuss my plans for improving client service (for example, my plan to implement new technology to make recordkeeping easier).

>> Share my contributions as an active member of the community (to show I'm a nice person).

>> Explain why I love my work and/or want to know my new clients personally.

>> Offer to meet all, or most important clients, one-on-one.

TIP

Notice how few items on the list speak to professional credentials. Contrary to many examples I see, an introductory letter is usually *not* best viewed as an opportunity to detail your accomplishments and qualifications at length. Most people overestimate others people's interest in credentials. As long as you provide some basic information about your experience, people typically take it for granted that you are qualified. Supply a highlight version of your professional history and spend the rest of the space communicating how life will be even better when the client works with you. And how nice you are.

Once you've outlined your substance, the letter nearly writes itself. Most often aim for a friendly but somewhat formal tone. Fashion your lead: a down-to-earth simple opener that explains why you're writing is fine. It may help to visualize your favorite client (see Chapter 2). One version:

> Dear Ms. Wish:
>
> I'm happy to introduce myself as the new Managing Partner of Pembroke Tax Accountants, Inc. As you may know, my good friend and colleague Tom Marx retired in June. I want to assure you that my goal is to give you the same level of personal service and counsel you're accustomed to, in every way.
>
> I have been an enthusiastic tax consultant for 22 years . . .
>
> I discovered my passion for this work when . . .
>
> Most recently, I managed tax services for . . .
>
> I had the privilege of serving . . .

I am especially proud to contribute to our mutual community, which was recognized by . . .

I am working on additional ways to make your tax experience pleasant and productive with new technology that . . .

I would very much enjoy meeting you in person soon. If you are able to stop by at a time convenient for you, or would prefer a phone conversation, just let me know and I'll arrange my schedule to accommodate yours.

Sincerely,

Len

G. Leonard March

TIP

An introductory letter need not be reserved for taking over a business. If you worked for an accounting firm and advanced to the top spot, you'd be wise to write a similar letter. If you're a freelancer in new territory — geographically, or because you're undertaking a new line of work — introduce yourself to the community and potential customers. If you join a consulting firm, an introductory letter is a good way to tell clients and prospects how your presence expands the firm's capabilities. If you work for a nonprofit, use letters to announce your new role to grant-giving organizations, major donors, relevant government offices, and other stakeholders.

A well-written letter is easily adapted for secondary audiences. If the tax specialist hopes to bring clients over from his former situation, he can reslant the content to them (if he has the legal right to solicit them). He can also quickly adapt it to reach new prospects.

WARNING

If you're part of an organization or representing one, make sure introductory letters are in line with your organization's culture and that the contents won't surprise your higher-ups.

An introductory letter may be delivered via email, the post office, an advertisement, a conference center exhibit, your website, or many other venues. Before you dismiss introductory letters as archaic, consider two examples from my own experience.

Example 1:

A letter, delivered by mail, from a medical specialist taking over the practice of a doctor I'd gone to for years. After a standard lead sentence stating his reason for writing, he supplied three long, dense paragraphs naming every disease that he customarily treats; every stage of education; and all his professional affiliations and journal articles.

My reaction: I did not look forward to becoming his patient. He failed to communicate that he cared about people and would provide a comfortable experience.

Example 2:

A letter placed on my doorstep by a contractor engaged to work on a nearby house:

> *Dear Neighbor,*
>
> *You may already be aware that the Fine family will begin a home renovation project shortly.*
>
> *As the family's general contractor, I wanted to take a moment of your time to introduce myself. My name is Gary Rand and I, or one of my project managers, will be on site every day. Having completed numerous projects in the community over the years, I am very sensitive to the effects a project of this scope can have on the neighborhood.*
>
> *I intend to deliver a quality, on-time project to the customer, and also, ensure the least possible impact on the neighborhood. My subcontractors thoroughly understand my expectations of unfailing courtesy and respect.*
>
> *Inevitably some minor damage may occur to the sidewalk. We will restore any such damage at the project's end and for your assurance, have levied a surety bond with the town.*
>
> *Please contact me in person, by cell phone, or email if any aspect of this project concerns or adversely affects you.*
>
> *With best intentions,*
>
> *Gary Rand, ABID, CPBD, UCLS*

My reaction: I will hire this contractor if I renovate. I had no idea what the certifications after his name signify, and didn't care. I trusted him upon reading because he understood residents' worries and probable resistance so well, and then addressed them not with clever language, but tangible proof of caring — the surety bond. People talked about the letter way past our street and Gary was on top of everyone's A-list for home improvement.

TIP

You create value in your communication when you base it on understanding other people and what they need. A message like Gary's addresses both heart and mind. It triggers a positive emotional response and supports a rational decision. It's remarkable what can be accomplished with thoughtful writing. No one I've talked to has ever received a letter like Gary's from a contractor, or similar situation. Think creatively about whether your work offers an opportunity to be the first in your neighborhood.

REMEMBER

Our digital environment does not preclude the usefulness of a traditional letter, direct mail, local marketing initiative, or print media. In fact, the entire digital world is trending toward personalization: curated and tailored content, individualized messages, micro-segmented target audiences, strategies to generate active participation, and word of mouth.

Writing to Pitch Your Services

If you're a solopreneur or partner in a small business, you may regularly need to write pitch letters or deliver cold-call messages. Typically, your goal is to bring you, or your product or service, to someone's attention and ask for an in-person meeting.

Such letters are important for professional specialists of many kinds. One approach is covered in the proposal section of Chapter 2. Here is another, which I illustrate via a specialized professional.

Sarah, a professional historian, knew that a county preservation office would soon need someone to organize an application to obtain landmark status for a local building. Aiming for an appointment to present herself, Sarah drafted a letter.

Try This: Imagine you're the government official Sarah is addressing. How would you react to this letter? And in context of this book's advice, how might you improve it?

> *Dear Mr. Johnson:*
>
> *I had the pleasure of meeting you last July when I accompanied Jane Maxwell of the city preservation office and architect Roger Brown on a site visit to Marigold House. At that time, Jane and Jeremy were working on the city's new Local Landmark designation for properties of historic and cultural importance outside the Big City Historic District. The Pritchard Building was officially approved by the City Council on November 28. Robert Brown was the consulting architect on that project, and I served as the consulting historian, preparing a historical title search and the land use, cultural, and biographical information necessary to establish the significance of the health center.*
>
> *The nineteenth-century Marigold House has more than 300 years of stories to tell and a number of them are nearly unknown. For example, the eighteenth-century correspondence of Margaret Green and Eleanor March; Mary Jennings' 1810 book of poetry, recently discovered; the autobiography of the slave Emelia, who escaped to the north on a boat in 1814. All of these and more contribute to your property's historical and cultural significance.*

I would like to research the title and history of Marigold House and prepare the significance portion of its application for Landmark designation in conjunction with Lisa and Roberta and the city preservation office. Can we schedule some time to talk about this?

Sincerely, Sarah Jones

Did you have trouble getting through this? I did, and assume Mr. Johnson would have too had he received the letter.

Here is the revision I suggested. How does it compare with your idea?

Dear Mr. Johnson:

We met at Marigold House last July when I accompanied Jane Maxwell of the City Preservation Office and architect Robert Brown on a site visit. I'm taking the liberty of writing now because as a professional historian, I would very much like to work with Jane and your office to research the property's title and history for its application as a designated landmark.

This eighteenth-century house has more than 300 years of wonderful stories to tell. For example:

- *The correspondence of . . .*
- *Mary Jennings' 1810 book of poems . . .*
- *The first-hand account of the slave Emelia who escaped . . .*

All these stories contribute to Marigold House's historical and cultural significance, but only a few of them are now part of the official registries.

I would like to prepare the significant portion of the application and include these stories and many more.

I've previously worked with Jane to develop the city's new Local Landmark designation regulations and I served as the consulting historian to establish the significance of Margaret Field . . .

I am the former resident historian for . . .

Can we schedule some time to talk? I will welcome the opportunity to explain my qualifications to research Marigold House and support its application for Landmark status.

Sincerely, Sarah Jones

Here are the guidelines derived from comparing these two versions:

>> **Say what you want ASAP so the person knows why you're writing.** When you have a personal connection, begin with that because it positions you, establishes trust, and builds instant connection.

>> **Format the letter to be quickly read and easily understood.** In the revised letter, the short, bulleted list breaks up the copy and gets the examples across more effectively. Paragraphs and sentences are shorter and less dense to encourage reading.

>> **Make the most of what's interesting, relevant, and/or close to the reader's heart.** Sarah showcases her qualifications with specific details in the bullets. This show-not-tell technique is far more effective than saying, "I am an expert historian and know many interesting stories."

>> **Use a writing style that relates to the audience and your goal.** In this case, the writer is addressing someone with an academic orientation similar to her own, so a slightly formal tone feels right.

>> **Cite credentials, but not necessarily up front.** They are often not your best sales points, as I explain in the previous section, "Introducing Yourself in Writing." People respond more to your understanding of their challenges and what you can do for them, rather than what you've done in the past. This isn't really counterintuitive: Knowing how to bridge your expertise to other people's problems is a top trademark of professionalism.

TIP

If you came up with a different version you like better, good for you. Editing and writing are far from scientific. It might be nice to think you can follow formulas or use templates, but "canned" approaches come across as overly general and boring. Practice thinking each challenge through with a goal-plus-audience framework in mind, address head and heart, and you'll get the results you want more often.

Creating Letters That Sell

Writing "cold call" letters to sell a product is a work staple for professional copy-writers, and for good reason. So many pitches compete for attention today that people are automatically skeptical, impatient, and bored with the piles of "buy me" mail that overwhelms in every form, from direct mail missives to emails, videos, and social media. While today's online environment offers extraordinary opportunities to create and deliver a marketing message, don't expect to do so off the top of your head. Here are some ideas to draw on.

>> **Define your goal and know your audience.** Don't expect someone to respond to a single communication by putting a check in the mail. More realistically, aim to pique the reader's interest, begin to establish trust, and entice her to the next step. An initial message should say just enough to interest your reader in going further.

If you're selling, it's your job to know the organization well enough to understand its challenges and explain how you can help. Think also about the particular person you're writing to — that person's goals, pressures, and role, which I talk about how to do in Chapter 2.

>> **Make a connection.** People trust people who appear to be from their own worlds. This isn't prejudicial; it's just hard to trust strangers. When you automatically have a connection, cite it: "We met at the such-and-such event" is good. More possibilities:

- We have a friend or professional connection in common.

- I talked to your company rep at a trade show or conference.

- We work with a client you know.

- We won an award for achievement in our industry.

Or perhaps you read a blog the person wrote, or heard her speak, or read about her in the business journal. Dig as you must.

>> **Start strong.** Try to combine both a personal connection and your problem-solving capability in a single opening sentence, such as:

Chuck Smith suggested I contact you to explain how I solved his most pressing problem, one I'm sure you share with him: reducing government audits of overseas investments.

Alternatively, lead with a story, a hot button, an unusual benefit or offer, a surprising fact or statistic. It's nice to be catchy, but don't make yourself crazy trying to be clever or funny. Better not to tell a joke than one that falls flat or could be misinterpreted. Knowing your value and how you can benefit the other party puts you on sure ground toward making the match.

>> **Remember "the ask."** If you want the reader to check out your website, request a free ebook, sign up for your blog, or ask a question — all in the interest of collecting contact information — say so. If you want a face-to-face meeting, say so. It's smart to set a time frame: offering to establish your value in 10 minutes, for example, is more attractive than requesting an open-ended commitment and suggests you're focused and won't waste the person's time. Ask about the reader's convenience, rather than saying "I'll come at 4 p.m. on Thursday."

>> **Prepare to be checked out.** Keep in mind that an interested reader will likely look you and your organization up on the Internet. Your website and LinkedIn profiles, among other platforms, should be in good shape to support your marketing message. And if you can find any embarrassing posts related to your personal life, rest assured a sales prospect will, too. Clean up your act — and screen yourself in the future to avoid losing opportunities you want.

Writing Difficult Messages

A guiding principle of this book is to see everything you write as an opportunity to advance relationships. New clients are hard to get, even for big corporations, and they are expensive to replace. If you're self-employed or operate a small business, balancing your desire to retain a client with your need to communicate something uncomfortable can be hard.

Here are some ideas for using your writing skills to both protect your own interests and handle problems proactively while minimizing the risk of relationship damage.

Spelling out services performed

Like all people, clients often have short memories. When I worked for a public relations agency that specialized in crisis communication, the bread and butter work was saving clients from disaster. The effort was intensive and the firm usually succeeded, but client gratitude often proved brief. The CEO's directive: Bill clients immediately while the averted threat remained fresh in their minds. A month or two later, safe and secure, they might review the invoice and find it exorbitant. An unpleasant effort to collect followed.

TIP

In addition to filing your invoices ASAP after completing the terms of an agreement, write a detailed account of what you did. For example, if I write a marketing publication for a project fee, I don't say:

> For writing service rendered — Marshall & White overview brochure

My invoice reads more like this:

> For Marshall & White overview brochure: 16 pages, 4-color glossy to serve as linchpin for major marketing campaign:

- Meetings with Executive Team (June 1, June 8, June 22, July 7)
- Ongoing telephone consultation
- Presentation to Board, June 14
- Concept development: delivered three creative strategy ideas
- Full treatment of chosen concept: 16 pp. mockup
- Content recommendations: 6- page "Ideas" executive letter
- Interviews with 9 staff members, 7 clients
- Coordination with graphic design

And much more. Notice that the list doesn't yet include copywriting.

Even well-intentioned clients only see the tip of your work iceberg. They observe a product, like a finished brochure or a workshop, and because the work is distant from their own specialization, have scant idea of what went into it. They also may overlook that preparing for and attending meetings consumes a lot of time (it's just part of their fully paid workday), and that creative work involves a lot of thought that doesn't stop at 5 p.m. Few clients like to pay a consultant for thinking, even though that's often the crux of the service.

Keep track of all the tasks you accomplish for the cause and put them right into the invoice. And if what you provide is intangible — like consulting — spell out as many tangibles as you can: creating the survey instrument, the 32-page report, the PowerPoint, the graphs for the website, and so on. If you can cite early evidence of the project's success, work that in, too.

Collecting on your invoices

No matter how carefully invoices and contracts are written, every consultant, freelancer, and entrepreneur has trouble collecting money at times. How to maintain a good relationship while pressing for payment?

Minimize the risk of losing your money and/or customer by asking for a retainer on signing, no matter how much you trust the person you're dealing with and how steady a client she has been. People are known to leave jobs and those who replace them have been known to prefer suppliers of their own, or bring the work in-house. Companies have been known to go out of business and file for bankruptcy without warning. You may also encounter disputes about whether, in the buyer's opinion, you delivered to the standard expected.

No one with honest intentions will ever fault you for acting in a businesslike way to protect yourself by requiring an advance. And don't lay the groundwork for cheating yourself if the nature of the work means you'll do a major portion in the beginning, like coming up with ideas or creating the blueprint. Set up the payment schedule to cover this aspect of the job should the agreement dissolve. A contract is only as good as the parties' willingness to live up to it. If a client doesn't like what you produce, legal enforcement may not be desirable or practical.

When payment is running a little late, minimize resentment by saying as little as possible in a perfectly neutral, blame-free, impersonal tone. Make the person you're writing to a partner in the collection effort:

Subject: Can you help?

Dear Tardee,

My payment for the Tyler project hasn't come through yet, though the work was finished two months ago. Is it possible for you to nudge the machinery a bit on my behalf?

I'll appreciate it very much. —Marty

Or:

Subject line: Friendly reminder

Dear Tardee,

I'm wondering if it's possible to speed up the processing of my second check for the Curio Design work. In line with our agreement it was due September 4 but has not arrived.

I'll appreciate your help with this.

Thanks, Marty

TIP

There's never a reason to plead poverty. Don't say you need the money to pay your bills. Late payment messages, unlike most I talk about in this book, work better when they are impersonal. The same minimalist approach is useful when you bear some responsibility. A friend was embarrassed to discover that she had neglected to deposit a check and it was too old for the bank to accept. She wrote to the client:

Dear Mr. Black:

In tracking invoices and payments for tax purposes, bookkeeping has brought to our attention that your check #9174 written on January 12 of this year was rejected by ABC Bank due to endorsement requirements.

Our records indicate that the check was not redeposited.

Attached is a copy of the check that was not credited to the Marketing Pro account.

Would you please issue a new check to replace the one that was originally provided?

We apologize for any inconvenience this may have caused.

Thank you,

Marcia White

Assuming the editorial or kingly "we" along with the formal tone depersonalizes the request and presents it as a glitch between bureaucracies, though the writer runs a very small company from a virtual office.

Sometimes, however, a true "letter of record" is called for to document an event or problem or present your claim more formally. This kind of letter may have legal implications that involve lawyers. That's beyond my scope, but I can share a strategy to keep in your back pocket for severely late payments and other confrontational situations: a chronological accounting. Here, it's all about the facts.

Marshal all the relevant bits and arrange them in a timeline. Then create a letter that simply marches down each item on your list in a dispassionate, matter-of-fact way: no frills, no flowery adjectives, no emotion. Start each item with the date.

Suppose you're an independent graphic designer and a client hasn't paid your last bill, which was due six months ago. He now hints that the work wasn't done to his satisfaction and won't take your phone calls. You don't want to go to court, but you do want your money.

Your letter can go this way:

> Dear Mel:
>
> On July 6 of this year, you contacted my firm, MorningGlory Design, to inquire about website services for your firm, Thompson, Ltd.
>
> On July 8, we met at your office for two hours to discuss Thompson's needs and goals.
>
> On July 15, I sent you a summary of our conversation with our suggestions for a website to meet your specifications. You called and said "I like the approach very much, go ahead."
>
> On July 22, I sent you an agreement specifying that MorningGlory would provide the services outlined (see attached contract pages 1 and 2) at a proposed fee (see attached contract page 3) and a schedule of payments.
>
> On July 22, we both signed the contract. You remitted the one-third payment due.
>
> On August 10, I presented the preliminary design. You said "with some revision it would be exactly what I want" and that you'd mail the second payment at week's end.
>
> On August 19, I presented the revised version based on your input. You said, "It looks fantastic, let me take a more careful look with my staff, and I'll check about the payment you didn't receive."

And so on. Further entries might include the dates the invoices were sent, when the new web design went live, and every other relevant detail — the more, the better. The close:

> In sum, I have met every obligation of our contract in a timely manner and with your full approval. The site is online exactly as I designed it. But six months later, you have not

paid two-thirds of the fee to which you agreed in writing. Kindly remit the balance owed immediately.

Very truly yours, Natasha

This may be the only place in this book that I recommend a stilted, formal language with an archaic tone. Such a letter sounds as if a lawyer is advising you. Or at the least, your reader will recognize that you have a good case and are prepared to seek legal redress. If Mel doesn't come through and you decide to take the legal route, your letter becomes part of that process and serves you well.

The approach works just as nicely when you're on the other side of the fence. Moreover, if you don't want to pay an unfair bill and clearly state that you have no intention of paying, the other party's recourse may be limited, depending on the state you live in.

Underscore your letter's legal undertones by mailing it — or better yet, certify it and require a signature to prove receipt.

Raising your fee structure

Most freelancers I know hate talking about money. Often, writing is a good way to do it. You can marshal your thinking points and articulate them more effectively without the person present, and give them breathing space to consider your request as well. Clients typically don't enjoy these conversations any more than you do, and may blurt out a negative response that's hard to reconsider.

Many successful consultants sidestep cost questions before presenting a proposal because they can write out all the work involved (similar to the invoice structure I suggest in the "Spelling out services performed" section). Writing also enables them to analyze and define the larger value of the proposed work to the company. This sets the stage for a better conversation.

One challenging need is a request for a fee increase. Most people who hire independent workers are content to continue in the same groove forever. I can't recall hearing of any instances where a freelancer was offered a raise. Ask you must, whether your business and living costs are going up like everyone else's, or because you've experienced "scope creep" — that is, you find yourself investing more time than your fee structure covers fairly.

The approach for collecting on invoices also works for this problem. List your possible content points. You will have specifics according to the situation, but here are some fairly universal points to make in framing the message:

>> I'm raising my rate 5 percent.

>> I haven't increased my fees for three years.

>> My overhead and operating expenses go up inevitably.

>> My work is valuable to you, as proven by . . .

>> My service this coming year will be even better because . . .

TIP

The last point is optional, but if you can think of something that doesn't really cost you anything — like a staff expansion or new capability you planned on anyway, an offer to meet more often, or a way to repurpose your work for additional uses — you provide a mitigating factor that inclines the client to agree more easily. She's spending more, but getting more.

WARNING

Remember that a message like this will probably be passed up the managerial chain and reviewed by financial people, so supply your connection with information to help him win approval on your behalf. And use an impersonal but still friendly writing style.

When you spell out your basic points first, you spare yourself a lot of agonizing. Just follow the trail!

Dear Jed,

I'm writing to alert you, as a client of many years, that Marsh Sisters will raise our project fee rate by 5 percent this coming year.

I know you'll understand that just like Tailor Enterprises, our operating expenses steadily increase. We have not raised our rates for three years, and did so only once in the seven years we've worked together.

Of course, we want to continue providing Tailor with the best possible service. We were very proud to earn the March Association Award of Merit for the Chancellor Project this past year, and even happier to know our work played a part in helping Tailor increase its Blue Division revenue this past quarter.

We have plans to support you in meeting your business goals even more effectively. We're implementing a new software system right now that will give you more detailed reports, with even faster turnaround.

All of us at Marsh look forward to working with you this year and together, know we will achieve new heights.

Sincerely,

Maggie

Communicating as a Virtual Worker

Working from home and virtual teaming trend upward every year. In addition to the escalating numbers of people who work on a project or hourly basis, more employees than ever work from their home base part of the week. Many others do their jobs away from headquarters, and may be continents and time zones away, or crosstown. Teaming with people we never see has become a commonplace experience for many of us.

Communication technology opens up all these possibilities with ever-easier ways to work virtually. But few of us are trained to function well in a virtual environment. Strategic writing gives you a key advantage as a virtual team member or project leader.

REMEMBER

Except for occasions when we see our virtual coworkers on screen, interaction between virtual coworkers is generally by written messages and phone calls. This brings a host of drawbacks. You must collaborate without being able to read people's facial expression, body language, and perhaps, intonation. It can take much longer to understand people's perspective, establish trust, and know what to expect from each one so you can interact effectively. If you participate in short-term projects with new teams every time, developing a set of practices is especially important.

TIP

If you have a choice, try to start the collaboration off in person, or close to it. Meeting face to face with the team is best because spending some time getting to know each other pays many dividends. Video conferencing is choice two, or use Skype or a cloud video meeting ground like Zoom. The telephone is third choice.

However accomplished, your initial meeting should address good practice and set agreed-to guidelines for distribution in writing to everyone involved. This document should spell out the group's goal; individual responsibilities; mutual obligations; milestones toward the goal and timelines; and each person's availability, taking locations and time zones into account, as well as working preferences (for example, are folks reachable at night? On weekends?). Include a checklist to denote progress. Decide on sharing mechanisms, such as Google Drive, Google Docs, or Dropbox.

It's preferable to plan for periodic group meetings online if not in person to maintain momentum, address personality issues, and solve the inevitable roadblocks — all are handled much better face to face.

TIP

It's important to know who's in charge. If there's a designated project leader, his role should be fully spelled out. If "everyone is equal" and no one is centrally responsible, it's a good idea for the group to agree that a specific person will coordinate, keep everyone on track, and hold team members accountable.

A notetaker or communicator-in-chief should for designated for meetings. If this unpopular task is up for grabs, volunteer! In notetaking lies power. You'll know more: Everyone shares information with you. And when you're the reporter, you create the perspective.

Here are some ways to help you be a good virtual collaborator and a good team member in general:

>> **Communicate always in a positive, upbeat way that promotes relationship building.** Express appreciation for other people's good work or contributions in written notes, which are especially valued.

>> **Contribute appropriate personal notes.** Until you know people better, you can ask about mundane matters like the weather or someone's weekend away. Note that research on teaming finds that the "small talk" and good listening that build comfort and trust level characterize the most successful teams.

>> **Write considerate messages.** Respect your teammates by making all your writing clear, concise, to the point, and complete. Use the good email techniques I present in Chapter 6.

>> **Introduce a written repeat-it-back technique to confirm everyone is on the same page.** Doing so prevents misinterpretations, especially if there is a shift in direction. For example, confirm your own actions with notes such as, "To follow up on our conversation on Tuesday, I plan the following . . . ."

Pitching the Media

Coverage in print or online media is an attractive proposition for most businesses. It gives you free exposure, right? The catch is that everyone knows this, so gaining media space is competitive. On the other hand, every day, more outlets materialize and demand a steady flow of new content. You can find opportunities if you're ready to invest some time and energy. Keep in mind that today's magical Internet enables you to publish and distribute your own news. You can post it on your own website, distribute it by email or use a service such as PR Newswire (www.prnews wire.com), 24-7 Press Release (www.24-7pressrelease.com), and eReleases (www.ereleases.com). However you distribute it, your press release must look professional.

TIP

If you want space to promote your product or service in a print or online outlet, know that the bigger and broader its audience, the more it is flooded with professionally crafted media pitches. Even mid-sized organizations maintain in-house PR departments or hire agencies to do this work to the degree they see benefit.

If you run a small business, or a one-person operation, it is logical to conclude that:

>> **Your best target is local media.** Local editors see their role as giving people in the community opportunity to shine and, of course, share news of interest to their readers. In many locales, community and city newspapers, regional business publications, and local magazines are flourishing. Most publish online versions as well.

>> **Your best strategy is to pitch by email.** Or possibly by telephone, depending on the editor. If you study the media in which you're interested, you can easily learn what the organization looks for and figure out how to relate to those possibilities. Watch for perennial needs such as stories that relate to the season and holiday, and ideas that make readers feel good. Publications want to speak to the heart, too.

Informal releases that don't adhere to the traditional format can be fine, but many of your targets require the familiar approach. In any case, knowing how to write a formal release sharpens your thinking.

Writing traditional "press releases"

This traditional press release format works best when you have "real news" to share — meaning something of interest to a reporter or editor is happening. For example, it's of local interest if you're holding a benefit concert and a well-known performer will appear; you're being presented with a significant award; or your business is opening a new office. Such events are good fodder for a community newspaper or regional business publication.

If you're fishing for coverage of your event, bear in mind that a static meeting or speech or presentation is not worth a journalist's time. But you can provide an after-the-fact account yourself. If you handle this as a reporter would by writing in the publication's style and supplying a good photograph, and if the editor has space to fill in that issue, your event may earn some of it.

You can make even a static event interesting with specifics. If a notable CEO gave a speech, for example, reporting what he said, providing it had value, is much more appealing than simply stating he was there. If a high school student was presented with an award, exactly what did he do to deserve it? What did he say at the ceremony? What are his future plans?

A media release is traditionally structured as follows. Let's assume your subject is an event.

» Date and full contact information — a specific person reachable day, night, weekends!

» A compelling action headline.

» Subhead with supporting information.

» Lead focused on most interesting or relevant information *for the editor's audience.* Important: Is the public invited? Is the editor?

» A few paragraphs with essential information. The guidelines are to cover Who, What, When, Where, and Why and may include an interesting quote and any photo ops.

» How the editor should follow up. Is there a schedule of events?

» "Boilerplate" statement describing your business in a few lines.

Writing email pitches

A good alternative to writing a traditional release is the email pitch, and in fact, many editors prefer it. But it must be carefully thought through. *Know your story.* Here, too, you need a compelling headline for the subject line. Then you must construct a few tight paragraphs that make your happening interesting, important, and relevant, and also answer the who-what-when-where-why questions. For example:

> Subject: Clever Computers Help Disabled Nursing Home Residents Discover the Internet
>
> Dear Mike:
>
> Nursing home life is a lonely enterprise for many of our community's elderly. The busier family members get, the less they are able to visit, and many residents have few chances to leave the limiting premises.
>
> My colleagues and I at Clever Computers have been teaching nursing home residents how to socialize with family and friends on the Internet, and pursue their personal interests through online resources and online courses. But we discovered that a number of these seniors cannot handle the keyboard well enough.
>
> On Monday, July 24, we'll show ten residents of the Maple Tree Home who are unable to type how to access the Internet's wonders through voice control alone.
>
> We'd be delighted if you, or a member of your staff, can join us and witness first-hand how these senior citizens experience their power to open up the world for the first time.

Clever Computers (www.clevcomp@bgs.net) is a 14-year-old community-based company serving the business community with computer troubleshooting, networking systems, and training.

[Event time, place, date, directions go here]

Call me any time for more details. A photographer is most welcome.

Sharon Fisher, CEO

A somewhat more structured approach is to invite coverage with a Media Alert at least a week before your happening:

From:

Contact:

Event: (Headline)

Event date:

Place:

Description of what will happen and its significance, who the organizer is (total three short paragraphs)

More information about organizer (with website address)

Direct invitation to attend

A local publication (unlike a national one) is likely to respond to either form of pitch. Local newspapers, regional magazines, and business publications are increasingly short-handed and show up only at high-priority events. Therefore, the editor may invite you to send a write-up after the fact, or a high-resolution photo and caption. Then, the better you do the reporter's work and deliver well-written, ready-to-use material, the better your chances of gaining some media space.

If you want to contribute a full-fledged article, or columns based on your special expertise, it's wise to pitch the idea in the same manner before writing. If interested, the editor will provide guidelines to help you produce what she needs. My advice on writing blogs in Chapter 12 can help.

Don't overlook your local online news channels, which are always starving for news. And consider local television. But to draw a video crew to the scene, you must be able to promise strong visuals. Because video technology grows so much better all the time, you might be able to produce acceptable footage of the event yourself and submit it. Or hire a local videographer.

Finding ideas for the media

TIP

You may have thought in reading this section that you don't have interesting activities like teaching nursing home folks to use the computer, or running a charity concert, or opening a new office. Companies and nonprofits identify good ideas in two basic ways: First, they constantly keep eye and ear open to notice what the organization and every member of it is engaged in that is share-worthy. Second, they create activities that merit publicity.

Clever Computers, for example, might have decided to initiate its nursing home program because someone recognized the need. Or, they might have thought about what they could contribute to the community that would be of value and justified media attention. The desire for publicity is a motivating force behind many wonderful programs. Every enterprise today wants to be known as a good community member and looks actively for ways to connect with that community through good causes.

TIP

If you are doing something wonderful or truly innovative in your industry, look to the wider range of possibilities. Trade and professional publications need material, too, and if you have something to offer, their doors may open. Pitch editors as I outline in the foregoing sections, taking account of your suggestion's value to the audience.

REMEMBER

News venues also thrive on relationships. Do your homework and become familiar with your local outlets: what interests them, their presentation style, their scope. Find out how to reach editors and reporters. On a local level, find opportunities to talk to them. On the national and regional level, remember that most major publications today scout for ideas and accept pitches through social media. They're happy to connect if you can offer them something of value and demonstrate an understanding of their needs. Follow them on Twitter and Facebook and learn about them on LinkedIn, and you're much better equipped to connect productively.

Next we look at applying the writing techniques we looked at in earlier chapters to typical management writing challenges.

Chapter **14**

Writing Well to Manage Well

Most great leaders are admired for their powerful communication skills. Not a surprise: How else can you inspire, motivate, and persuade? But alas, most people's direct experience is with managers who are not leaders and who fall short on this skill set. Gallup, the premier polling group, reports that two-thirds of American workers identify themselves as "unengaged." Done every year, the report has consistently pinpointed poor relationships as the main cause, which often translates as poor manager communication.

Seen from the organization's perspective, this rampant disengagement generates mistakes, misunderstandings, inefficiencies, and high turnover. A workplace with low morale is an unproductive one. Why so many organizations allow this huge limitation to persist connects with misplaced values, structures that reward people counter-productively, and lack of training.

While these problems can't be solved easily, if you are a manager or aspire to join those ranks, this chapter can help you manage better by communicating better. All the techniques for writing and speaking I cover in earlier chapters give you useful tools to work with. Here the focus is on applying those ideas to typical management writing challenges, from thank-you's to no-thank-you's, good news to bad news, inspirational to critical.

This chapter also covers communicating to manage up, because we all report to someone, whether a department or division head, a CEO, the governing board, or a set of clients. We need to communicate gracefully with both those below and above us in the hierarchical chain of command. Fortunately, the guidelines are similar. Like so much of successful living, it's all in the attitude, so that's where I start.

Communicating as a Manager

You may think that the higher you ascend the management ladder, the more you can issue orders, and the less you need to care about the feelings of those who report to you or rank lower on the company totem pole. Big mistake! Even if you hit the top, autocratic ways of managing are both unpopular and ineffective in today's work environment.

TIP

If you want people to work hard for you, help you perform well, feel enthusiastic about their work, and say nice things about you and the company, the word is: You must be more courteous, accommodating, and considerate than ever. This outlook should show in both your in-person communication and in what you write.

I do realize first-hand that the boss's lot is not an easy one. The messages can be hard: "No, you don't get the assignment or promotion or new office you wanted . . . No, the company won't pay for your MBA . . . Sorry, I can't let you work at home three days a week . . . The company had a bad first quarter so no confer-ence requests this year . . . Everyone's taking a 3 percent pay cut, well, maybe not everyone." And then there are the routine written performance evaluations and critiques, which are seldom fun.

And those are just messages to subordinates! You must write with great care to your own supervisors and find ways to express your viewpoint even when they don't want to listen. You must represent "your people" and try to protect them from any negative impact from higher-ups.

You're expected to feed the chain of command's need for better data or sales fig-ures or productivity so higher-ups can, in many cases, take credit for your team's accomplishments. You must win support for programs and innovations by writing reports and proposals they will only skim. You are probably required to explain and implement directives you don't agree with. And you may have a host of new audiences to address: management peers, board members, donors, suppliers, and more.

Where to start on all this? *Tone.* To write strategically — that is, to accomplish your goals with people on different levels — it's especially important to gauge your audiences as individuals, not just as cogs in a corporate machine. You can be most successful by relating to each person above and below you, both within terms of his or her role and personal perspective. Let's look first at communicating with your staff.

Relating to your team members

If you head a department or work unit, you are fully responsible for how the group interacts and operates. This carries some ramifications that all too many managers appear to forget. When you're the boss, you're the role model; don't look for any vacations from that. How you treat people and communicate with them is echoed in how they interact with each other. Remember also:

>> **You're always in the spotlight.** People are intensely aware of any perceived unfairness, inconsistency, or favoritism on the boss's part.

>> **You set the standards for level of commitment and respectful behavior.** Hard work, courtesy, and consideration are contagious when coming from the top.

>> **You establish value.** People naturally strive to perform in ways they observe the boss to value — if you write well, for example, they typically write more carefully, too.

>> **What you say and what you write may be given far more weight than you credit or intend.** Careless statements can have unintended consequences. Remember all those movies where a VIP said, "If only Smith wasn't around to bug up the works . . ."?

>> **Your communication style affects what your employees choose to share with you and how honest they will be.** This also affects to what degree they'll express their opinions.

>> **Your tone in communicating has lasting impact.** A badly thought-out or mean-spirited message may negatively affect your whole unit, while positive messages inspire and motivate.

Here's an important corollary of the foregoing principles: *Your responsibility as a manager requires you to control your own feelings and short-sighted reactions.* If you want to be respected, letting negative emotions like anger, frustration, or bad moods rule will always work against you. The boss is key to the whole spirit of our work environment. We need her to be positive, cheerful, and even happy so we can feel secure and supported.

REMEMBER

The best advice I've heard is that whatever the work, aim to build a team around yourself. Never get so lost in the numbers, pressures, or urgencies that you forget this basic commitment or run out of time to handle it. Use everything you write to foster good feelings and commitment.

Set the stage for yourself by looking at your staff members as individuals. Build a profile for each with the tools presented in Chapter 2. Take special account of what motivates each person, his strengths and aspirations, and how he relates to the team.

TIP

Creating profiles of those under your authority gives you a super tool for deploying your forces well and promoting team spirit. Always cherish the differences. If we all had the same skills and enthusiasms, and looked at the world the same way, life would be a lot duller and organizations way less productive than they can be. The better you know your team, the better you can frame your written messages to each person as well as the full group. Let's look at some helpful general guidelines.

Writing to inspire and motivate

The harder your staff works, the more you accomplish, the better you do your job, and the more kudos you gain. What's not to like? Many ways of motivating people come down to surprisingly basic ideas. But they are so often ignored that it is easy for you to absorb them and stand out. Here are some communication-related guidelines:

>> **Share information regularly.** People like and need to know "what's going on." A new edict coming down from on high? Tell your staff as much as you can ASAP, and what it means to them. If people know they can depend on you to share important news, you diminish opportunities for gossip and wild surmise.

>> **Give people the big picture.** It's motivating to know how the department and your own work fit into the organization's goals. Keep your staff in tune with how the company is doing, and perhaps industry trends, to help them feel valued and make them better equipped to do their jobs.

>> **Make the most of good news — and don't hide bad news.** If you're recognized for an achievement that took a team, share the glory and celebrate. If there's bad company news, tell it. The news will come out anyway so share it early rather than late if you want to maintain trust.

>> **Keep a positive, upbeat attitude in all your communication.** This projects that you like your job, know you do it well, and expect the best from everyone. Extend trust and most often, people will be trustworthy.

>> **Let people know you are monitoring their work and holding them accountable.** Beyond keeping them on track, this helps people feel valued and leads them to aim higher.

>> **Actively encourage your staff to share their own information, ideas, and suggestions.** Everyone complains about writing reports, but if your staff includes more than eight people or so, how else will you know what's going on?

>> **Show appreciation often: for work well done, an over-and-above contribution, and good writing!** People repeat and amplify behavior that brings praise, while an unacknowledged good deed may remain a lonely one.

REMEMBER

Always keep in mind that good communication is a two-way street. Technology has changed us: We expect to interact online, not just read, and we want to contribute ideas and opinions and be heard, rather than just listen and follow orders. People want to be part of the action rather than just recipients of information from on high. Practice the old one-way-trickle-down style (colorfully called "cascading") at your own risk. Your most valuable people will not put up with it. Stay on the lookout for opportunities to encourage active participation.

TIP

This is especially important in managing Millennials and the younger Generation Z (Chapter 2). They value "the experience," chances to learn, and knowing the why of everything. Such opportunities are more important than money to many young people, and they may quickly disappear themselves if kept on the periphery.

Let's try these concepts out first with messages no one likes to write: bad news.

Delivering bad news

Suppose the head of technology, Hal, has been told that poor company profits for the past quarter mean there will be no raises this year. He's been given a lot of profit-and-loss (P&L) statistics, but not much else to help explain the situation to his department. He knows that top management came close to cutting staff and will no doubt consider doing so should company performance not soon improve. He must break the news to his ten-person team.

First consideration: Should Hal deliver the news in person or in writing? When the news is bad, or you must criticize, always consider face-to-face interaction first. People often feel it's cowardly to hide behind a written message in business — and they're right, just as it's cowardly to break off a personal relationship with a Snapchat post.

TIP

On the other hand, in many negative situations, a written message can be a good opener. It enables you to think through the facts and their meaning, and communicate them in a more controlled way that helps readers digest the information before reacting, or over-reacting.

In this case, Hal's *goal* is to deliver the unwelcome news and minimize the bad feelings it will naturally produce. He considers his *audience* and his team members' probable responses. This mental scan suggests that probably at least one person will respond with quick anger that will infect everyone else and set a bad tone for a conversation. Emotions are communicable! He envisions the whole group dwelling on the injustice of it all, making the situation worse.

Hal's decision: Communicate the basic message in writing and follow-up face to face, with a short delay that gives everyone time to absorb the news and come to the meeting with relatively open minds.

Try This: Before reading the following version of the memo Hal might write, think about how you would write it. How would you generate a positive outlook without sacrificing honesty? Then read this version:

Subject: Next year salaries and planning

Dear Ellen, Jerry, Marsh, Quinn, Larry, Jackson, Emery, Jenny, Bob, Sue:

At the Leadership Team meeting yesterday, I learned that the company will award no salary increases for the coming year. This decision was reluctantly made by top management because our Q4 earnings fell 7%, in large part because the Mister Magic launch fell well below expectations.

The decision-makers could alternatively have chosen to make up the deficit with layoffs. While we all feel justifiably disappointed not to receive raises, I for one am grateful that the decision was to maintain full employment. So, none of us is now at risk, and we need not fear for our colleagues, nor worry about extra work burdens falling upon us.

I can also share that this year will see three new product launches. Our decision-makers are hopeful that results will be strong, the P&L picture will rebound, and we'll all reap the rewards down the line. I'm optimistic — but I can't tell you that we should be complacent.

What can our team do at this juncture?

I see a real opportunity for us to prove our value on a broader scale. My idea is that in the coming months, we could push ourselves to move above and beyond our own territory. I would love to see us share our project management know-how with other departments and help them adapt our systems to improve their own productivity. This helps the whole company, of course, and gives us a chance to spread the word on how valuable our work is and how well we do it.

Let's meet on April 10 to brainstorm ideas. At that time, I'll also reserve 10 minutes to talk about the wage freeze and answer any questions to my best knowledge. I'll share the P&L statements if you want to see them.

Meanwhile, please think about my plan and bring your best thoughts to the brainstorming. Let's identify departments that can benefit from our practices and create a preliminary plan of action.

I'm proud of the team we've built together, and I believe we can use our combined skills to contribute more and be valued more. —Hal

Why it works: Hal takes the "us" perspective throughout — we're a team and we're all in this together — but there's no question about who is in charge. He strategizes his content and writing style to accomplish the goal and uses a matter-of-fact, low-key tone. The message acknowledges that readers will feel unhappy, but doesn't dwell on it. He makes the likely assumption that people will not much be interested in the P&L statements, so gives that a light reference that he will supply the material if wanted. He spends the most time framing the bad news in a more positive light by:

>> **Conveying confidence in the company:** He points out that decision-makers could have made a less humane and acceptable choice, firing people, which suggests that the company cares about employees.

>> **Creating a silver lining:** Hal tells his people that though things are not as they would wish, they're okay — and moreover, they can help underwrite their own prospects by pitching in above and beyond now.

>> **Reframing his team's attention from the inevitable "so unfair" complaints into an action possibility:** The idea that as a team, they can work to demonstrate their value is energizing, and sets a positive tone for a think-tank session.

In such situations, it's important to create a perspective shift without misleading people or offering false assurances. In many instances, it might seem hard to find a silver lining — but with a little creativity, you may be surprised at how often you do.

TIP

Notice that the message puts the bad news right up front — bottom line on top applies to bad news just as it does to cheery news. Delivering an unwelcome message in a "sandwich" framework used to be popular. For example, "We have really liked working with you. Unfortunately, we're not renewing your contract. But we had some good times together, right?"

Today's readers don't react well to such tiptoeing. Get the bad news done and then move on to some kind of mitigation, insofar as possible. It must be genuine, or don't do it at all. For example, if you're turning down a job candidate, you might end with, "Here is the contact information of someone who I believe might like to know about your skills," or "We'll hire a new set of interns in August and would be glad to review your application again at that time." Such offers mean infinitely more than, "We had so many great candidates but could only choose one."

What if you have 1,000 applicants to turn down, or just don't have anything help-ful to say? Then just close simply but firmly. "Thank you for applying. We very much appreciate your interest in our company."

WARNING

Even worse than the sandwich technique is trying to obscure bad news in a torrent of irrelevant information, or news that's good for people other than the reader. The CEO of a major international corporation made a fool of himself a few years ago by announcing big layoffs in an email that meandered on for seven pages about the company's great future, then got around to announcing that a whole division was eliminated in the interest of this rosy future. Outraged employees immediately hit their share buttons and the whole world jeered.

The CEO overlooked this book's governing principles — know your audience, know your goal, and strategize content within that frame. In announcing layoffs or other news that is calamitous to some, those at the top may forget that these messages have multiple audiences with different self-interests.

If you fire 500 people in writing, which is often the chosen medium, what's the message to all the colleagues you hope to retain? Your goal for the laid-off folks should be to minimize their distress and hatred of you as a callous employer. Those slated to remain need to know that the company isn't going under, and there's good reason to stick with it and soldier on. The general public and media are only a click away, so you're inevitably delivering the message to them as well. Therefore, you need to demonstrate that the firm is on solid ground, has made a difficult but valid decision, and isn't unfeeling toward those losing their jobs.

How would you write such a letter, or email, telling 500 people they are laid off?

Try This: If you've been faced with a challenge like this or can imagine one in the future, use this approach: Combine the goal-plus-audience strategy (Chapter 2) with the talking points technique (Chapter 8). Here's how it might work if you're responsible for letting those 500 people go:

1. **Define your audiences.**

   Your primary audience is the 500 people you're laying off. Your secondary audience is the remaining staff and everyone they might share the message with (the board, the media, the public, stockholders, competitors).

2. **Define your goals.**

   Inform the 500 people that they are unemployed soon as sympathetically as possible. Reassure the remaining staff that the company is in good shape and that their jobs are currently secure and they will not be adversely affected. Reassure the other audiences and in doing so, avoid any suggestion that the company is mean or vulnerable.

3. Brainstorm to create talking points.

The talking points for this situation may be:

- Decision was made by the CEO and Executive Leadership Team
- They regret the need for making the cut
- Reason: closing down of unprofitable division that is behind the times technologically
- Remaining staff are secure in jobs but must pull together
- Each laid-off employee will receive a generous severance package reflecting service time
- The company is retaining a career counseling firm to help identify new opportunities for all the laid-off workers and counsel them one on one

Once you've articulated your audiences and clarified what you need to accomplish, the talking points give you good substance to work with. Here's one way to use the points:

> Dear ___:
>
> I am sorry to share that the AeroWing Division will cease operation April 3 of this year, and that all division staff will be laid off. We highly value your nine years of service and regret that we will not be able to continue employing you as of that date.
>
> I made the decision in close consultation with the Executive Leadership Team. We are responding to the division's steady decline over the past five years, primarily because this product has been technologically outpaced by new competitors. We've concluded that unfortunately, the company is unable to support these losses and further invest in this arena at the expense of our other product lines, which continue to grow.
>
> We want to offer you as much support as we can at this time. You will receive a compensation package reflecting your time with Aero that I am sure you will find generous. The Talent Management Office will shortly contact you to arrange a personal consultation.
>
> Also, we are retaining a professional firm, BetterNextTime, to provide every member of the AeroWing team with one-on-one counseling. Ten counselors will work on-site for six months to help everyone affected find appropriate opportunities, and their full resources will be available to help you with your next career step.
>
> I hope you will accept my personal good wishes for your every future success, and my appreciation for all your contributions to a division in which we will always feel enormous pride.
>
> Sincerely,
>
> Jack
>
> John C. Berry, CEO

Why it works: The CEO and Executive Leadership Team take responsibility for the decision, and the CEO delivers the message in his own name. This may seem like a small point, but taking ownership matters to people. What is more annoying than bad news delivered in statements such as, "It was decided that . . ."?

The tone is low-key and matter of fact, but also somewhat formal, which is befitting the subject matter. The CEO expresses sympathy to an appropriate degree; going overboard with warm feelings would accomplish little and might be taken as hypocritical. The bottom-line reason for the layoffs is clearly stated in a way that doesn't involve other parts of the company. The primary audience can't argue with the numbers, and few will be interested in more detail.

Secondary audiences, such as the media and stockholders, may well want to see the financials, however, and the company would be wise to have backup material ready. More detailed information should also be tailored for a set of press releases, announcement on the company website, and other channels this company uses to communicate with its full range of stakeholders.

TIP

Writing with the structured approach I recommend always helps you think more analytically. In considering "audience" for this sample message, until I wrote the organized list, I overlooked the importance of stockholders and the company's board of directors. Major clients might also need more tailored messages, as well as strategic partners and government agencies. If the organization is a nonprofit, a major announcement should be directed to supporting foundations, private donors, and volunteers. This suggests a broad principle.

WARNING

When you're responsible for communicating with a number of audiences, don't forget them in reporting on an important event. Identify each audience and brainstorm how to customize the message for each: content, level of detail, language, tone. Keep WIIFM in mind — what's-in-it-for-me.

And, know how to reach every audience. Board members may need hand-delivered information packets, different employee groups may prefer social media or email or printed memos, stockholders probably want a letter from the CFO. All too often, organizations unintentionally focus on communicating with a few audiences via their traditional channels, and overlook other venues more likely to reach other audience segments.

TIP

Research indicates that effectively handling bad news messages, such as announcing layoffs, makes a difference in how those who are losing their jobs react. Follow-up studies showed that departed employees who felt respectfully treated and understood the business situation harbored little bad feeling toward the company. Those who were treated carelessly remained angry — and found many ways to share that resentment.

Writing good news messages

Certainly, it's a whole lot nicer to share good tidings, but you may have found that in fact, positive messages are difficult in their own way. But "thank you," "good work," and "congratulations" belong in the good manager's portfolio, and this writing skill should be exercised often.

TIP

Many supervisors dwell on the need to criticize rather than offer messages of appreciation. But in many instances, appreciation is a better way to encourage behavior we want and wean people away from what we don't want. Most employees aim to please their bosses and live up to expectations or exceed them. All too often, the problem is that supervisors fail to adequately communicate what they want! Many employee surveys highlight this unfortunate gap.

Writing is an ideal tool for making this connection. It feels more official and special when you deliver a written compliment rather than a spoken one, which is fleeting, and may not in the moment be well expressed.

REMEMBER

The key to composing good thank-you and job-well-done notes is specificness. It's easy to orient yourself to be specific if you apply the goal-plus-audience framework. Suppose your subordinate, Allie, has done a good job preparing a slide deck for your client presentation. You know a thank you is in order. Off the top of your head, you might say,

Hi Allie — Thanks so much for the slide deck, show went well. —Chuck

But this is short-sighted. If you more deeply consider your main goal — to encourage future good work — you'd probably see the challenge more concretely:

>> Reinforce Allie's enthusiasm for such assignments.

>> Acknowledge her extra effort — she worked on this over the weekend.

>> Help her feel she's a valued member of the team.

>> Help her feel good about working for me.

Here's one way of meeting these goals:

Dear Allie,

I presented the show last night, and it went very well! I noticed that Bob, the prospect's division head, smiled all the way through, and 20 minutes of good Q&A about our campaign ideas followed. It's too soon to say if the account is ours, but I'm happy that we gave it our best shot.

So, thanks for helping me do that. You pulled the deck together on a tight deadline and translated the packaging ideas into effective visuals. The transitions you came up with tied it all together nicely.

Glad to have you on my team. —Chuck

REMEMBER

Does this message sound like overkill — perhaps too effusive? As always, adapt the ideas to your own style and comfort zone. You don't want to write notes like this every day, of course. But observe what a few minutes of strategic writing accomplishes. In telling Allie exactly what she did well and the results this helped achieve, Chuck shows Allie she is valued as a contributing member of the team; her hard work is appreciated by the person who matters most, her boss; and that boss is a great person to work for. Remember, relationship-building is an underlying goal for *every* message (see Chapter 2).

As Allie basks in feeling appreciated, her motivation can only grow. Will she work even harder to merit further praise? Put in extra time as needed? Come up with more creative ideas? Probably. Well-delivered praise is the best available way that you, as a manager, can promote alignment with staff members and get future work done outstandingly. But it only works when it's specific and concrete.

Criticizing with kindness

It falls to the manager's lot to coax team members to meet standards and perform better. Many supervisors are uncomfortable with this demand, but it's essential to the role. The good news is that often you can accomplish your goals with a positive approach.

When I began presenting workshops early in my career, I realized that often when someone gives a speech, or reads an assignment to the group, listening to feedback is a terrifying experience. Although group input was always meaningful, at times people were unthinkingly (or thinkingly) cruel in their responses. The result was hurtful rather than helpful.

TIP

I stumbled across two techniques that mitigate these harmful interactions. First, invite the spotlighted person to review his own performance with a question such as, "How do you think you did? Anything you'd like to do differently next time?" Next, require that the group deliver only positive comments. I found that more was accomplished when following this positive-only rule than with open criticism. When everyone engages in looking for the good, strengths are highlighted, there are no worries about hurt feelings, and everyone learns more.

Try This: Telling someone what he did right reinforces the behavior you desire. Further, positive input generates ideas for improving in a more natural and friendly way. Often the process leads the "target" person to come up with better ideas himself. In a one-on-one meeting, you first might ask, "What did you feel went well with the project?" and then follow up with, "Looking back, what do you think you could have done better?"

TIP

Written messages, obviously, lack this back-and-forth potential. But the non-blaming spirit of the idea is nonetheless useful. Suppose Allie had not done a good job on her slide deck assignment. You didn't like all the visuals, the transitions were uneven, the flow was shaky, whatever. You need to hold her accountable, yes, but the overarching goal is for her to improve next time. It's probably counterproductive to tell her all of this, as crushing her initiative and confidence doesn't accomplish any purpose at all.

Considering this, you might say:

> *Allie, I appreciate that you got the show done on such short notice. I know that was tough.*
>
> *However, I had some problems with the deck. I don't know what else is in your portfolio now, but your work is usually better. Let's talk about it to understand what happened.*
> *—Chuck*

REMEMBER

A brief, less specific message does the job better. Unlike when you deliver compliments, when it comes to criticism, reviewing specifics often is best accomplished in a private conversation rather than in writing. The foregoing memo to Allie prepares her for a thoughtful discussion aimed at helping her improve.

You may need a "nudge" memo that is stronger, according to your judgment of the persona and situation. Here's an example:

> *Gwen, you edited the workplan, but you missed a lot. I would have expected you to ask questions if some of the material was unclear to you. Here's my own rewrite — let's discuss.*

An important exception to this less-is-more approach is when you need to create a written record of insufficiencies, such as for legal documentation. Then write in excruciating detail. A lawyer or HR person is probably available to give you these guidelines.

Writing requests and giving orders

The same principles of thoughtful communication apply when you assign work. Routinely see everyday messages as building blocks toward better performance and good relationships. Which request in each of the following memos would you prefer to receive from your boss?

> *Jake, here's the material for the Collins report. Due date Wednesday, no fail! Better, get it on my desk Tuesday for review. Thnx.*

> *Jake:*

> *Here's everything you need for the Collins report. I believe all the sections are covered, but please take a look at the attachments and let me know ASAP if you find anything missing.*

> *This is high priority, and I count on you to get the full draft to me Tuesday. Then I'll do a quick review for delivery to the client on Wednesday. If you run into any problems call me, day or night.*

> *I know this deadline is tight. Thanks for pitching in.*

The second message tells Jake why he's doing the work on short notice and that it's for the team. He feels respected and included. Who doesn't want to feel that way? When I talk about this in workshops, often someone says, "But that's my assistant's job! Why do I have to cajole him into doing it?" You don't. But if you want the work done with enthusiasm and resourcefulness, perhaps with unacknowledged overtime, you need to care how the person feels.

TIP

Make it a habit to visualize whom you're writing to (see Chapter 2) so the person is real and individual to you. Decide to use every message to build that team around you. People work harder for a manager who cares about them and tells them why their assignments matter.

I know a young, successful department head who frames every request to staff this way: "Would you do me a favor and . . . ." "Of course they have to do it," she explains, "and they always say 'sure.' When I put it like that, it sets a tone that says I appreciate what they contribute. They're happier to 'help me' than if I just said, 'do this.' So, I just give all my orders that way."

Writing to Higher-Ups

You don't need me to tell you that when you write to a superior, every message should be carefully thought out, well written, and scrupulously edited. If your boss sends you cryptic, confusing, or non-explanatory messages (such as, "No!" or "Not now!"), do not take that as a reason to write abrupt, careless messages yourself.

REMEMBER

I recommend developing a written profile of your supervisor, drawing on the approach I detail in Chapter 2. You can much more successfully present your requests, suggest ideas, and build trust when you take the time to understand the person, especially his communication style and decision-making preferences. Does he want a lot of detail, the big picture, or the bottom line? What problems does he want to solve, what keeps him up at night? What's the best time of day to ask for something you want? (Research says that many people are most well-disposed and open after lunch.)

See through the boss's eyes and you'll automatically find the right words and persuasive framework. The same process I present in earlier chapters for writing emails, reports, and proposals apply when the audience is your manager. But pay close attention to some characteristics that I am 98 percent sure your boss possesses by virtue of position. She feels:

>> Always short of time

>> Pressured to show results for her domain

>> Faced with conflicting priorities

And, of course, she reports to a boss of her own, with all the attendant challenges.

WARNING

Remember that an email or document sent to your supervisor may work its way up the management line or be included in a report or other material. So even if you enjoy a comfortable relationship with your boss, as a guiding principle, assume all upward-directed messages may have a larger audience and use your best thinking and skills. Let's look at how to take account of the three common characteristics I cited for bosses.

Most often, with variation based on your profile of your supervisor, your best strategy is to write brief, straightforward emails that stick to one subject. Long detailed emails may be skimmed or not read at all, especially if the subject line and lead don't get to the point right away. In general, any time you're addressing a higher-up, such as board members, donors, executives, and government regulators, aim to:

>> **Be direct.** Begin by clearly stating your reason for writing and end with a call to action — what do you want?

>> **Take a positive tone and position.** Better to be perceived as a problem-solver than a problem-bringer or complainer. Stay upbeat and sound objective and in control; provide solutions or alternatives when you can.

>> **Write super-concisely.** Don't include extraneous thoughts or words. Use simple language and short words, sentences, and paragraphs.

» **Write correctly.** Use full sentences, good grammar, correct spelling and punctuation, and clear transitions. Be suspicious of abbreviations and beware of emoji!

» **Create self-contained messages.** Include just enough context so your multitasking reader doesn't have to look up previous material, do research, or ask basic questions.

» **Write with extreme courtesy.** Take time not to sound abrupt or as if you're issuing orders or calling him to account.

» **Employ good visuals.** Make the information easy to access and grasp. Draw attention to important points with subheads, bold lead-ins, and plenty of white space. A plain typeface in the 12-point range is best.

Here's an example of an email that follows these guidelines.

Subject: Hiring consultant by Thursday

Hi, Elaine:

Here are the three best responses to our RFP for a benefits consultant on the Chandler Project, filtered from 39 candidates. It would be great if we can announce the decision by Thursday; then we can put the paperwork through in time for board approval on June 4.

If you want to talk this through, just let me know. I believe all three candidates are strong and would meet our needs.

If you are able to get back to me by end of Thursday, it will be very helpful in moving forward on schedule.

Thanks. —Sam

Guarding your tone

WARNING

The most frequent complaint upper echelon managers make about employee writing — especially when done by younger people — is that they are "tone deaf." In other words, they address VIPs, including clients and top executives, in the same spirit and language they might use writing or texting to friends. This doesn't come across as respectful. If you feel that respect must be earned, not automatically awarded for reasons of age or relative importance, I won't argue with you. But you can damage your prospects. You'll gain more respect for yourself by communicating in line with the high standards most upper-level people expect, or insist on.

Try This: If you need to develop your ear for tone, make a practice of reading your emails aloud and consider: How does it sound — like my natural voice? Does it give the impression that I'm annoyed or frustrated? Or don't like the person I'm writing to?

TIP

Be especially mindful of how easily a piece of writing can communicate actual feelings such as anger or dislike. Choice or words, cadence, and sentence structure can almost magically give away negative feelings. Notice when you read messages from other people that you sometimes intuit an emotion without being able to pinpoint what carries it. The takeaway for you: Try not to betray negative emotions!

WARNING

Should you fake respect or good feelings when they're not genuine? Yes, sometimes. When you communicate in ways that lead others to feel badly, rejected, or disrespected, it may never be forgotten or forgiven, especially if you do it in writing. You need to build relationships, not undermine yourself.

Try This: Accept that your negative reactions, or assessments of other people, may not be always be fair or balanced. We all have limited perspectives and can misperceive other people's words or actions. Experiment with giving difficult managers — and everyone in your work environment — the benefit of the doubt. Treat others with generosity, even when you don't like them or think they've offended you, and you may find yourself bringing out their better side.

The bottom line: Monitor your tone in every message to see if it's negative or can be misinterpreted in any negative way by the reader. When it's important, ask a trusted colleague to review what you wrote. Do you need more incentive to read between your own lines? Consider that your superiors won't let you near a customer, client, or VIP of any sort if they can't trust you to be in control and represent their interests well.

Here are some extreme examples.

Version 1:

> *Marge, didn't I already ask you five times to review the draft I spent 23 hours writing and give me your input? Remember? I'm at a standstill! If I don't hear from you by 3:30 tomorrow, I'll assume you have nothing to say and go ahead on my own. —Matt*

Version 2:

> *Marge — I'm still waiting for your input on the draft I sent Tuesday. This is creating problems. Any chance you can get back to me this week? —Matt*

Version 3:

> *Hi, Marge,*
>
> *I know what a busy time of year this is, but we'll really appreciate your input on the Marshall draft. You may recall we promised to deliver it Monday. Is it possible for you to take a look by the end of the week?*
>
> *It will be a big help.*
>
> *Best, Matt*

I take for granted you don't write emails like Version 1. If you read it aloud, it sounds accusatory, impatient, whiny, and childish. If Marge is Matt's boss, she will feel attacked and regard him with suspicion henceforth. If he's a client, Matt may soon be job hunting. If Marge is a coworker, she'll feel angry and uncooperative.

Version 2 is less offensive but still has a negative intonation — I'd call it passive-aggressive. Marge may do as asked, but won't feel warmly toward Matt.

Version 3 is courteous and deferential. If you read it aloud, the tone is neutral and feels respectful. It carefully avoids casting blame. This message has the best odds of achieving its goal, to coax Marge to give the draft a few minutes' attention and regard Matt as perfectly reasonable.

Avoiding the blame game

Version 3 suggests another good strategy: finding a way to let another person, especially a VIP, save face if he or she errs. No one likes to feel chastised, belittled, or implicitly criticized by anyone, let alone someone on a lower level. If the boss or a client ignores your plea for a response, or fails to return a phone call, or even stands you up for an appointment, how can you handle it?

TIP

A good general principle is to let that person off the hook without relinquishing what you need. In Version 3, Matt does this by saying that he knows this is a busy time of the year for Marge. It can take a moment's thought to figure out an appropriate mitigating statement for the other person and use it to frame what you want in a more acceptable way. For example:

> *I know you've been traveling and how hard it is to catch up . . .*
>
> *This may have fallen through the cracks when so much is going on . . .*
>
> *I know everyone's pressing you for figures this week . . .*
>
> *It looks like we had a miscommunication . . .*

A person who feels well-disposed is much more likely to help you out or rectify an oversight than one who is put on the defensive.

REMEMBER

Don't overlook another tool in your strategy kit — the thank-you note. I talk about the value of expressing appreciation to subordinates earlier in this chapter, and the approach is equally effective with supervisors. Executives rarely receive compliments or thanks from people who report to them. Writing to thank them for good advice or a special favor makes you notable. A respectful compliment is also welcome. A message such as, "Tom, thanks for being such a great mentor and helping me grow so much," may be in order once in a while. More immediate compliments may be best delivered in person. For example, "I admire the way you handled the Burke problem and learned a lot from it."

Making it easy to respond

TIP

Here's another idea that gives you better results when you need something from a supervisor, VIP, or peer: Make it easy for that person. Recognize that realistically, your messages won't get much attention. Managers spend a lot of energy putting out fires, and the broader their perspectives, the harder it is to keep everything in mind and focus on detail. Here's a theory: In general, the higher up the hierarchy you go, the briefer your messages need to be. Or if not brief, the more easily grasped in record time. Aim to give your superiors just enough to make a good decision, ask important questions, or take other action.

See this demand for brevity as a compliment: These busy people trust you to decipher what matters, tell them what they need to know, and filter out the rest. Here are some techniques to help you do this:

>> **Be clear in each case what the manager needs to do — or what you want her to do — upon reading the message.** Make a decision? Take an action? Evaluate something? Stay up-to-date? Figure out what is necessary for that goal and include the right amount of background and detail.

>> **Pay attention to the visuals.** Even an email can use headlines, subheads, and bold lead-ins to direct attention to high points and support productive skimming. Dense material is uninviting and a challenge to absorb. Follow the rules for short sentences, paragraphs, and words.

>> **Lead with an executive summary.** What, for an email? Yes, if helpful. The reader may have a particularly short attention span; or you may want to set him up to read the body of the material in a certain light. If this is the case, compose a mini-version of an executive summary, which I cover how to do in Chapter 7.

>> **Keep a backup in your pocket.** Have a "stage 2" communication ready should the boss want more detail or context.

TIP

Another way to make it easy for a higher-up is to offer active help. Extending the example in the preceding "Guarding your tone" section, Matt could have improved Version 3 of his memo to Marge this way:

I know what a busy time of year this is, but we'll really appreciate your input on the Marshall draft this week. Would it be easier to talk about this by phone for a few minutes? I could then make the changes for you. If this would be helpful, just give me a call when convenient.

TIP

An ingenious supervisor I know reports to her own short-attention-span supervisor in a government office this way: She sends him an email and also prints it out. She brings the printed copy to the conversation and gives it to him. He reads it in her presence, talks about it as inclined, asks questions, and makes notes on the printout. She is thus assured that he read the message thoroughly and is well-equipped for a decision. His annotated printout gives him a secure platform for proceeding.

APPLYING MANAGER-THINK TO LONG-FORM DOCUMENTS

The examples in this chapter focus on email and other everyday messages, but the same principles also apply to "big" documents such as reports and proposals. Some particular points that take management perspective into account:

- Create good, complete executive summaries, bearing in mind that decisions may well be made based on the summary alone.

- Present information in order of importance and highlight important portions to capture attention.

- Use supportive graphics; clear subheads with an action feeling, not labels; and easily grasped charts and graphs as suitable.

- Include backup material such as history and research in specific sections so they can be read as desired but ignored without repercussion.

- Arrange the document in a clear, logical sequence, presented in an upfront Table of Contents.

- Make clear recommendations in the conclusion, and perhaps in the executive summary.

Chapter 7 covers developing long-form material in depth.

Writing Backup Memos

When communicating with subordinates, superiors, and peers, it is often smart to confirm mutual understanding in an email or other internal communication format. This can save a great deal of hassle later if those involved emerge with a different memory or interpretation of the matter at hand. Make these memos concise and to the point.

For example, to a supervisor:

Subject: Confirming action on Melody

Dear Luke:

Thanks for taking the time to talk through the Melody account with me this morning. Here is my understanding:

We will recommend two possible courses of action for our client, Gray Builders:

- Option A is to start the project in June.
- Option B is to delay project start until October.

To flesh these alternatives out, I will:

1. Ask Terry Thompson in Accounting to crunch both sets of numbers for us.
2. Put my staff to work researching the permits from the EPA, municipal authorities, county housing office, etc.

If any of this doesn't accord with your understanding or needs further thought, please let me know. Otherwise I'll proceed on this basis early next week.

Thanks, Jenny

Take a similar tack when assigning something significant to a staff member, and in addition, consider whether the person you're writing to is fully equipped for the task. Does he need specific instructions? A way to learn something? Connection to necessary resources? Access to people or files?

REMEMBER

If you want your team to function efficiently and with confidence, provide easy access to more information and a comfortable way to ask questions. Avoid forcing people to guess what you want or how you want them to do it: Take the time to brief them fully and then trust them to deliver. But encourage your team to bring problems to your attention at any point in time, as soon as possible.

It won't surprise you that one of the most empowering things you can do for your staff is to set a good example as a communicator, in both what you say and what you write. In addition to the example you set by demonstrating this skill set, consider an appropriate level of training. Your employees will thank you as they discover the value of better writing, and they will do you credit.

And this, dear reader, is where I leave you. Now you have it — the A to Z of business writing I promised, starting with the often overlooked but important emails you produce every day to your staple business documents, spoken communication, online presence, and special communications challenges.

But don't go away quite yet: The following "Part of Tens" chapters give you three sets of quick helpful insights about using your writing skills to advantage.

I hope you will take the foundation this book gives you to enjoy writing, practice it in your daily work life, and keep learning. I know this investment will always reward you — often in unanticipated ways.

6

The Part of Tens

Learn how to use the résumé writing process to understand who you are, where you've been, what you've done, and what you're ready for.

Discover how you can to use your writing to stand out in the business world and build the professional image you want.

Learn the techniques for creating effective video, whether promotional videos created for public relations or marketing reasons or more low-key how-to and self-introductory videos for your website or video blogs.

Chapter **15**

Ten Ways to Advance Your Career with Writing

Good writing helps you succeed. Despite the business world's growing need for effective communications, good writers are ever more difficult to find. So, use writing to stand out and build the professional image you want. When you write every message well, over time you are seen as authoritative, reliable, and resourceful. Draft, review, edit, proofread. This chapter gives you ten specific ways to use your skill to your advantage. And all the ideas presented here are fully covered in the relevant chapters of this book.

Write to Build Relationships

Many written messages today help you interact with people you don't yet know — and may never meet. Consciously use business email and correspondence to personalize your messages, as appropriate.

Get friendly gradually. A first message should be fairly formal. If your correspondent mentions a vacation or a personal milestone, perhaps inquire about that in subsequent correspondence. Or fall back on the weather or vacation time, as you do in face-to-face conversation. Once you create a relationship, foster it with written contact, typically via email or social media.

REMEMBER

Many cultures expect more formality than the North American culture you may be accustomed to, but may also see relationships as prerequisites to business. Write with formality, but be sensitive to the other person's cues — like moving to a first name basis, for example, or inquiring about the family.

Write a Great Elevator Speech

Introducing yourself well at meetings, industry events, and public occasions can open doors magically. To craft an effective 15-second pitch, focus on your own value to the people you want to meet: How can you help them? This 15-second speech should say who you are, what you do, and what makes you unique.

TIP

Once you own a message you like, practice, then take it on the road. Find out where prospects, investors, collaborators or anyone else you want to connect with get together in person. If you're under 35, you may see a few of your cohorts showing up and are likely to find yourself welcomed with open arms.

Write Your Own Long-Range Career Plan

If you don't know where you want to be next year, or in five years, or ten, use the power of writing to catalyze your planning. First write down what you'd most like to achieve in your chosen time frame. Then look at where you are now and write down the steps that can get you where you want to go. Do you want to acquire training? Take on certain assignments? Find intermediary jobs that qualify you? Meet particular people?

This thinking helps you recognize the opportunities you might overlook and make better decisions. But write it down. Otherwise, your thoughts revolve around the same old paths, and moving ahead looks like too big a step. Expect to make adjustments along the way as you refine your journey.

Write an Ad for Your Dream Job

Another good way to channel your thinking about the future is to create an ad for your ultimate job. Put yourself in the employer's place and figure out what he is looking for. Describe the job in detail and list every relevant responsibility, credential, and personal quality you can think of. This shows you how well you currently match up and what you need to work on. Go a step further and write a cover letter as if you were applying for the job right now.

Go Out of Your Way to Thank People

The busier people feel, the more they forget to be polite, let alone appreciative. Make a good impression by saying thank you, in writing, when someone does you a good turn — an opportunity, referral or reference, advice, introduction, or interview.

A good thank you reflects what the other person values hearing. Be specific. For example, "Your virtual introduction helped me understand the profession better, and also, how to prepare myself for it." For extra points, send a hand-written note.

Take Notes to Control the Conversation

Write things down. Later, you may be the only person who knows what actually happened. People forget quickly when they have a lot going on. It's hard to argue with someone who knows when something was done or what everyone's assignment was. Most people duck the role of note-taker at meetings, but writing the recap gives you the chance to articulate the main points and decisions. It also puts you in the loop for new information.

Use Social Media Strategically

Focus your online participation by developing a plan to promote your goals, whether you want to network, build a following for your blog, find job opportunities, or establish your expertise. Always write thoughtfully online and with a positive tone. See everything you post as a chance to showcase your skills. Your online presence lets people evaluate you almost as if they're eavesdropping. Remember that everything you post is part of your résumé today and will never really go away.

TIP

Think your ideas through. Express them well. Edit out misspellings, bad grammar, and anything that suggests you are less than the person you want to be.

Know How to Explain Your Value

Always be prepared to tell other people what you contribute and the value of your department's work. This enables you to articulate your value to a prospective employer or new boss and field unanticipated challenges.

Be clear on how you fit into your department's work and the organization as a whole. Aligning with company goals helps you do a better job — and you may well be noticed. To better engage employees with their "mission" is a big driver for most organizations.

TIP

If you're self-employed, be ready to speak about your value to customers or clients. You never know who may be a prospect for your services, and spelling out to yourself what makes you outstanding enables you to adapt the conversation to the other person's concerns.

Profile Your Higher-Ups

Creating written, detailed profiles of your supervisors shows you how to communicate with them better, ask for what you need, and perform to higher expectations. Create a list of applicable factors, such as management style, communication style, how he makes decisions (ideas? statistics? impact on people?), and values and priorities (efficiency? teaming? bottom line? new technology?).

Think also about your boss's hot buttons, his positioning in the company, his biggest problems and ambitions, what he cares about, and what keeps him up at night. You may be surprised at how much you know and can intuit, and how much the information helps you when you want something or wish to contribute more and be recognized. You may be able to turn a relationship around because you can see interactions from the other person's perspective.

Create Talking Points

Politicians do it, CEOs do it, celebrities do it, Boy Scouts do it. So can you: Prepare. Instead of going into interviews, presentations, and challenging situations cold, develop a page of talking points by brainstorming first the main points you want to make, and second, the questions you may be asked — especially the worst-nightmare ones. Review your points before the event. Having a firm grasp on what you want to say and how you answer tough questions makes you 100 percent more effective and confident. You're also ready to handle the unanticipated.

Chapter **16**

Ten Ways to Energize Your Résumé

Actively use the résumé-writing process to understand who you are, where you've been, what you've done, and what you're ready for. The good news is that while this effort can be agonizing at times, finding the language transforms your sense of yourself. In figuring out how to prove yourself to prospective employers, you prove your qualifications to . . . you! You feel reaffirmed and ready for the next step — and prepared to sail through the interviews. Here are ten ways to smooth the process.

Don't Apply for the Job You Have Now

People often make the mistake of writing a résumé as if they're applying for their current job. That's probably because it's easier to describe where you've already been than where you want to go. The best résumés read as if the candidate has spent his or her whole career preparing for the new opportunity: not just any new job, but this particular opening. It makes customizing your résumé essential when you're seriously interested in the job. Spend some time identifying the match points between you and the employer's want list. Imagine the ideal candidate: What do you have in common with that theoretical person? Can you orient your experience and qualifications to show you're the one to hire, and that your past history proves you're ready?

Adopt the Employer's Language

Read the ad 20 times to absorb the company's perspective and understand more deeply what those who hire are looking for. Try to find the problem to be solved or the credentials and qualities that will be most valued. Read between the lines: Does the job posting repeat a word more than once, like "resourceful" or "reliable"? Maybe these qualities were lacking in previous job holders. Does the ad ask for anything specific, like the ability to multitask or work on team projects? These are clues that you should cite proven skills and provide evidence. A close read also helps you identify the best keywords and search terms to use. Don't slavishly repeat what the ad says, but adopt enough of the wording to show you're on the same wavelength.

Write Clearly and Concisely

Use tight wording and short, simply structured sentences. You don't need full sentences; you can be somewhat telegraphic and cut unnecessary words whose absence won't interfere with meaning. For example, say "Supervised nine people during vacation seasons," rather than "I was responsible for supervising nine people in the absence of the supervisor." Cut little words — prepositions and articles like *the, also, and, a,* and *an* when possible. But don't distill the thoughts down to mysterious fragments that make readers guess at what you mean, such as "Ran office, vacations, nine people." Note that the simple past tense usually works best, but for ongoing activity in a current job, present tense may be better.

Communicate What You Actually Do

Rather than getting lost in official or "insider" descriptions of your work, take the time to figure out how to explain it to your grandmother or to a 10-year old. Think: How do I spend my day? What am I proud of? What skills do I call upon? What problems do I solve? What do people depend on me for? What have I accomplished? Try to quantify your accomplishments in terms of saving time or making money.

TIP

Go through as many thinking stages as necessary to make what you do concrete and real. If your job title doesn't really represent your responsibilities, or you want to more strongly connect your experience with the posting, give yourself a suitable job title, but refer also to the company title this way: "Manager, In-House Video Production (official title: Administrative Chief, Visual Services Unit, Communications Office)."

Write Narratives, Not Just Bullets

Bullet points are handy for concise presentation, but don't rely on them to tell your story on their own! Think of them as examples and points of evidence that back up your narrative explanations. Write a strong positioning statement to introduce yourself at the top of the page (see Chapter 10). For each significant job, begin with a few lines that give a big-picture overview of your role, and then use bullets to cite projects, proof of success, initiatives, and so on, as appropriate. Start each point with the same part of speech, preferably a verb (for example, catalyzed, reorganized, introduced). Remember that it's hard for readers to absorb more than seven bullets.

Sidestep Jargon and Business-Speak

REMEMBER

When you use jargon, even people in the same industry may not understand it. If you're applying to a somewhat different industry, you're doubly muffing it Often jargon becomes invisible after you're working somewhere a while, so ask someone to read your résumé and to tell you if he understands what you mean. If he doesn't, explain the meaning behind the words until you get down to the basics and that person does understand you. Take your cues from there. Also, avoid the empty rhetoric that characterizes so much business writing. A statement such as, "designed a breakthrough innovative scalable interface," doesn't cut it.

Use Action Verbs to Prove What You Accomplished

Launched, streamlined, originated, chaired, generated, instituted, rejuvenated, mobilized, originated, revamped . . . there are hundreds of high-energy verbs to choose from, and you can easily find them by Googling "action verbs." They're even broken down by industry. Build with action verbs to show how you've made a difference in the jobs you've held rather than being someone who just fills a role passively. Avoid phrases that start, "responsible for . . ." or "duties include." Go for accomplishment and facts. "Managed purchasing for office" can be better stated as "Systematized departmental buying and saved 3 percent of total budget." Of course, tell only the truth.

Write in a Confident, Positive Tone

How do you feel when you assume your best posture and walk around that way for a few minutes? Probably more confident and just a little assertive. Not boastful or combative. Review your résumé with this feeling. You want it to breathe quiet self-assurance and capability. Avoid hedgy, wishy-washy words like sometimes, might, seems, probably, almost, and possibly. They diminish your stature and raise doubt about your value. And keep away from empty descriptive words like extremely, incredibly, and amazing. Communicate a quiet strength. Also, communicate your intelligence and trustworthiness by eliminating every mistake by proofreading thoroughly. Failing to do so carries a high price. Fairly or not, many recruiters and hiring managers toss a résumé at the first spelling error.

Incorporate Keywords

Keywords are critical to getting past digital screening or junior-level readers, and they also make you findable. Recruiters today looking for the best candidate search the Internet using their pet search terms. Identify keywords and search terms in the job post you're answering.

TIP

Look for keywords in job descriptions, industry material, social media sites, and the free Occupational Outlook Handbook published by the U.S. Department of Labor (www.bls.gov/ooh).

Make It Look Good

Appearance counts! Aim for an inviting, accessible presentation that reads easily. This means:

» Keep good margins and plenty of white space rather than cramming in more information that few will read.

» Use a plain, legible typeface in at least 10-point type for body copy and the same, or one other coordinating typeface for headings.

» Don't use fancy fonts that may not even translate between platforms, especially for your name.

» Arrange your elements in a logical way; a standard format is fine if well used.

Chapter **17**

Ten Steps to Creating Video

I f you're creating mini-videos with your smartphone, you're probably shooting spontaneous moments to share with friends. While you want to take advantage of better picture quality and special effects as the technology develops, you may not need to plan much.

But it's different when you have a business goal. Then you need an overall plan for producing a "show" that achieves your business objectives and engages your target audience. A promotional video done for public relations or marketing reasons demands good production values: interesting and well-lit video, quality sound, good graphics.

Between the spontaneous smartphone video and marketing production is a wide range of in-between videos — the how-to demo for YouTube; your self-introduction for your website; video blogs; your short commercial for an email offering; Snapchat and other social media posts. How good do these videos need to be? That's up to you. But whatever use you make of video, and even if you're doing it completely by yourself, it's helpful to know how professionals work. You can adapt some of their techniques to your own needs. In this spirit, here are ten guidelines based on traditional video production.

Know Your Goal, Know Your Audience

The stage prior to actually shooting new material is preproduction — planning — and it's critical. Start by developing a clear idea of why you're producing your video, whether it's mini or maxi in nature, and what you want it to accomplish. How does it fit into the rest of your marketing? Whom do you want to see it? What exactly is your message? Try crystallizing the message in one sentence, Hollywood style: "This video will show that this startup is the most fun place to work in the world and the best programmers want to be here." "Our new gizmo is the ideal gift for people with limited hearing." Know ahead of time how and where you will show your production.

Plan Your Production Style and Content

Consider your options: You may envision a balance of live action and interviews, for example. If you're promoting a product, you might show it in use, how it's made, and testimonials by users. A nonprofit might want to depict its work in action, supplemented by interviews with staff members, volunteers, and beneficiaries of the service. Set parameters: How long will the video be? What do you need: live sound? Narration? Still images? Music? Graphics? Special effects? Animation? Brainstorm how to best tell your story and balance your vision against the practical realities of time, money, team skills, specialized staff, and equipment.

Write a Word + Picture Script

Once you've set your goals and parameters, take a sheet of paper or electronic equivalent divided vertically down the middle. Label the left-hand column "Picture" and label the right-hand column "Words." Microsoft Word's Insert Table tool works nicely for creating simple grids within word-processing documents. A split page keeps you focused on your video's parallel needs and time frames. (You can also use a storyboard like many professionals still do. And you can use specific screenwriting software, but it's expensive and not necessary.) It's smart to leave a narrow column on the far left to record time codes, essential to the editing process; and a narrow area on the far right for notes to help you remember things such as "save for lead."

Create a Shot List

After you have a rough script that includes your ideas for words and visuals, create a shot list that covers every scene you need: live action, specific people, scenery, or whatever else you need. Ultimately the shot list should also include all the logistics the camera crew (or you) needs to set up, shoot, and move between locations, in a carefully thought-out time frame. Especially if you're hiring professional cameramen and more, you want as little down time as possible. Setting up lights and sound takes time in every new scene, so that needs to be built into your timetable. Professionals always scout the locations to make sure they can access sufficient electric power and plan for their needs. Ultimately you may decide to shoot for two hours, 10 days, or anywhere between. Budget probably rules.

Lights, Action, Camera

At last, you've reached the production stage. Even when you're well-prepared, it's often stressful. Carry out your shooting plan and be alert to other opportunities to supplement it. You need to shoot "B roll" — secondary material like pans of the room, close-ups of relevant objects, people walking in, and so on. Video eats up a lot of footage! And you need variety.

TIP

Be sure to prepare people for the action scenes and interviews — ideally before you show up. Even if you want a documentary-style video, you still need to tell your "talent" what you want them to do and what kind of statement you want them to make. Bring a prepared list of questions that are likely to elicit the answer you want. And pose them in the tone you want reflected back: enthusiasm, appreciation, happiness, thoughtfulness. Stay open to the unexpected and recognize that your script keeps evolving as you shoot and edit. Juggling between words and pictures is a continuing process right until the end.

Review Your Shoot and Other Resources

Now you're in postproduction. Totally familiarize yourself with the video footage and other materials, too, such as existing footage from your files or outside resources and still photos or graphics. You must know what's on hand for the "Picture" side of the ledger. You can never have a blank screen. Identify all your best shots, which may be quite different from what you expected. Don't be surprised if you have to adjust the script a lot because you ended up missing some of what you wanted, or found good material you couldn't have planned for. Now you can decide what story you can successfully tell.

Find a Good Lead

REMEMBER

Never underestimate how easy it is to lose an audience. Look for something intriguing or interesting about your subject and lead with it if possible. Make sure you have a good visual to carry the words. You may find a natural big-picture opening, whatever the subject. For example, start a how-to video with the problem: *"Nothing feels worse than lower-back pain from computer hunch. Have you tried all kinds of meds and they don't help? Or exercises that just make it worse? I'm going to show you how to feel great by investing only six minutes per day."* Or just start with the strong visual. Sometimes a startling fact or statistic or quote works well as an opening graphic, and it can be shown on-screen without words for a powerful opening, especially with music. If you shot a strong testimonial, you might start with a short clip of the best bit.

Match Picture and Words

Work your way through your script section by section, matching up picture and words. Aim to narrate or explain as little as possible and let the picture tell as much as it can. Don't repeat orally what's self-evident visually. At this stage, thanks to your cohesive planning, you often find ways to whittle down the words much further than your original script. But think before eliminating the words altogether, even if the style is documentary. You don't want your viewers to wonder why they're looking at something or trying to piece meaning together for you. Use the narration to keep things in perspective, connect, explain, or amplify, as necessary.

Craft the Right Words

For narration, aim to distill the essence of the idea or fact into as few words as possible, but don't overlook chances to use graphic, evocative language. Depend on short, easily pronounced words and simple sentences. Break grammar rules freely. Fragments are fine, as are one-word sentences if the result sounds good and meaning is clear. Avoid complicated literary or other deep thoughts. Distill, distill, distill. *"Computer hunch. Pain. Misery. Frustration. It's the twenty-first century's way of saying take a break! Here's how."*

TIP

Edit, edit, edit until the narration reads like liquid. Have someone else read it, listen and edit, and rephrase. If you record narration before editing, listen carefully and rewrite again if your narrator stumbles or sounds awkward. If you're working with professional editors or other specialists, listen to their suggestions, too.

Let Me Entertain You

When we watch video, we expect to be entertained. A marketing video must have good production values. A nonprofit's video should touch viewers' emotions or sense of idealism, if there's a potential for that. A how-to video also gains by incorporating visual variety and good sound. People may seek out an instructional video when they want to learn how to do something, but they probably have a good many choices and may scan around to find an appealing one. The human eye in particular is a fickle thing, and when it gets bored, it looks for an escape. Try for some visual variety rather than just one or more talking heads without a change in camera angle all the way through. Or keep such a video very short.

Index

About the Author

Natalie Canavor is a business writer, communications consultant, and workshop leader. As a national magazine editor-in-chief, she was responsible for four start-ups. Subsequently she directed communications for a major educational agency and built a 12-person creative department.

Natalie has also worked in public relations, sales promotion, and nonprofit communication. Her byline has appeared frequently in the *New York Times, Newsday,* and a number of publications for businesspeople and communication professionals. She has won more than 100 national awards for her publication work and videos.

At each career stage, Natalie noticed that many people were losing opportunities and failing to meet their goals because of poor writing. She began developing workshops and courses to teach adults practical techniques for writing more powerfully and strategically. Ultimately, she taught advanced writing seminars for NYU's Master's Program in Professional Communications, and now helps colleges improve their business writing programs.

She continues her magazine work as editor of *Impact,* an award-winning magazine published for Israel's Ben-Gurion University of the Negev. And in addition to this book, she is the author of *Business Writing Today* (Sage Publications), a college textbook going into its third edition; *The Truth about the New Rules of Business Writing* (FT Press), coauthored with Claire Meirowitz; and *Workplace Genie: An Unorthodox Toolkit to Help Transform Your Work Relationships and Get the Most from Your Career* (Skyhorse Publishing), coauthored with hypnotherapist Susan Dowell.

Natalie lives in New York and Annapolis, Maryland. Reach her at: www.canavor communications.com.

Dedication

Dedicated to the next generation of learners: Talia, Noa, Coby, Jackson, and Allie

Author's Acknowledgments

I am happy to acknowledge how much better this book is because of my enthusiastic Wiley editor, Amy Fandrei, and my sharp-eyed (but sensitive) project editor, Katharine Dvorak. Thank you!

Publisher's Acknowledgments

Acquisitions Editor: Amy Fandrei

Project Editor: Katharine Dvorak

Technical Editor: Michelle Krasniak

Sr. Editorial Assistant: Serena Novosel

Production Editor: Magesh Elangovan

Cover Image: © Palto/Shutterstock